Space Law

The Emerging Trends

The space law started to emerge as a separate branch of international law. During 1960s and 70s, five major treaties were entered into the field of outer space under the auspices of the United Nations. However the progressive development of space law halted after the Moon Agreement in 1979 due to the divergence in the opinion of the States. Now in the 21st century, with the entry of private sector into space activities, commercial use has emerged as a single largest use of outer space. This has made the world community to rethink on the existing space law which is directed towards the regulation of traditional State activities in outer space and not towards the regulation of modern commercial activities.

With the entry of private players into the realm of space activities, we find the existing international space treaty regime is inadequate to deal with manifold nuances of space activities. This brings forward the question—what steps need to be taken to deal with the emerging trends in space activities?

The nature of different emerging activities in outer space has been studied, which include space tourism, space transportation, space research, exploitation of space resources, and human habitation in outer space. Also the inadequacy of current legal regime to regulate these activities needs to be explored to suggest a working model for regulating and channelizing space activities.

Hence, an attempt is made through this book by the contributors who have explored the possibilities of legal regulation of emerging trends in space activities through concerted effort at both national and international levels.

Contributors

B. Sandeepa Bhat
Eligar Sadeh
Sohini Banerjee
Arindrajit Basu
Amrisha Tripathi
G.S. Sachdeva
Savithran Ramesh
Aditya Prasad
Deva Prasad M.
Pranjal Srivastava
Biswanath Gupta
K.D. Raju
Shraddha Srivastava
Sourav Kumar
Bayar Goswami
Venkatachala G. Hegde
Malay Adhikari
Kumar Abhijeet

Space Law

The Emerging Trends

On the occasion of celebrating the
50th Anniversary of Outer Space Treaty

GENERAL EDITOR

B. Sandeepa Bhat LLM, PhD
Professor of Law, W.B. National University of Juridical Sciences
Member, International Institute of Space Law, Paris, France

KOLKATA NEW DELHI
EASTERN LAW HOUSE

Published and processed by
EASTERN LAW HOUSE PRIVATE LTD.
54 Ganesh Chunder Avenue
Kolkata 700 013
Tel: (033) 4063-2301
Email: mail@elh.co.in
www.elh.co.in

New Delhi Branch
EASTERN LAW HOUSE PRIVATE LTD.
Govind Bhawan, 3rd Floor, Room No. T-2
4384/4A, Ansari Road, Daryaganj
New Delhi 110 002

First Edition 2018
Reprint 2026

ISBN 978-81-7177-331-2

Printed at
Sarat Impressions Private Ltd.
Kolkata

Preface

Space law is one of the fast growing branches of law in the twenty-first century. While the initial stage of space developments has been more in terms of scientific activities, the developments in the twenty-first century are more commercial oriented. The norms that are developed in the twentieth century under the auspices of the United Nations have started to become outdated with this shift. Currently, we are witnessing a number of legal issues relating to commercial activities in outer space. These legal issues need urgent solution, since they are capable of overturning the gift of technological growth into a curse. Moreover, the speed with which the space technology is growing is indicating a possibility of chaos in outer space if we are not futuristic in our approach. Hence, this book is an effort to highlight the emerging trends in space activities and need for developing laws to regulate them.

This book consists of fifteen chapters contributed by space law experts from India and abroad. The book starts with the chapter titled, *Answering the Legal Challenges Posed by Recent Developments in Space Activities*, which is authored by Prof. Dr. B. Sandeepa Bhat. This chapter provides an introduction to the entire book by highlighting the legal issues involved in the current day space activities. It encompasses the issue of private space financing, liability and insurance in private space activities, legal aspects of space tourism, governance of space inventions, celestial property rights and resource exploitation, and space dispute settlement mechanism. The author concludes that with the slow progress in the development of space law and rapid developments in space technology, there requires a lot of efforts to be made in a short span of time to develop legal norms to channelize space activities.

The second chapter of the book is titled, *Public-Private Partnerships for the Development of Space Activities,* which is contributed by Dr. Eligar Sadeh. This chapter highlights the need for cooperation between the State and the private players for promoting commercial space activities. The author deals with different partnership models that are available for State and private players to adopt. Attempt is made to probe into various models that are operative in the United States and to find out how effective they are. Working of Antrix Corporation in India is also discussed as an illustration of public private partnerships being in operation in Indian space sector. The chapter concludes with a note that the combined efforts of both the sectors are the need of the day.

The third chapter is on *Extraterrestrial Habitation and Space Law,* which is written by Ms. Sohini Banerjee. With the exiting plans of human habitation on the celestial bodies several legal issues have cropped up in the space law circle. The author starts with the analysis of problems associated with the possible claim of sovereignty by the States over celestial bodies, which may ultimately lead to colonization. She then proceeds to address the requirement of separate laws to govern the personal status of space inhabitants. In the next part, the author probes into the aspect of extraterrestrial real estate and its feasibility under the current international law. Finally, the author provides an overview of Indian position with respect to extraterrestrial habitation.

The fourth chapter is on *Regulatory Mechanism for the Exploitation of Natural Resources in Outer Space and Celestial Bodies,* which is contributed by Mr. Arindrajit Basu. This chapter starts with the analysis of recent efforts to extract and exploit natural resources in outer space. The current legal framework of non-appropriation and interpretational concerns in the provisions are discussed in detail. While the author supports the exploitation of space resources, he advocates for a proper regulatory mechanism for exploitation to prevent misuses. He analyses different regulatory systems and suggests a three-pronged model for regulating the exploitation and cater to the interest of all.

The fifth chapter, contributed by Ms. Amrisha Tripathi, is on *Commercial Mining of Lunar Resources*. The chapter begins with the discussion on seven segments involved in the space resource mining. It further analyses the economic and technical prospects of lunar resource mining. It discusses the uncertain legal regime relating to lunar resource mining and attribution of responsibility on the States for commercial mining even though carried on by private entities. The author argues that neither under the Outer Space Treaty nor under the Moon Agreement there is any prohibition for commercial lunar mining. However, according to the author, there is a need for developing a new regime to regulate lunar mining in the interest of the world community.

Dr. G.S. Sachdeva has authored the sixth chapter of the book, which is titled, *Space Tourism—Some Legal Implications*. Undoubtedly, space tourism is at the top of the list on next generation fascination. The author finds that space tourism would primarily involve space transportation and space hospitality – each of which requires specific set of rules to have space tourism in a sustained manner. The author looks into the aspects of technical feasibility, commercial viability, public response and safety standards involved in space tourism. While discussing the legal implications, the author addresses the legality of private commercial activities, determination of liability, safety aspects, status of space tourists, need for travel documents, governance and public order in space, space hospitality norms and security aspects.

The seventh chapter of the book is jointly authored by Mr. Savithran Ramesh and Mr. Aditya Prasad. It is titled, *Regulating Space Exploration and Tourism—A Study of SpaceX and Blue Origin*. The authors start with a brief discussion on the development of space law and subsequent growth of commercial space industry. Activities of SpaceX and Blue Origin, two private space companies, are discussed in this chapter. The authors argue that the current space treaty regime is utterly inadequate and there is a need for reforms. While suggesting for reforms, the authors have focused on the need for change in liability norms and emergency assistance to foster the growth of private commercial space activities.

The eighth chapter is on *Regulating Space Tourism and Space Habitation—Significance of Sustainable Development Concept*, which is authored by Dr. Deva Prasad M. The author starts discussion with space tourism and its legal implications. Safety of passengers and protection of environment are found by the author to be the two major issues in space tourism. Then, he moves on to discuss space habitation, wherein he finds property rights and environmental protection as the two major concerns. Since the environmental protection is the common major concern, the author discusses the principle of sustainable development as a tool to regulate space tourism and space habitation.

The ninth chapter is titled, *Obligation Towards Debris Remediation vis-a-vis Space Contamination and Fault Liability*, which is contributed by Mr. Pranjal Srivastava. The author starts with the current position of space debris before discussing the relevant provisions of space treaties. He has tried to connect the aspect of debris to fault liability regime under Article III of the Liability Convention. According to him, the fault liability regime would be useful in pressing for debris mitigation and removal. The author argues for a more comprehensive construction of fault liability under Article III to find solution to problem of space debris.

The tenth chapter is jointly authored by Mr. Biswanath Gupta and Dr. K.D. Raju. It is on *Liability Sharing Mechanism for Commercial Outer Space Activities*. Since this chapter is on the norms of liability for private space activities, the authors start with the discussion of the liability regimes prevailing in different space-faring nations like, United States, Russia, Australia, United Kingdom and France. They argue that the concept of limited liability found in these jurisdictions is advantageous to promote private space activities. Requirement of compulsory insurance in these jurisdictions is also found advantageous to ensure compensation to the victims in case of damage caused by space activities. Finally, the authors advocate for bringing into force a space liability regime in India by incorporating the above aspects.

The eleventh chapter on *Space Insurance* is jointly contributed by Ms. Shraddha Srivastava and Mr. Saurav Kumar. The chapter first elaborates upon the evolution of space insurance market by highlighting the ups and downs in the market. The risk and returns factors in the current space insurance market is analysed by the authors with respect to the different types of space insurance. Liability of the States under space law and insurance as a mechanism to shoulder it is explored by the authors. The authors conclude by stressing upon the need for expanding insurance coverage as well as space insurance market for the benefit of all stakeholders.

Mr. Bayar Goswami has contributed the twelfth chapter of the book, which is on *Settlement of Disputes Arising in Space Activities*. The author begins the chapter by highlighting the multiple possibilities of disputes arising between different stakeholders like States, intergovernmental organizations and private players while carrying on space activities. The author finds that while consultation and cooperation between the States are the major means of dispute settlement under the space treaties, the Liability Convention provides for establishment of Claims Commission for settlement of disputes. However, the decisions of Claims Commission are not binding unless the parties agree. Hence, exploring better models of dispute settlement for space activities is found necessary by the author. In light of this the author details out the available mechanisms under general international law, ILA's Draft Convention and Permanent Court of Arbitration Optional Rules.

The thirteenth chapter of the book titled, *Regional Approaches to Space Cooperation—Creation of SASA* is contributed by Prof. Dr. Venkatachala G. Hegde. The author begins with the argument that SAARC is one of the most significant regional organizations having huge potentiality for cooperation. He looks into the SAARC framework and finds that it is broad enough to accommodate all cooperative endeavours including a Space

Charter. Need for regional space cooperation in Asia, especially in the field of disaster management is argued to be most significant. Finally, the chapter concludes with the proposal for creation of South Asian Space Agency and contours of it.

The fourteenth chapter is titled, *Establishing International Space Organization—An Indian Vista,* which is written by Dr. Malay Adhikari. The author starts with the development of institutionalization in the Indian space sector. Contribution of great personalities like Meghnad Saha, Homi Bhabha, Vikram Sarabhai and Satish Dhawan is discussed in detail. The developments in the governmental and private levels in respect of institutionalization are also discussed. Finally, the author ends with the need for moving towards regional and international institutionalization for catering to the common interest.

The last chapter of the book is on *Bangalore Declaration–A Beacon for National Space Legislation for India,* which is authored by Mr. Kumar Abhijeet. This chapter begins with the analysis of need for national space legislation. The author highlights commercialization and privatization, safety and security, compliance with international and constitutional obligations, encouraging investments etc. as primary factors in this regard. Then he proceeds to analyse fourteen issues that need to be covered in the national space legislation for India, which are identified under the Bangalore Declaration.

Thus, all fifteen chapters of this book are focused towards addressing the emerging legal trends in space activities. It is expected that this book would not only be useful for practitioners, academicians, students and researchers but also for policymakers. Moreover, the public sector undertakings and private sector space investors would also be benefitted out of this book.

Kolkata
10th August 2017 B. SANDEEPA BHAT

Contents

Chapter 1

Answering the Legal Challenges Posed by Recent Developments in Space Activities

B. SANDEEPA BHAT*

Introduction

International norms on the space activities are the creations of efforts during 1960s and 70s. Five major treaties entered during this phase of outer space law-making are Treaty on Principles Governing the Activities of States in the Exploration and Use of Outer Space, including the Moon and Other Celestial Bodies (Outer Space Treaty) 1967, Agreement on the Rescue of Astronauts, the Return of Astronauts and the Return of Objects Launched into Outer Space (Rescue Agreement) 1968, Convention on International Liability for Damage Caused by Space Objects (Liability Convention) 1972, Convention on Registration of Objects Launched into Outer Space (Registration Convention) 1975 and Agreement Governing the Activities of States on the Moon and Other Celestial Bodies (Moon Agreement) 1979. With the absence of consensus in UNCOPUOS,[1] space treaty-making ended in 1979. This inevitably

* LLM, PhD, Professor of Law, Coordinator-Society for Studies in Outer Space Law, The West Bengal National University of Juridical Sciences, Salt Lake, Kolkata. Member, International Institute of Space Law (IISL), Paris, France.

1 United Nations Committee on Peaceful Uses of Outer Space.

resulted in confining the application of space treaties to the then prevalent State oriented space activities. With the shift from State oriented space activities to private sector oriented space activities, questions are posed on the adequacy of existing space treaties to regulate new trends in space activities. Though some States have resorted to national space legislation to fill-in the existing void, such efforts are minimum and scattered. Thus, the moot question to be answered today is- are we heading towards chaos in outer space?

In answering the above question, we need to probe into manifold recent developments consequent to private space activities. To start with, challenges posed by private space financing attain significance. Second aspect to be looked into is the concern of liability for private space activities and viability of space insurance as a solution to liability concerns. Moving forward, the nuances of commercial space tourism under the existing space law need focused discussions. Space inventions and consequential problems under the traditional patent regime require special attention. Testing the claims of private property rights and resource exploitation in outer space under the gamut of existing space law is indispensible. Further, it is also equally significant to examine the ways to develop a strong dispute settlement mechanism to deal with ever-increasing space related disputes.

Private Space Financing

Despite the entry of private sector into space activities, the space investments are considered to be less than the expected level. Element of risk involved in space investments is the reason behind reduced space investments. While the natural risk of satellite failures cannot be prevented, the creditors are concerned about the manmade risk of debtor's refusal/failure to pay back the borrowed sum. Asset-based financing[2] is currently used as

2 The assets that are financed themselves are used as collateral in asset-based financing. See Ruwantissa Abeyratne, *Asset-Based Financing and Leasing of Aircraft and Equipment*, Journal of World Investment, 2001, pp. 831–856 at pp. 831 & 832.

the mechanism to finance the private space activities, which involves the creation of a non-possessory security interest in the space asset.

The multibillion investments in space activities necessitate cross-border investments by several investors from different countries. In the event of debtor's failure to pay back the loan, difficulties are faced in terms of zeroing down the jurisdiction and applicable law to decide the rights of creditors. Such a determination has far-reaching consequences, since some of the jurisdictions may not recognise non-possessory security interests, and some others may recognise partially.[3] As the space assets are tangible movables, traditionally principle of *lex situs* is applied in determining the applicable law. This gives sufficient scope for the debtor to misuse by making default when the space asset is in a jurisdiction that doesn't recognise non-possessory security interest.

In the absence of any reference to private space financing laws under the space treaties, UNIDROIT[4] made an effort to bring a regime governing space financing. It devised a two tier system consisting of a base convention[5] and area specific protocols[6] to deal with financing of different mobile equipment, which move from one jurisdiction to another. The UNIDROIT

3 Roy Goode, *Transcending the Boundaries of Earth and Space: The Preliminary Draft UNIDROIT Convention on International Interests in Mobile Equipment*, Uniform Law Review, 1998, vol. 3, Issue 1, pp. 52–75 at pp. 54 & 56.

4 International Institute for the Unification of Private Laws is an intergovernmental organisation, which functions from Villa Aldobrandini, Rome. As stated in its website, the purpose of UNIDROIT is "to study needs and methods for modernising, harmonising and co-ordinating private and in particular commercial law as between States and groups of States and to formulate uniform law instruments, principles and rules to achieve those objectives". Available at <http://www.unidroit.org/about-unidroit/overview> last visited 14 January 2017.

5 Convention on International Interests in Mobile Equipment 2001 (popularly known as Cape Town Convention).

6 There are three protocols relating to aircraft equipment, railway rolling stock and space assets respectively. Protocol to the Convention on International Interests in Mobile Equipment on Matters Specific to Space Assets 2012 (Space Protocol) is designed to govern space assets.

system tries to build the confidence of creditors in financing space activities by providing for creation and registration of international interests, laying down rule of priority amongst competing creditors, ensuring default remedies and protection of creditors during insolvency of debtors.

Though the UNIDROIT system was drafted with much expectation, it failed to come into force with respect to space assets.[7] Of course, there are certain inherent limitations in the UNIDROIT system, which have resulted in creating an imbalance amongst competing interests of different stakeholders. Moreover, the primacy of UN space treaties[8] also brings doubts about the practical implementation of the UNIDROIT system. In light of these factors, there is an immediate need of revisiting the UNIDROIT system to make it operative in the field of space assets. Until this herculean task is accomplished, the onus is on the States to deal with the space financing issues comprehensively in their national space legislation to protect the interests of space investors.

Liability and Insurance in Private Space Activities

Shouldering the liability for damage caused by private space activities is a significant area of concern. The space treaties advocate for the liability of 'launching State/s' for any damage caused by space activities.[9] In the absence of a separate liability regime governing the private space activities, States are burdened with the liability for any damage caused by private players. Since such an imposition of liability on the States happens irrespective of their fault, every State is concerned of it. Despite the treaty obligations, shouldering liability for private space

7 The Space Protocol has failed to receive even a single ratification till today. See the current status at <http://www.unidroit.org/status-2012-space> last visited 14 January 2017.

8 Space Protocol, Article XXXV: The Convention as applied to space assets shall not affect State Party rights and obligations under the existing United Nations outer space treaties or instruments of the International Telecommunication Union.

9 The Outer Space Treaty, Article VII and the Liability Convention, Articles II and III.

activities by the States results in compromising the public good to promote private good. Hence, the States are compelled to devise mechanisms to shift the liability for damage caused by private space activities.

Search for a mechanism to shift the liability has resulted in the birth of space insurance as a pre-requisite for grant of licence to carry on private space activities.[10] While satellite insurance, liability insurance and launch vehicle insurance are the three types of space insurance, the liability insurance is mandated by almost all existing national laws.[11] However, despite such a strong insistence on space liability insurance, problems in the field are not yet over due to some concerns in space insurance.

To start with, the space insurance has always faced the problem of risk evaluation, since there is no objective criterion to determine the magnitude of risk. The line of demarcation between a successful and a failed space mission is blurry. Moreover, a failed mission may result in huge amount of losses, much beyond human imagination. This operates as a deterrent factor in providing insurance coverage to liability arising out of space accidents.[12]

There are also certain key aspects of contract of insurance, which are difficult to comply with in space insurance. Duty to disclose in good faith, for example, may pose challenge to the insurance seeker especially in light of confidentiality associated with space technology. Similarly, satellite recoupment under the right of subrogation by the insurance provider (after payment of compensation) would bring forward concerns to the insured

10 C. Gaubert, *Insurance in the Context of National Authorisation,* in Frans G. Von Der Dunk (ed.), *National Space Legislation in Europe,* 2011, pp. 163–178 at p. 165 (The Netherlands: Martinus Nijhoff).

11 United States, Russia, Australia, United Kingdom, South Korea, Austria, France, Netherlands, China, Japan and Singapore are all the examples of States that have incorporated the requirement of liability insurance in their national legislation.

12 Such trend has already been evidenced in the history of space insurance. Ilias I. Kuskuvelis, *Space Insurance* in K. Tatsuzawa (ed.), *Legal Aspects of Space Commercialization,* 1992, pp. 60–75 at pp. 62 & 63 (Tokyo: CSP Japan).

in terms of technology transfer and intellectual property rights. In addition, the discharge of duty to mitigate damage, a duty of the insured, is also difficult to prove in the absence of any due diligence standard applicable to space activities.

Due to above concerns in space insurance, the insurance providers have resorted to defensive practices in providing space insurance. Several exclusion clauses are inserted by the insurers to limit the scope of their liability,[13] much to the detriment of insured as well as third-party victims of space accidents. Hence, it is prudent to find an alternative to space insurance with a view to enduringly solve the problems of liability for damage caused by private space activities. Drawing parallel from nuclear liability funds,[14] creation of a space liability fund with the contribution of private space players seems to be the best available option in this direction.

Commercial Space Tourism

Space tourism is emerging as the next generation fascination for those who are capable of affording its exorbitant cost. With the potentiality for a lucrative market in sight, the private sector has shown interest in developing orbital and sub-orbital space tourism. Virgin Galactic has reached very close to the point of operating commercial space tourism with its successful testing of SpaceShip II in December 2016.[15] Hence, the dream of space tourism is blossoming into reality in this fast changing world.

While the scientific achievements in realising the common man's dream of outer space entry is commendable, such space

13 See for example <https://www.cpic.com.cn/cx/upload/Attach/infordisclosure/46444786.pdf> last visited 19 January 2017.

14 Convention on Supplementary Compensation 1997 establishes international fund for compensating nuclear damage. Similarly, in the municipal level, United States has created Price-Anderson Fund under the Price-Anderson Act 1957, and India has setup a Nuclear Liability Fund under its Civil Liability for Nuclear Damage Act 2010.

15 Alex Patrikios and Sam Rkaina, *Virgin Galactic Spaceship Completes Successful Test Flight Two Years after Fatal Crash*, available at <http://www.mirror.co.uk/news/uk-news/virgin-galactic-spaceshiptwo-test-flight-9392614> last visited 18 January 2017.

entry is not free from problems. Use of aerospace vehicles in space tourism brings forward the fundamental questions about the demarcation of airspace from outer space, and the consequential debate on the applicable law. Since the fundamental principles of aviation law are different from that of space law, clarification on the applicable law is absolutely necessary to avoid uncertainties in space tourism.

In the absence of clarification on the applicable law, one of the major problems would be in terms of certification and continued supervision of space tourism. Under aviation law, the Chicago Convention 1944 requires the State of registry to issue all licences and certificates.[16] However, under space law, the Outer Space Treaty mandates the 'appropriate State' to grant licenses and continuously supervise space activities.[17] Thus, the States recognised under both the regimes may be different. Added to this, the difference in the liability norms stands as another problem. While under space law, liability is attributed to the launching State/s,[18] aviation law attributes liability on carriers and operators,[19] who are primarily private players.

Next significant question in space tourism is about the status of space tourists in case of emergency. While the astronauts and personnel are entitled to protection under the space treaties in case of emergency or unintentional landing of space objects,[20]

16 Certificate of airworthiness and licenses to the aviation personnel, for example, are to be granted by the State of registration of aircraft under Articles 31 and 32 of the Chicago Convention respectively.

17 The Outer Space Treaty, Article VI: ... The activities of non-governmental entities in outer space, including the moon and other celestial bodies, shall require authorization and continuing supervision by the appropriate State Party to the Treaty...

18 The Outer Space Treaty, Article VII and the Liability Convention, Articles II and III.

19 Carriers' liability is towards the damage caused to parties to the contract in civil aviation under the Warsaw Convention 1929 and its amendments as well as the Montreal Convention 1999. Operators' liability is towards damage caused to third parties by civil aviation under the Rome Convention 1952 and its amendment, the Montreal Protocol 1978.

20 The Outer Space Treaty, Article V and the Rescue Agreement, Articles 1-4.

the status of tourists is in limbo. Protection to astronauts and personnel are consequent to the principle of "astronauts as envoys of mankind" as envisaged under Article V of the Outer Space Treaty.[21] Since they represent the mankind in outer space, the obligation to rescue and return them to launching State is unconditional. Moreover, the rescuing State has no claim for reimbursement of cost involved in rescue and return of astronauts or personnel as they are considered to be representing the rescuing State as well. However, such logic would not apply for the space tourists who enter outer space for pleasure and not for doing anything to further the interest of mankind. Hence, the rights of space tourists during emergency or unintended landing are unclear.

Another serious concern in developing space tourism industry is its adverse impact on space environment. Existing regime to protect the outer space environment is the weakest limb of the space treaties. Only Article IX of the Outer Space Treaty and Article 7 of the Moon Agreement are the direct provisions on the environmental protection in the space treaties. Article 7 of the Moon Agreement is very limited in scope both in terms of obligatory nature[22] as well as sphere of application.[23] On the contrary, Article IX of the Outer Space Treaty is more oriented towards the protection of earth's environment as against the outer space environment. It only prohibits the 'harmful contamination' of outer space, which is construed to be very narrow.[24] Hence, a better regime of space environmental protection needs to be adopted before proceeding forward with

21 Steven A. Mirmina, *Astronauts Redefined: The Commercial Carriage of Humans to Space and the Changing Concepts of Astronauts under International and U.S. Law*, FIU Law Review, 2015, vol. 10, pp. 669–678 at p. 671.

22 Only 17 States have signed and ratified the Moon Agreement. Many of them are not even space-faring nations. See <https://treaties.un.org/pages/ViewDetails.aspx?src=TREATY&mtdsg_no=XXIV-2&chapter=24&clang=_en> last visited 18 January 2017.

23 Moon Agreement is applicable to moon and other celestial bodies but not to entire outer space.

24 Y.M. Kolossov, *Legal Aspects of Outer Space Environmental Protection*, Proceedings of the Twenty-Third Colloquium on the Law of Outer Space, 1981, pp. 103–106 at p. 104.

large-scale commercial space tourism. Any lapse in doing this would be detrimental to the future of space exploration.

Rights in Space Inventions

With the establishment of International Space Station and future plans to establish similar stations in outer space and celestial bodies, space inventions are bound to happen in the near future. Since outer space environment is conducive for breakthroughs in medicine, researches are going on in outer space to find cure for many human diseases.[25] This invariably brings forward several questions relating to patent rights in outer space inventions. In light of the fact that the patent's regime advocates for monopoly rights and outer space treaties speak about common rights in outer space, the first question in the field of outer space inventions would be; whether a monopoly right like the patent right be granted for an invention conducted with the help of common resource like outer space? Despite the arguments against monopoly rights in outer space, granting of patent rights for space inventions is inevitable.[26] In the absence of patent rights, investments in the space inventions would dry up, resulting in a standstill in intellectual creations.

If the patent has to be granted for space inventions, the next question would be; to whom it has to be granted? Going by the prevalent system of first-to-file for granting patent rights may be prone to misuses in case of outer space inventions. Since every activity in outer space is monitored from ground control facility, persons in ground control facility would be having access to inventions conducted by researchers in outer space. Hence, they may misuse their position to collect all documents relating

25 Possibilities of finding cure for cancer, emphysema, diabetes and immune system disorders are expected out of space research. See The *International Space Station: An Overview*, NASA Facts, June 1999, available at <https://er.jsc.nasa.gov/seh/issovw.pdf> last visited 20 January 2017.

26 Anna Maria Balsano, *Intellectual Property within Public International Research Organizations. The Example of European Space Agency*, Proceedings of the Thirty-Sixth Colloquium on the Law of Outer Space, 1994, pp. 3–19 at p. 4.

to invention and file a patent application before the actual researcher returns from outer space. Addressing this concern in space inventions is crucial to protect the interests of space inventors.

While above are the concerns in granting patent rights for inventions in outer space, there are more pressing concerns relating to infringement of earthly patents in outer space. When a patented invention is infringed in outer space, two prominent questions to be addressed would be on the determination of jurisdiction and applicable law to try the infringement. Article VIII of the Outer Space Treaty advocates for the jurisdiction of State of registry on space objects and personnel thereof.[27] This jurisdiction is a combination of quasi-territorial and personal jurisdiction without setting any hierarchy between the two. Given this fact, there may be a conflict between these two jurisdictions in certain circumstances, which may result in either two States concurrently claiming jurisdiction or both of them refusing to exercise jurisdiction by pointing towards each other to exercise jurisdiction.[28]

Applicable law to deal with the patent infringements in outer space is complicated to determine, since there is no *lex situs*[29] to apply just like earthly instances of patent infringements. Until an international patent regime is developed, transportation of earthly patent laws to outer space to deal with the patent infringements is the only option available to us. However, the

27 The Outer Space Treaty, Article VIII: A State Party to the Treaty on whose registry an object launched into outer space is carried shall retain jurisdiction and control over such object, and over any personnel thereof, while in outer space or on a celestial body...

28 This primarily happens when one State sends an astronaut into outer space on board its registered space object, and the astronaut enters a space station in outer space registered by another State. His activities after the entry into space station are linked to the first State through personal jurisdiction and to the second State through quasi-territorial jurisdiction.

29 Law of the place where the infringement takes place is the traditional norm applicable in case of patent infringements. However, there is no separate law relating to patent rights in outer space.

national patent laws cannot be randomly picked for application to patent infringements in outer space. It has to be done on the basis of appropriate connecting factors. While nationality[30] and registration[31] are considered as the only two known connecting factors for the extraterritorial application of domestic patent laws to outer space infringements, both of them are not free from problems.[32] At times, they also result in absurd consequences to deprive the rights of patent holders. Therefore, internationalisation of patent laws to deal with the patent infringements in outer space seems to be inevitable.

Property Rights and Resource Exploitation

Claim of private property rights on the moon and other celestial bodies has been one of the recent developments witnessed by the world community. This has even led to sale of property in moon and other celestial bodies by persons like Dennis Hope.[33] One of the main arguments of private property rights advocates is that the Outer Space Treaty prohibits only national appropriation and not individual appropriation.[34] However, this is not the correct proposition, since neither under the common law system nor under the civil law system such claims can be maintained. Under the common law system, State owns the entire territory and private property rights are conferred to the

30 Nationality of the infringer.

31 Registration of space object.

32 Sandeepa Bhat B., *Inventions in Outer Space: Need for Reconsideration of the Patent Regime*, Journal of Space Law, 2010, vol. 36, No. 1, pp. 1–17 at pp. 11–14; see also Bin Cheng, *Liability Regulations Applicable to Research and Invention in Outer Space and their Commercial Exploration*, in Sa'id Mosteshar (ed.), *Research and Invention in Outer Space-Liability and Intellectual Property Rights*, 1995, pp. 71–94 at pp. 75 & 76 (Dordrecht: Martinus Nijhoff).

33 See <http://www.lunarembassy.com/> last visited 20 January 2017.

34 The Outer Space Treaty, Article II: Outer space, including the moon and other celestial bodies, is not subject to national appropriation by claim of sovereignty, by means of use or occupation, or by any other means. See Alan Wasser and Douglas Jobes, *Space Settlements, Property Rights, and International Law: Could a Lunar Settlement Claim the Lunar Real Estate it Needs to Survive?*, Journal of Air Law and Commerce, 2008, vol. 73, No. 1, pp. 37–78 at pp. 43–47.

individuals by the State. Since under the Outer Space Treaty, States are barred from claiming property rights over the moon and other celestial bodies, they cannot grant title to their individuals. In the civil law system, property rights are conferred on the individuals who occupy and develop an area that does not belong to anyone else (*res nullius*). However, the moon and other celestial bodies are not *res nullius*, rather accepted as province of all mankind.[35] Hence, an individual from civil law system is also debarred from establishing any property right in the moon and other celestial bodies. Moreover, the establishment of individual property rights in outer space would go against the fundamental tenet of common rights advocated by the space treaties, which is also accepted to be an established principle of customary international law.[36]

Despite the legal impediments, private property claims have become a fascination in the absence of appropriate actions from States. While Dennis Hope's business of selling extraterrestrial property has continued unabated over last two decades, persons like Gregory Nemitz[37] and Sylvio Langevin[38] have even moved to the courts of law to establish the validity of their extraterrestrial claims. Though the decisions in these cases were against the claimants, neither of them reflects the position of higher judiciary of the respective State. Since the property claims on the moon and other celestial bodies are made by the

35 The Outer Space Treaty, Article I: The exploration and use of outer space, including the moon and other celestial bodies, shall be carried out for the benefit and in the interests of all countries, irrespective of their degree of economic or scientific development, and shall be the province of all mankind.

36 Virgiliu Pop, *Who Owns the Moon?*, 2009, p. 38 (Berlin: Springer).

37 In *Nemitz* v *United States* 2004 WL 3167042, the District Court of Nevada had to deal with Nemitz's ownership claim over asteroid 433 Eros. However, the Court summarily dismissed his petition to hold that neither the US ratification of the Outer Space Treaty nor its failure to ratify the Moon Agreement has conferred property rights to Nemitz on the celestial body.

38 *In Re Langevin* 2012 QCCS 613, the Superior Court of Quebec addressed the property claim of Langevin on several celestial bodies and concluded that such a claim is not legally tenable.

individuals, it is prudent to say that the respective States need to take appropriate actions to regulate such illegal activities. Support to this line of argument can also be derived from Article VI of the Outer Space Treaty, which attributes responsibility for private space activities to appropriate State.[39]

Exploitation of space resources is closely connected to the issue of property rights. However, can we afford to argue against the permissibility of exploitation of resources in light of absence of private property rights in outer space is a debatable issue. The current need for economic development to uplift the standard of living, especially in the developing countries, would necessitate lateral thinking in terms of space resource exploitation. Moreover, the earthy environmental concerns in the exploitation of currently available limited resources further indicate the requirement of alternative sources to meet human needs in terms of development.

It is clear that the bounties of nature in outer space may be used for human developments. However, it is to be kept in mind that such exploitation needs to be in accordance with the principles of sustainable development and for common benefit. One of the celebrated concepts in this regard, which has been sidelined by the developed countries over the years, is the concept of common heritage of mankind. Article 11 of the Moon Agreement incorporates the concept of common heritage of mankind to the regime of outer space and elaborates upon its application in eight paragraphs. While it advocates for collective rights and equitable sharing of benefits on the one hand, it also imposes an obligation to protect and preserve the resources for future generations on the other hand. Hence, it is advisable to revisit this concept to develop a sustained regime of space resource exploitation.

39 The Outer Space Treaty, Article VI: States Parties to the Treaty shall bear international responsibility for national activities in outer space, including the moon and other celestial bodies, whether such activities are carried on by governmental agencies or by non-governmental entities, and for assuring that national activities are carried out in conformity with the provisions set forth in the present Treaty...

Space Dispute Settlement Mechanism

Developing a strong dispute settlement mechanism is one of the most significant aspects in any area. Space law is certainly not immune from it especially in light of inadequacy of the existing setup of dispute settlement. Under the current state of affairs, Liability Convention provides for settlement of disputes through diplomatic negotiations and upon failure, by establishing 'Claims Commission' in the international level.[40] It is apparent that such a setup is directed towards the settlement of disputes between the States in the realm of outer space. Moreover, the reference to International Court of Justice, in accordance with the provisions of its statute, is also an option available to the States.

With the increased private space activities, search for appropriate forum for the settlement of private disputes relating to space activities has started. Though resorting to domestic courts having appropriate jurisdiction to try the disputes is an option available at present, it is not suitable for technical and high-stake space disputes. While the lake of expertise of judges in the ordinary courts of law would take away the predictability of decisions, the painstaking and lengthy judicial process would cause serious detriment to the parties to the disputes. In a multibillion dispute like space disputes, every day of a delay might cost dearly to the stakeholders. Hence, it is prudent to develop a speedy and cost effective dispute settlement mechanism administered by the experts in the field.

Adopting the speedy and effective non-adversarial dispute settlement mechanism[41] is most suitable for space disputes. Increasing number of private space activities require cooperation

40 The Liability Convention, Article XIV: If no settlement of a claim is arrived at through diplomatic negotiations as provided for in Article IX, within one year from the date on which the claimant State notifies the launching State that it has submitted the documentation of its claim, the parties concerned shall establish a Claims Commission at the request of either party.

41 Judy Gutman, *The Reality of Non-Adversarial Justice: Principles and Practice*, Deakin Law Review, 2009, vol. 14, No. 1, pp. 29–51.

from different players. In the absence of such spirit of cooperation, there would be chaos in the exploration and use of outer space. Court based litigation, which is adversarial, would result in the distortion of cordial relationship between the parties. Hence, we need to move from adversarial to non-adversarial dispute settlement mechanism for resolution of outer space disputes. Since most of the litigants in space disputes are technically sound, online mediation and negotiation may be better suitable for settlement of space disputes. Grooming the skilled mediators and negotiators in this field is an immediate task to be accomplished to prevent the outer space from being the region of conflicts.

Conclusion

Space activities are increasing at an alarmingly high speed. With the fast-growing technology, more and more commercial uses of outer space are found on regular basis. Private enterprises entering into the realm of space activities have brought forward several legal concerns to the world community. Private space financing itself is a concern at present due to the failure of international efforts made by UNIDROIT to harmonise conflicting finance laws. Reviving talks on setting right the mistakes in the UNIDROIT system to bring predictability in space financing is of utmost significance to protect creditor interests. Similarly, to protect the States' interest, efforts are required in the direction of shifting their burden of liability for damage caused by private space activities through a proper mechanism. As established above, the existing mechanism of space insurance is not suitable for balancing and protecting the interests of different stakeholders. Gradual move towards creation of space liability fund seems to provide durable solution to the problem of liability for damage caused by private space activities.

Commercial space tourism may be one of the most fascinating and lucrative businesses of the future. However, implementation of it would require clarifications on the applicable regime, status of space tourists during emergency and stringent norms on space environmental protection. Similarly, the most awaited space inventions require a suitable regime to deal with the conferment and infringement of patent rights. In the absence of it, the benefits derived out of space inventions would be outweighed by the concerns associated with them.

Preventing the legitimization of individual property claims in outer space is of utmost significance to further common interest in outer space. Proactive steps from the States in this regard are urgently required to prevent the outer space from being the victim of space property race. Though such prohibition is not advisable for sustained exploitation of resources in outer space, need for regulation of exploitation is undisputed. The concept of common heritage of mankind envisaged under Article 11 of the Moon Agreement has to be interpreted in the right spirit to balance the conflicting interests of developed and developing countries.

Finally, it is to be borne in mind that bringing into force any regime would require a strong dispute settlement mechanism to interpret norms and decide the rights and obligations of parties. In the absence of this, the regime is bound to fail in practical terms. Hence, the focus should be shifted to create expertise in handling complex space related disputes emerging out of present and future developments in outer space. Lack of current legal developments in the above discussed aspects of space activities has ultimately left us a herculean task to accomplish in a relatively short span of time. However, if we still don't wake up from our slumber to set right the problems, our future in space would meet a fatal end.

Chapter 2

Public-Private Partnerships for the Development of Space Activities

Eligar Sadeh*

Introduction

The dynamics between governmental and commercial space sectors are changing in fundamental ways. One area of significant change is the privatization of space activities that were previously conducted by national governments. Historically, this trend emerged with the privatization of telecommunication satellites, and more recently, in commercial space launch and remote sensing. These trends are characterized by the ways in which national policies and laws ensure the viability and support of space activities in both sectors, governmental and commercial. Of relevance, what are public-private partnerships (PPPs) and how they are structured and applied towards the development of space systems and activities?

This chapter first identifies a range of PPP models directed at the development of space systems whereby the government provides risk reduction, technology and knowledge transfers, and capital formation programs, as well as establishing political and legal regimes, which enable space commerce to support both national space programs and privatization of space

* PhD, Educator and Aerospace Professional, serves as President and Technical Consultant with Astroconsulting International. Editor, *Astropolitics*.

activities. The PPP concept entails the existence of political support and government funding, and aspects in commercial development that provide for a business case and attract private capital. The issue is how to fashion a synergistic relationship between the government and private sectors that effectively crosscut political, legal, financial, market, and technical risks inherent in the formulation and implementation of PPPs for the development of space systems and activities.

Following this, PPP models enabling commercial space launch in the United States are probed. Relevant PPP models encompass more traditional governmental contracting of private industry by negotiations, and governmental acquisitions of systems that are commercially developed, operated, and owned. United Launch Alliance's (ULA's), Evolved Expendable Launch Vehicles (EELVs), the Atlas V and Delta IV, and Space Exploration Technologies' (SpaceX) Falcon 9 are analyzed. The scope of this chapter is evaluated and relevant lessons for national space programs are ascertained. The applicability of these lessons is highlighted with the PPP example of Antrix Corporation in India.

This chapter addresses the dynamics between the governmental space sector and the commercial space sector with an emphasis on public-private partnerships. These partnerships are directed at risk reduction, capital formation, technology and knowledge transfers, and political and legal regimes that enable space commerce to support both governmental and private space activities. Specific public-private partnership models are investigated in the case of space launch systems in the United States. One model focuses on governmental contracting for development by private industry, and the second model involves acquisitions by government of systems that are commercially developed, operated, and owned. Political and legal aspects of pubic-private partnerships, implications for national space programs, and the applicability of these implications for public-private partnerships in India are discussed.

Public-Private Partnership Dynamics and Models

The government, whose motivation is to act in the public interest and create public value, can undertake the risk for research and development (R&D) and formulate appropriate political and legal regimes that facilitate PPPs for commercial development. One major barrier to commercial space activities is the inability of private firms to raise the capital needed for implementation of business plans. Important factors related to this barrier are the lack of credible near-term revenue markets for commercial activities, and political and legal uncertainties associated with commercial ventures. In other words, the private sector cannot be confident that it will realize and accept return-on-investment (ROI) solely on the basis of private markets. As a result, the commercial space sector partners with the government to share in the technological and capital risks. Figure 1 below illustrates this dynamic.

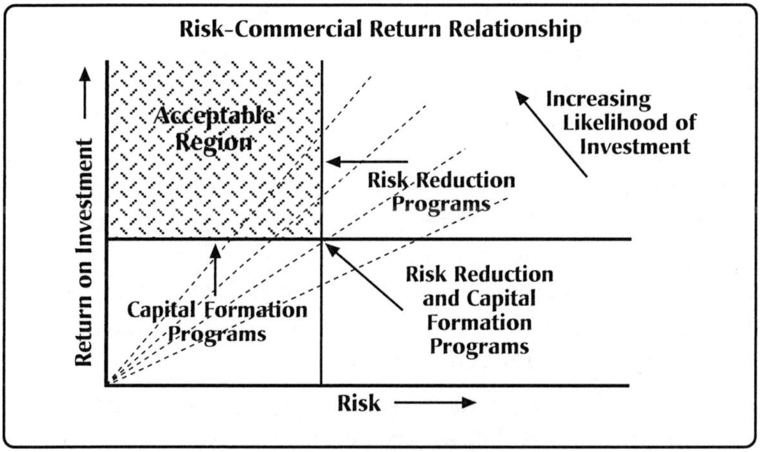

Fig. 1: Public-Private Partnerships and Risk to Commercial Return Relationship

SOURCE: DEVELOPED BY AUTHOR

An important role for the government in PPPs is to reduce as many risks as possible. This is accomplished through formulating policy and legal actions so that the government does not constrain the development of the private space industry, providing a role for government in capital formation and technology and knowledge transfers in developing commercial space technology, and by off-loading governmental space activities to the private sector. These actions reduce risk and enhance possibilities of ROI for private entities that then commercialize the technologies. An acceptable region for this commercialization exists when there is a favorable benefit-to-cost ratio where ROI is greater than risk. This characterizes the evolution of space commerce in telecommunications, launch vehicles, and remote sensing.

The traditional approach of governmental contracting of R&D deals with risks inherent in the development of new and innovative technologies. This approach is augmented with transfers of technology for commercial use. The PPP equation implies that the government not only contracts for R&D and facilitates the transfer of the developed technologies, but also addresses additional risks encompassing political, legal, and market ones. The viability of PPPs depends upon the extent to which the government reduces all these risks for the private sector. For example, the successful commercialization of telecommunication satellites, space launch vehicles, and remote sensing satellites in the United States became possible because the government not only contracted for the R&D of these technologies for its civil and military space use, but also facilitated the transfer of these technologies to the private sector, established laws that provide a licensing and regulatory regime, and promoted the development of markets that sustain these areas of space commercialization.

There are a number of PPP models encompassing governmental subsidies or ownership stakes, governmental relations with the private sector through contracting for hardware and services, and policies and laws that the government formulates and implements, which foster private sector development. The scope of PPP models include: (1) R&D based on governmental contracting ("contracting by negotiations"); (2) governmental purchasing and acquisition of commercial services and items ("acquisition of commercial items"); (3) technology transfer and licensing; (4) diffusion and sharing of technical knowledge; (5) intellectual property rights; (6) contractual rewards; (7) prizes for technology innovation; (8) subsidies; (9) loans, and tax benefits and credits; and (10) governmental corporate ownership.[1]

In this chapter, the first two models listed above are explored in the case study of commercial space launch in the United States. The first model entails negotiated contracts (between government and industry) for technology development and entails various applications of cost-plus contracting, fixed-price block buys (usually for services and not technology), competitive acquisitions, sole-provider acquisitions, and cost-sharing approaches. The second model is one where the government acquires technology (and services) as commercial items. With this commercial approach, funded and unfunded public-private agreements provide for government capital and expertise to private industry for technology development and operations. On this basis, operational launch vehicles, for example, are available for government use under fixed-price arrangements. The intent of the second model is to realize the goal of an "acceptable region" of meeting both governmental and commercial interests, and lowering risk for commercial development while realizing ROI as was explained earlier and shown in Fig. 1. ULA's Atlas V and Delta IV are assessed as examples of the first model, and SpaceX's Falcon 9 is presented as a case of the second model.

1 Eligar Sadeh and *et al.*, *Public Private Models for Lunar Development and Commerce,* Space Policy, 2005, vol. 21, pp. 267–275; J.A. Alic, *Policies for Innovation: Learning from the Past,* in V. Norborg-Bohm (ed.), *The Role of Government in Technology Innovation: Insights for Government Policy in the Energy Sector,* Belfer Center for Science and International Affairs, Harvard University, October 2002, pp. 21–36; Lewis Branscomb and Philip Aureswald, *Taking Technical Risks: How Innovators, Managers and Investors Manage Risk in High-Tech Innovation,* 2001 (Cambridge, MA: MIT Press); Joseph Corn (ed.), *Imagining Tomorrow: History, Technology and the American Future,* 1986 (Cambridge: MA: MIT Press); Michael H. Gron, *Harnessing the Genie: Science and Technology Forecasting for the Air Force, 1944-1986* (Washington D.C.: Office of Air Force History), 1988; and Vernon W. Ruttan, *Technology, Growth and Development: An Induced Innovation Perspective,* 2000 (Oxford University: Oxford University Press).

Contracting by Negotiations

Governmental contracting by negotiations for technology development is the traditional procurement and acquisition approach. In the government's traditional relationship with industry, the government pays for technology development on a cost-plus basis that covers total cost for industry, as well as an additional amount for industry profit. In this model, the government is responsible for cost overruns and schedule delays. Of note, approximately 90 per cent of the work effort on space programs and projects in the United States are contracted out to industry under this model. NASA and the U.S. Department of Defense (DoD) are the key government organizations in this regard.

There are extensive regulations in place for government oversight and compliance that directly affects development and management of space systems intended for government use, including space launch systems. These regulations are provided by U.S. Federal Acquisition Regulations (FAR), Part 15 (FAR 15), which imposes governmental legal requirements that must be followed by industry under strict supervision of civil servants.[2] Nevertheless, the government possesses limited insight into contractor costs since government contracting officers cannot require cost or pricing data even though the government is responsible for all costs, including cost overruns and schedule delays. This is a key issue since both NASA and DoD experience cost overruns and schedule delays in the majority of their programs as a result very often of governmental cost management that lacks the discipline needed to ensure that project life-cycle estimates are reasonable. Essentially, government within a context of the need for public value, as well as budgetary constraints and politics, underestimates costs. This leads to underfunding and cost overruns, placing programs at risk of being reduced in scope or requiring additional funding to meet their goals.[3]

2 Part 15-Contracting by Negotiations, available at <http://www.acquisition.gov/far/current/html/FARTOCP15.html> last visited 27 April 2016.

3 *NASA: Lack of Disciplined Cost-Estimating Processes Hinders Effective Program Management*, U.S. Government Accountability Office, GAO-04-642,

NASA counter-measures to these issues encompass more cost estimating management practices, “best practices,”[4] entailing full-cost accounting over the entire life-cycle development of programs and projects, placing cost management as a critical part of project management, strengthening center (e.g., cost analysis division at NASA Headquarters) and field center cost-estimating capabilities, and basing cost estimates on work breakdown structures that encompass both in-house and contractor efforts. To ensure implementation of these ‘best practices’, NASA developed project management guidelines for cost estimating that aligns costs in project management with accounting and budgeting, project life-cycle development, and risk assessments.[5]

In the case of DoD, acquisition management practices define ways in which the contracting by negotiation model is applied. DoD guidelines for acquisition policy, regulations, and management are the Defense Federal Acquisition Regulation Supplement (DFARS) and DoD Instruction (DoDI), known as DoDI 5000.02.[6] The most recent DoDI 5000.02 of 2013 establishes overall acquisition strategies and models with a focus on cost estimating and quality controls during systems development, operations, and sustainment. Overarching objectives of the 2013 DoDI, which updated and replaced the previous 2008 version, are to incorporate streamlined rules, emphasize program and project management process and

---

28 May 2004, available at <http://www.gao.gov/products/GAO-04-642> last visited 27 April 2016.

4 *GAO Cost-Estimating and Assessment Guide: Best Practices for Developing and Managing Capital Program Costs,* U.S. Government Accountability Office, GAO-09-3SP, March 2009, available at <http://www.gao.gov/new.items/d093sp.pdf> last visited 27 April 2016.

5 *2008 NASA Cost Estimating Handbook*, available at <http://www.nasa.gov/pdf/263676main_2008-NASA-Cost-Handbook-FINAL_v6.pdf> last visited 20 June 2016.

6 DFARS, available at <http://www.acq.osd.mil/dpap/dars/about_dfarspgi.html> last visited 20 June 2016; and Interim DoD Instruction 5000.02, Operation of the Defense Acquisition System, 25 November 2013. This instruction updates and replaces DoDI 5000.02 from 8 December 2008.

planning, put forward systems engineering guidelines, and provide product-tailored acquisition models.

Space systems are difficult to execute and easy to derail. In space program and project development, one must get everything right the first time as there are no recalls or second chances. This problem creates a potential for significant wasted resources and program and project failures. For the EELV program, for example, this led to an emphasis in project management to trade-off costs to achieve technical performance directed at "assured access to space" that the DoD requires.

Further, the development of military space assets exists within a "less money, more mission" environment. This leaves the U.S Government vulnerable to sharp programmatic cost increases from year-to-year as the budget for military space swings up and down with implications for programmatic continuity and sustainment. The DoD's Future Years Defense Program (FYDP) assessed that there exists a gap in resources between the demands placed on DoD's military space programs and the projected budgets for military space spending. In fact, there is the risk of cost growth with all DoD space programs and projects by as much as 40 per cent in any one year, and even risks of a doubling in costs over a five year period or longer.[7] In a U.S. Government Accountability Office's (GAO's) assessment of EELV, program costs are projected to be $70 billion through 2030, which are $35.7 billion more than the previous estimate from 2012.[8] "Several causes for this cost growth were identified including extension of the program life-

7 *The Long-Term Implications of Current Plans for Investment in Major Unclassified Military Space Programs,* U.S. Congressional Budget Office, 12 September 2005, available at <http://www.cbo.gov/sites/default/files/cbofiles/ftpdocs/66xx/doc6637/09-12-militaryspace.pdf> last visited 20 June 2016; and *Long-Term Implications of the 2014 Future Years Defense Program,* U.S. Congressional Budget Office, November 2013, available at <http://www.cbo.gov/sites/default/files/44683-FYDP.pdf> last visited 27 April 2016.

8 *Defense Acquisitions: Assessments of Selected Weapons Programs,* U.S. Government Accountability Office, GAO-14-340SP, March 2014, available at <http://www.gao.gov/assets/670/662184.pdf> last visited 27 April 2016.

cycle from 2020 to 2030, procurement of 60 additional launch vehicles, the inherently unstable nature of the demand for launch services, and space industrial base instability."[9]

In the acquisition management of space systems, escaping the "death spiral" is an essential challenge as shown in Fig. 2. This death spiral is a failure to achieve programmatic and project goals, avoid significant overcharges, and curb wasteful spending. In order to avoid these outcomes, program and project managers must be prepared to detect the distinct warning signs of impending failures, especially as to cost and technical performance, and to take management actions to confront them.

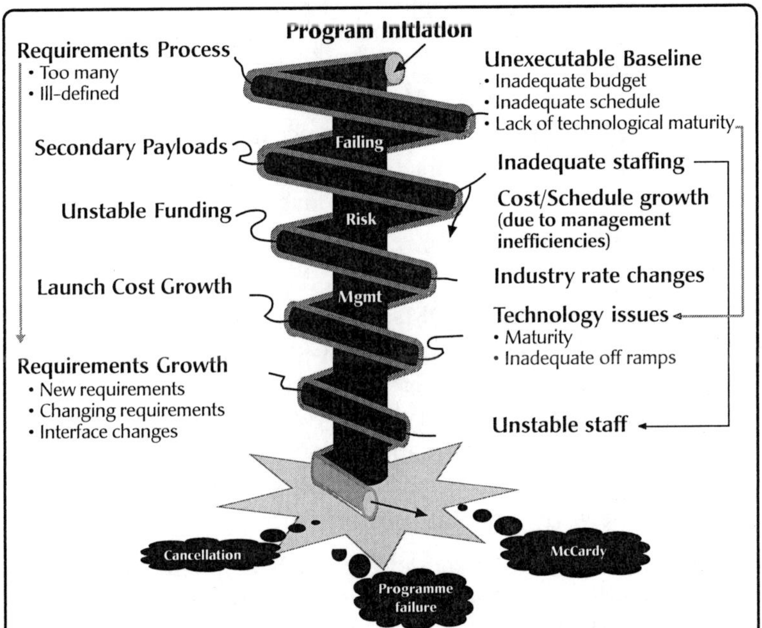

Fig. 2. Acquisition Death Spiral

SOURCE: "ESCAPING THE SPACE ACQUISITION DEATH SPIRAL", AIR FORCE SPACE COMMAND, AUGUST 2011

9 *Defense Acquisitions: Assessments of Selected Weapons Programs*, U.S. Government Accountability Office, GAO-14-340SP, March 2014, available at <http://www.gao.gov/assets/670/662184.pdf> last visited 27 April 2016.

In the EELV case, launch cost growth, as previously mentioned, is a key issue. Since the program was started in 1996, there exists a high degree of technology maturity and the program is in a sustainment phase since 2006 with initial operational capabilities achieved. In the system development process, there were shared costs between government and industry. Over the course of development, investments totaled $1 billion on the part of DoD and $4 billion to $6 billion on the part of ULA.

Costs for the EELV program until 2011 were largely managed under a "cost-as-an-independent-variable" (CAIV) model. CAIV allowed for project managers to trade-off costs to achieve technical performance directed at assured access to space; under CAIV, program acquisition unit costs for the EELVs grew by 358 per cent.[10] On the other hand, the EELV programs exhibits a near-perfect record of operational space launch including some of the heritage systems used beforehand. Although several anomalies in launch took place, the last outright launch failure took place in 1993.

DoDI 5000.02 and associated Acquisition Defense Memoranda of DoD (ADMs) institutionalized several key changes to address cost growth issues inherent with the EELVs and other major programs. First, a Better Buying Power model (BBP) aimed at "affordability" as a requirement that is on par with operations and performance was put into place. This model replaced CAIV with the intent to mitigate the trade-off of cost management with technical performance.

Second, a block buy model for EELV acquisitions of space launch services based on firm-fixed pricing was established; DoD acquired 36 launches from ULA in a block buy that covers 2012 to 2017. This replaced the procurement of single launch units used previously, albeit EELV launch capability (the rocket technology) continues to be acquired on cost-plus basis for the

10 R. Royce Kneece, *et al.*, *Implementing Effective Affordability Constraints for Defense Acquisition Programs*, Institute for Defense Analyses, IDA Paper P-5123, Alexandria, Virginia, March 2014.

36 core rocket boosters. Fixed-price contracting exhibits lower cost growth because of their application to more mature, lower-risk technology that characterizes the EELV program.[11] The combined approach in contracting for EELVs is highlighted in Table 1.

Table 1. Cost-Plus and Firm-Fixed EELV Contracting

	EELV Launch Capability	EELV Launch Services
Contract type	Cost-plus incentive fee.	Firm-fixed price.
Purpose	Acquire launch capability based on the strategy of assured access to space (requires a fixed, high-cost labor force).	To acquire launch hardware.
Terms covered by contract	Mission integration, systems engineering, production and management, propellants, transportation, and labor for launches.	Launch vehicle hardware, production, and direct labor.
Number of active contracts	One contract active at any time.	Multiple contracts.
Length of contract terms	Contract covers one year of launch capability.	Varies: contracts for one launch or multiple launches, and some contracts are for multiple years.

SOURCE: DEVELOPED BY AUTHOR

Third, in an effort to advance affordability, DoD established a model of competitive launches. The goal is to use competition to spur the development of additional technology, maintain performance excellence, and contain costs. DoD established management procedures for this approach (FAR 15 competitively negotiated source selections) based on a "best value" model that covers two approaches to a competitive

11 *Performance of the Defense Acquisition System, 2014 Annual Report,* U.S. Department of Defense, Under Secretary of Defense, Acquisition, Technology and Logistics, 13 June 2014, available at <http://www.acq.osd.mil/docs/Performance-of-Defense-Acquisition-System-2014.pdf> last visited 20 June 2016.

acquisitions strategy. The first one is trade-off source selection between non-cost and cost factors to account for other factors (not *per se* the lowest cost or the highest technical); and the second one is lowest price technically acceptable source selection that bases on selections primarily after cost assuming technical requirements are met.

The competitive model certification standards for DoD's space launches are stated in the New Entrants Certification Guide (NECG) issued in 2011. The NECG outlines the risk-based approach DoD uses to certify the capabilities of new launch companies to compete for DoD space launches. NECG adopts a common standard framework for certification based on NASA certification criteria for space launch services risk mitigation according to NASA Policy Directive (NPD) 8610.7D.[12] The NECG allows for DoD interpretation and certification requirements to differ as to number of launches to be competed (e.g., 14 are planned from 2012 to 2017), number of successful launches to be completed prior to certification (commercial launches are acceptable), standards for common space launch vehicle configurations that are acceptable, data and information sharing standards, and the overall order in which certification phases take place. DoD's launch directorate at the U.S. Air Force (USAF), Space and Missile Systems Center (SMC) is responsible for granting launch vehicle certification under NECG. The NECG certification covers a number of features.[13]

12 *Coordinated Strategy Among the United States Air Force, the National Reconnaissance Office and the National Aeronautics and Space Administration for New Entrant Launch Vehicle Certification* [undated memorandum of understanding], signed October 2011; and *Launch Services Risk Mitigation Policy for NASA-Owned and/or NASA-Sponsored Payloads/Missions*, NASA Policy Directive (NPD) 8610.7D, available at <http://nodis3.gsfc.nasa.gov/displayDir.cfm?t=NPD&c= 8610&s=7D> last visited 27 April 2016.

13 Phases are drawn from the NECG. The NECG document is unavailable to foreign governments due to U.S. export controls policies and laws. For insights on the NECG, see *Launch Services New Entrant Certification Guide*, U.S. Government Accountability Office, GAO-13-317R, 7 February 2013, available at <http://www.gao.gov/assets/660/652037.pdf> last visited 27 April 2016.

- Prior to NECG consideration, USAF must approve an implementation plan with schedules. Plans are realized through an approved Cooperative Research and Development Agreement (CRADA) between industry and USAF, and must include planned for capabilities to integrate national security payloads with the launch vehicle being considered for use.
- Based on the CRADA, which contains that vehicle's planned capabilities, a formal "Statement of Intent" to certify a vehicle is required. Capabilities must include at least 9000-kilogram (kg) low earth orbit (LEO) lift capacity and the capability to launch at Cape Canaveral Air Force Station and Vandenberg Air Force Base in California.
- Launch certification can occur following approval of milestones and completion of activities outlined in the NECG. New entrants submit a formal "certification plan" that outlines the tailored certification approach through which a new entrant intends to achieve certification.
- A separate certification plan and process is required for each launch vehicle configuration. Additionally, if a certified launch vehicle undergoes changes that "substantially affect" certain factors outlined in the NECG, such as operating time or engine thrust profile, that vehicle must re-enter the certification process from the beginning.

The NECG provides the standards of risk that are acceptable for certification. There are three risk categories drawn from NASA definitions based on NPD 8610.7D. These are defined as 1, 2, and 3 categories based on the risk associated with that vehicle, i.e. more risk with 1 and less risk with 3. To be certified for operational mission launch with the NECG a level 3 of risk is required, which represents the most proven, lowest risk launch vehicle. Risks for launch vehicles are also matched with payload risks. DoD operational mission launches represent Class A payloads that require category 3 with the space launch vehicle. Higher risk launch vehicles can launch for the DoD, but only with payloads that are of a technology demonstration type (non-essential to current military operations). Of note as well is that launch failures do not invalidate previous launch vehicle certification if an engineering review board concurs with cause and corrective actions are undertaken by industry on this basis.

Acquisition of Commercial Items

In contrast to the contracting model, there is government acquisition of commercial items for technology and services. The 1998 Commercial Space Act specified that commercial space transportation services be acquired as commercial items whenever the government requires such services. Current US National Space Transportation Policy (2013) and amendments to the Commercial Space Launch Act of 2004 established in US policy fostering the space transportation industrial base, as well as encouraging the promotion and development of a viable commercial space transportation industry for both cargo and crew.[14]

The policies and laws regarding commercial space transportation are implemented under FAR 12 regulations. These regulations define "commercial items" as those items that evolved under government solicitation and are used for non-governmental purposes in addition to governmental use. Key criteria important for commercial space launch under FAR 12 include the financial wherewithal of industry to develop and commercialize the items, in addition to technical merit and performance. FAR 12 regulations prescribe procedures for the acquisition of commercial items, which includes the use of firm-fixed price contracts and other provisions to streamline the acquisition process and regulatory framework. This political

14 *National Space Transportation Policy*, President of the United States, 21 November 2013; and *Commercial Space Launch Amendments Act of 2004*, available at <https://www.faa.gov/about/office_org/headquarters_offices/ast/media/PL108-492.pdf> last visited 27 April 2016.

and legal regime captures the dynamics of PPPs described earlier; namely, the goal of commercial space systems and programs realizing viable ROIs to support both governmental and commercial space activities.

Specific to commercial space launch, a performance oriented, fixed-price based approach under FAR 12 is used in combination with funded Space Act Agreements (SAAs) that NASA is administratively empowered to engage in by the National Aeronautics and Space Act of 1958 and subsequent congressional authorizations. Of note within this arrangement, is that additional work to meet performance criteria, including cost overruns, are borne by industry. In this SAA FAR 12 model, government payment is made to industry when performance is met by industry. NASA's Commercial Crew and Cargo programs are based on this approach.[15]

In NASA's Commercial Orbital Transportation Services (COTS) example (cargo program), performance milestones were established for design and development, test and production, and flight demonstrations covering external cargo delivery and disposal, internal cargo delivery and disposal, and internal cargo delivery and return. SAAs were applied for development[16] and FAR 12 contracting for LEO cargo transportation services to/ from the International Space Station (ISS). Benefits of the SAA FAR 12 model are stated below:

- Enables governmental portfolio investment in multiple, diverse commercial partners to reduce risks.

15 NASA Headquarters acknowledged this new way of business by revising NASA Policy Directive (NPD) 1000.5, the Policy for NASA Acquisition. This new approach required NASA to "consider the full spectrum of acquisition approaches", including procurement, grants, cooperative agreements and Space Act Agreements. See *Commercial Orbital Transportation Services*, NASA/SP-2014-617, February 2014, available at <http://www.nasa.gov/sites/default/files/files/SP-2014-617.pdf> last visited 27 April 2016.

16 NASA is not acquiring a good or service for the agency's direct benefit. Therefore, COTS is not traditional procurement; neither is it a grant nor a cooperative agreement often used when NASA provides funding to a university.

- Companies selected on the basis of NASA's level of confidence in their ability to meet both technical goals and execute business plans.
- Leverages NASA investment with additional company provided capital.
- Application of corporate based R&D.
- Enables known and limited cost and risk using pay-for-performance milestones. Governmental pay to industry is contracted and pre-negotiated, and remains fixed. Cost overruns are incurred by industry.
- Limited termination liability. NASA may not unilaterally terminate the agreements for its convenience (termination only for failure to perform). In this regard, scheduled delays and cost overruns are not causes for termination. The key aspect is technical progress that is acceptable to NASA.
- Mitigates cost impacts due to evolving requirements. SAA partnerships permit the evolution of system requirements as system development takes place.
- Compliance with top-level system performance, goals, and objectives.
- Companies are free to innovate and optimize their system per their capabilities, and apply management and life-cycle design methods. Commercial partners are responsible for the overall design, development, manufacturing, testing, and operation. NASA intentionally limits participation in the commercial programs to enable maximum use of innovative, cost-effective commercial practices. NASA's primary role is to monitor the progress through an assessment of the milestones and to make payment for successfully completed milestones. NASA provides and transfers expert technical assistance and technology as requested or where considered necessary.
- Discrete mode for oversight. Validation and verification of requirements are milestone, performance-based

("burden of proof" of demonstrated capability on industry).

- Enables streamlined and flexible acquisition processes (avoids the "death spiral" shown in Fig. 2).
- Simplifies program management and oversight with objective milestone success criteria.
- Use of informal day-to-day communications with partners.
- Reporting requirements are performance-milestone based and through key technical reviews (e.g., critical design reviews).
- Performance incentives to manage cost and schedule.
- Commercial-friendly intellectual property and data rights. Special provisions for minimal government retention, licensing and use of intellectual property developed by industry under agreements. Companies retain the benefit of their investment.
- U.S. Federal Aviation Administration (FAA) licensing, liability, indemnification, and enforcement. Given the commercial nature of space launch for NASA's Crew and Cargo program (i.e. not government activities), legal jurisdiction falls under the FAA. Congress and the FAA adopted a strategy to foster the commercial spaceflight sector—enforcing safety where necessary, but also remaining cognizant of the need to critically examine rules and regulations to foster and not hinder or constrain, commercial spaceflight.
- Since 1988, the government provided indemnification to commercial providers of launch services. In the case of an accident, the company will be only financially liable for what has been determined through the licensing process as "maximum probable loss." Any further amount will be the responsibility of the government. Both government indemnification and the moratorium on regulations are intended to encourage the industry and make companies successful and more competitive.

- The Commercial Space Launch (Amendments) Act 2004 included a "learning period" from 2004 to 2012 that limited the FAA's ability to impose regulations for crew and spaceflight participants, which the U.S. Congress extended. FAA also provides open lines of communication with industry representatives and coordinates closely with NASA Commercial Crew and Cargo Program.

Notwithstanding these benefits, the NASA Office of the Inspector General found in 2014 that NASA's use of SAAs lacked adequate transparency, accountability, and oversight. As a result, NASA agreed to revamp its procedures and policies for SAAs. Of concern, is an accounting for total costs and incorporating them in the closeout process for SAAs. Overall, there are four types of SAAs: (1) funded where NASA provides funding to its partner to undertake a program (e.g., commercial crew and cargo); (2) reimbursable where the partner reimburses NASA for all or part of the program; (3) non-reimbursable where NASA and its partners provide their own resources used for R&D projects; and (4) international used for establishing joint programs with foreign partners (though, NASA uses executive-level memoranda of understanding and intergovernmental agreements for international cooperation).

Essential to this model are streamlined regulatory and acquisition practices. This entails industry control on meeting performance criteria, i.e. "commercial partners, not NASA, establish their own requirements and are responsible for the design, development, and testing of their spacecraft;"[17]

17 NASA Headquarters acknowledged this new way of business by revising NASA Policy Directive (NPD) 1000.5, the Policy for NASA Acquisition. This new approach required NASA to "consider the full spectrum of acquisition approaches", including procurement, grants, cooperative agreements and Space Act Agreements. See *Commercial Orbital Transportation Services*, NASA/SP-2014-617, February 2014, available at <http://www.nasa.gov/sites/default/files/files/SP-2014-617.pdf> last visited 27 April 2016.

simplified documentation requirements, such as the development of COTS' Integration and Interface Requirements Document (IIRD) to allow for ISS support for cargo resupply; discrete reporting and oversight as technical or management issues arose and to support major performance-based technical reviews (versus a model of continuous reporting requirements and oversight); and protections of industry proprietary know-how and data.

In addition, NASA works to promote and foster the commercial industries in the COTS program. In this vein, NASA provides technical expertise and project management know-how. Such a transfer of knowledge was essential in the success of SpaceX with COTS. For example, SpaceX encountered in COTS schedule delays at more than two years. NASA helped SpaceX in several ways to address this issue. First, NASA showed flexibility and determined that the partnership would continue to exist as along as technical progress on key elements, like the Falcon 9, were evident. This drove accelerated technology development at SpaceX from the Falcon 1 to the Falcon 9 space launch vehicle in that SpaceX abandoned efforts for an intermediary approach with a Falcon 5 launch vehicle that it had originally planned on developing. Second, NASA directly influenced SpaceX management through the adoption of integrated schedules, more extensive documentation and configuration management processes, and improvements upon manufacturing processes.

Analogous to the COTS model of acquisitions management is NASA's Commercial Crew Development program (CCDev) that was initiated in 2009. CCDev is focused on developing vehicles and technologies needed for crew transportation to LEO for support of ISS by 2017-2018. The fundamental challenge relevant for space launch is to ensure crew safety, i.e. safety requirements continue to be met and there is an established process for continuous improvement towards achievement of the safety goal.

Given this challenge, NASA made use of traditional cost-plus acquisitions under FAR 15 for initial certification purposes

(Certification Products Contracts). The intent was to ensure a greater capacity for governmental oversight to engage in the certification of technologies for the safety of crew. Following this, the SAA FAR 12 model was used in similar fashion to COTS with initial SAAs for overall development followed by FAR 12 contracts for systems integration capabilities. CCDev phase 3 was completed in September 2014 with Commercial Crew Integrated Capabilities (CCICap) FAR 12 contract awards to SpaceX, which will make use of Falcon 9 for launch, and Boeing that plans to use the Atlas V.

Specific to the certification of human spaceflight for CCDev is NASA's Commercial Crew Transportation System Certification Requirements.[18] With crew safety as a principal requirement, a much more rigorous certification approach was applied as compared to COTS. These requirements are based on NASA's Procedural Requirements (NPR) 8705.2B, Human Rating Requirements for Space Systems. NASA certification of a human spaceflight system consists of four separate functions: (1) validation of the technical and performance requirements and standards; (2) verification of compliance with those requirements and standards; (3) consideration of relevant operational experience; and (4) acceptance of technical risks.

The relevant NASA Program Manager is responsible for ensuring that the operational and design certification requirements and standards are met through agreement milestones, statement of work, contract requirements, and engineering and operations plans. At the discretion of NASA, modifications to existing space systems along with the appropriate milestone reviews can be requested. The certification process can also be accelerated and milestones can be combined based on flight history and heritage of systems.

18 ESMD-CCTSCR-12.10 Revision-Basic, available at <http://www.nasa.gov/pdf/504982main_CCTSCR_Dec-08_Basic_Web.pdf> last visited 12 September 2016.

Further, NASA evaluates all design, manufacturing processes and testing to verify the mission falls within the bounds of the certification and that anomalies are addressed. Mission authorization takes place through flight readiness certification and acceptable risk. During the operations phase, NASA monitors safety performance by evaluating risk based on any observed anomalies and by updating independent assessments of safety performance.

Clearly, human rating of the space launch vehicles selected by industry to support CCDev, Falcon 9, and Atlas V, is required. Human rating involves meeting all of NASA's certification requirements. These requirements are met by adopting an integrated approach (launch vehicle and human spacecraft). Acceptable risk per the NASA Launch Vehicle Certification Requirements discussed earlier must be at a category 3. Both SpaceX and Boeing are meeting certifications by evaluating requirements with Falcon 9 and Atlas V designs. This entails critical design reviews demonstrating the design maturity of the system architect, i.e. the integrated human spacecraft, launch vehicles, and ground systems.

Lessons

The analysis herein probed the dynamics regarding the development of space launch systems in the United States on the basis of PPPs. The effective use of the PPP model of "acquisition of commercial items" illustrates how traditional approaches rooted in government contracting for technology development can be augmented. This commercially oriented model further demonstrates how government can transfer capital and expertise to private industry for technology development and operations. In turn, commercial operations can then be applied for government use under fixed-price arrangements. Table 2 summarizes how the PPP models of contracting by negotiations and acquisition of commercial items apply to the cases of EELVs and the Falcon 9.

Table 2. Public Private Models and Space Launch in the United States

<table>
<tr><th>PPP Model</th><th>Activity</th><th>Results</th></tr>
<tr><td>Contracting byNegotiations</td><td>EELV program development with dynamic acquisition strategies (cost-plus contracting, fixed-price block buys for services, competitive acquisitions, sole-provider acquisitions, and cost-sharing approaches).</td><td>Assured access for national security space assets achieved with EELV development with technical excellence (no launch failures with current EELV systems). Cost management issues led to block buy approach in acquisitions and a strategy of competitive acquisitions.</td></tr>
<tr><td rowspan="3">Acquisition ofCommercial Items</td><td>NASA Commercial Crew and Cargo Program.</td><td>NASA's Commercial Crew and Cargo Program is achieving success.</td></tr>
<tr><td>Falcon 9 for crew and cargo.

Atlas V with process of human rating.

Space Act Agreements.</td><td>NASA's Commercial Orbital Transportation Services program led to the successful development of commercial cargo services to LEO and the ISS by Space X. One successful result is a services contract between Space X and NASA to provide cargo transport to ISS (two additional service contracts are in place with Orbital ATK and Sierra Nevada Corporation).</td></tr>
<tr><td>Commercial services contracts.</td><td>NASA's Commercial Crew Program (CCP) is directed to Commercial Crew Development (CCDev) and Commercial Crew Integrated Capabilities (CCICap). CCDev phase 3 is complete and CCICap contract awards to SpaceX and Boeing.</td></tr>
</table>

SOURCE: DEVELOPED BY AUTHOR

Key lessons for national governments aspiring to develop commercially viable space industries lie less in the specifics of the U.S. case study as to the PPP models and more in the ways in which government structures the political, legal, and regulatory environment, and addresses capital, market, and technical risks inherent in any commercial project. A fundamental challenge facing space commerce today, with the exception of satellite-based telecommunications, is that market forces on their own are inadequate for space commercialization. This fact serves to highlight the critical importance and role of government in PPPs directed at space commerce. The chapter here demonstrated that an effective role is linked to a robust legal regime to facilitate optimal outcomes for both government and industry.

In the case of India, Antrix Corporation is illustrative. Government corporate ownership is the applicable PPP model as Antrix is a wholly government owned Indian company under the administrative control of the Indian Department of Space and Indian Space Research Organization. Relevant lessons from the analysis in this chapter suggest that a broadening of policy and legal frameworks are useful to foster greater levels of private investment and commercial participation in Indian space activities. This suggests a mixed use of the PPP models listed earlier and exhibited in this chapter. One strategy on the path to this end that worked effectively is that of off-loading governmental administrative and management control of space commercial activities to industry. This places the burden for program and project development on industry, allows industry to own and operate systems independent of government, encourages industry innovation and new practices for management and technology development, and facilitates greater levels of private capital.

Conclusions

The role of governmental, technical, capital, market, and business factors presented in this chapter offer approaches for commercial development on the basis of PPPs. The factors address the critical issues of risk and ROI. Ultimately, the viability of the PPPs depends on the extent to which ROI is greater than risk. The risks highlighted include political and legal risks; technological risks; and financial and market risks. The nature of the risks is identified and solutions for mitigation of risks were offered through the chapter in the case of commercial space launch in the United States. Neither the public sector nor the private sector independent of each other is likely to sustain successful commercial development; to realize this goal will take the combined efforts of both sectors. The more these efforts are synergistic, the more the risks can be alleviated and the more that commerce can remain viable.

It is vital for national governments to recognize and implement a far larger presence of the private industry in space development and activities. In this context, contractual authority must be bestowed to national governments for the purpose to reach broadly into the commercial communities. Further, national policy and law needs to provide incentives for entrepreneurial investment in space by creating and considering alternative models of commercial development, such as suggested herein. An obvious assumption is that national governments must collaborate with private industry. This is vital as the space industry is a major driver of new technology development and one source of competitive advantage in global markets. The insights from this study are useful for governmental policy-makers to craft the new business models needed to sustain and advance space industry both nationally and globally.

Chapter 3

Extraterrestrial Habitation and Space Law —A Socio-Legal Perspective

SOHINI BANERJEE*

Introduction

At the outset, let's talk a bit about the *The Martian*[1] – a 2015 American science fiction film based on Andy Weir's 2011 novel 'The Martian'. In the critically acclaimed movie, Matt Damon stars as an astronaut who is presumed dead and left behind on mars by mistake. The film depicts his struggle to survive and others' efforts to rescue him. Realising that he has enough food to last only 300 sols (roughly 309 days), Watney, a botanist, improvises a farm with Martian soil fertilized with human waste, water produced by extracting hydrogen from leftover rocket fuel then oxidized by burning, and potatoes saved for a Thanksgiving meal. He begins to modify the only functional rover, i.e. space exploration vehicle to make long journeys across mars. But who knows, this may become the regular way of life for many humans who decide to settle in space or other habitable landmass in space as soon as the next decade.

* LLM (Cantab), Assistant Professor, IISWBM, Kolkata. Guest Lecturer, Department of Law, University of Calcutta.

1 The Martian (film), available at <https://en.wikipedia.org/wiki/The_Martian_(film)>.

Space awes us. Space law deals with a wealth of issues – some are inchoate and some are strictly legal.[2] As we know, the space above earth may be divided into airspace and outer space. No State is authorised under any treaty to regulate the use of outer space. The boundary between the two regimes of airspace and outer space is as uncertain as the border between the territorial sea and the high seas in former decades. No composite agreement or codification exists on this.[3]

While Andy Weir's cornerstone entitled "The Martian" offers a vanguard insight into extraterrestrial habitation, legal issues raised by it can by no means be dismissed. Freedom of domicile or occupation is our constitutional right. This chapter proposes to explore the territorial notions of a sovereign State *vis-a-vis* outer space, national policies regarding the ownership of immovable property in outer space. Will these parcels of invaluable land cause a paradigm shift in the international markets on real estate? What are the legal consequences of having a permanent address in outer space? Would we require a slew of new legislations on conveyancing issues, and contractual law which must arise? Just like we have the international maritime law, will this new dimension in outer space entail newer legislations? Also is this going to lead to the genesis of a 'private space' industry and its *inter alia* leanings and trappings? What could be the possible sociological fallouts? Also what about the mechanism for accommodating various nationalities in this limited sphere? Will India be required to be a signatory to a fresh Outer Space Treaty, should this, as per Late Hon'ble President Abdul Kalam's vision soon become a reality in 2020? The colonisation of space by human beings is not a distant dream any more.

Today India is among the five countries that do not have a dedicated space law.

2 Nandasiri Jasentuliyana (ed.), *Space Law: Development and Scope*, 1992, p. 2 (Westport, Connecticut, London: Praeger).
3 D. Goedhuis, *Some Trends in the Political and Legal Thinking on the Conquest of Space*, Netherlands International Law Review, 1962, vol. 9, Issue 2, pp. 113–136.

But commercialisation and privatisation of outer space are issues conducive to national space legislation with a special focus upon acquisition of property. A slew of international space agreements which are beyond the comprehension of a layman, a few Articles from the Constitution of India, national laws, the Satellite Communications (SatCom) Policy of 2000, the revised Remote Sensing Data Policy of 2011 failed to raise the bar.

We might also recollect how a claim of sovereignty were made by some equatorial States over some parts of geostationary orbit above the earth.[4] This demand was summarily cancelled by the important space-faring nations. However, such dangers of one-sided claims to orbital regions near the earth do exist. But a consensus is lacking. But till now, no precedent of interception of spacecraft of one State by another when its flight path crosses the airspace of another has been noted. The Outer Space Treaty of 1967[5] cancelled the prospective of brightline zones. Flights in outer space occur through the atmosphere, orbit, deep space and celestial bodies; the areas merge.

But even then, a space station with a crew on the moon or one in permanent planetary orbit requires a separate legislation governing their status. What is the status of the space workers residing therein for long durations for work purposes? What if some of them wish to stay on along with a family? What if the instrumentalities of State and transfer of property decide to become a part of their existence? The question in such a possible scenario is, whether the freedom of trade and commerce should be a listed freedom in such a culture of space-oriented enterprise. As it is a customary law, or even an offshoot of public international law, how it should be reconciled with say, an Indian

4 Declaration of the First Meeting of Equatorial Countries (Bogota), 1976, by Brazil, Colombia, Congo, Ecuador, Indonesia, Kenya, Uganda and Zaire.

5 Treaty on Principles Governing the Activities of States in the Exploration and Use of Outer Space, including the Moon and other Celestial Bodies, Done at Washington, London and Moscow, 27 January 1967. Entered into Force on 10 October 1967, 18 UST 2410, TIAS No. 6347, 610 UNTS 205 (the Outer Space Treaty).

national establishing proprietary right over immovable property on a planet. Commerce is already percolating outer space. Private enterprise and free trade doctrines which inhere in the law of the sea may not be agreeable to a coexistent culture. Also the freedom of exploration that inheres in the Outer Space Treaty is not consonant with the concept of property acquisition. This again raises the issue of the freedom of access *vis-a-vis* a possible transfer of property in future. Article 9(2) of the Moon Agreement provides that, "Stations shall be installed in such a manner that they do not impede the free access to all areas of the moon ...". Again, Article XII of the Outer Space Treaty advocates open visitation on a reciprocal basis. A separate legislation is required to ratify concepts of ownership and possession envisaged by the various Acts on the Transfer of Property. The Indian Government may affect an extraterrestrial application of an existing legislation through a Central notification. It is suggested that States should not, however, make similar notifications as a subterfuge for monopolising and earmarking strategic positions for space stations.

It is evident that a private space habitat industry is not so far away. Soon, with advancements in science and technology, billions of people would be able to maintain a permanent residence outside the periphery of earth. As a legal concept, the freedom of domicile includes our constitutional right to choose where we want to live. But outer space is unfettered as far as the political limitations that govern State boundaries on this earth are concerned. Also a limited application of the concept of sovereignty may be a healthy option as far as the real estate scenario in space is concerned although the strict earthly territorial concerns may be diluted a bit.

Extraterrestrial Real Estate and the Law

Extraterrestrial real estate is defined as land on other planets or pockets of outer space that is officially sold through organizations, websites or individuals. This is not recognized by any authority. A few private individuals and organizations have claimed ownership of celestial bodies like the moon. Many are 'selling' parcels of celestial land through certificates of ownership termed as Lunar Deeds, Martian Deeds etc without any legal corroboration whatsoever.

Article VI of the Outer Space Treaty states that "The activities of non-governmental entities in outer space, including the moon and other celestial bodies, shall require authorization and continuing supervision by the appropriate State Party to the Treaty." The role and stance of the national governments therefore become very crucial in this case.[6]

Ownership of arbitrary parcels of outer space is a dicey issue as boundaries are inchoate on empty land. However, the national governments remain at liberty to dispute this.

Take the case-study of the website <https://www.lunarland.com>.[7] It states that: "LunarLand.com was formed for the direct marketing of real estate for Land on the Moon. As premier authorized agents of the International Association of Human Planetary Exploration (IAOHPE), our team of professionals is driven to make your purchase of Moon property a most pleasant and rewarding experience. Lunar Land is dedicated in keeping you up to date with the latest information concerning your purchase as well as special offers brought to you only by LunarLand.com. All records of Lunar Land Registry will be stored at the International Association of Human Planetary Exploration (IAOHPE)." It is known that they have no paucity of clients.

Many opt to call such a propensity to acquire extraterrestrial real estate as a rush for the New Atlantis.

In a similar vein, websites like <http://www.spacesettlement.org/> state with a dissipated state of mind: "Efforts to develop space settlements have almost stopped, primarily because no one has a sufficient reason to spend the billions of dollars needed to develop safe, reliable, affordable transport between the Earth and the Moon. Neither Congress

6 Status of international agreements relating to activities in outer space as at 1 January 2005, United Nations Office for Outer Space Affairs.

7 See <https://www.lunarland.com/> last visited 21 January 2017.

nor the taxpayers wants the government stuck with that expense. Private venture capital will support such expensive and risky research and development ONLY if success could mean a multi-billion dollar profit. Today, there is no profit potential in developing space transport, but we have the power to change that.

We have the power to create a "pot of gold" waiting on the Moon, to attract and reward whatever companies can be the first to assemble and risk enough capital and talent to establish an airline-like, Earth-Moon "space line" and lunar settlement. How? By making it possible for a settlement to claim and own — and re-sell to those back home on earth — the product that has always rewarded those who paid for human expansion: land ownership.

Lunar and Martian real estate is currently worthless. But that real estate will acquire enormous value after there is a settlement, regular commercial access, and a system of space property rights. Lunar or Martian property ownership could then be bought and sold back on earth, raising billions of dollars. This is a plan to be sure that money is used as an incentive and reward for those who invest in a way to get there and stay there."[8]

But the question is should there not be a national legislation in place to rein in such transactions which are in every way no different from our average real estate transactions?

The Legal Picture in the Indian Context–Article 246

No documentation whatsoever is necessary to stay aboard a spacecraft. No natural right is created therein. Any creature in the universe may avail of that status without any fetter whatsoever. No new law is required for this.

But mars and some other celestial bodies like the moon have become conducive to human settlement today. Occupancy creates a right *in rem* on unclaimed territory. As time progresses,

8 See <http://www.spacesettlement.org/> last visited 21 January 2017.

the States may want to start a campaign for individual sovereignty in space. Without compromising strategic interests, this raises the question that as people clearing forest land first are the first claimants to the proprietorship of the land, why will not this hold true for acquisition of property in space as well. Space tourism and sponsorship of space expeditions; do these give actual weightage to the nations sponsoring them?

In relation to property acquired by Indian subjects for settlement in space, in conformity with Article 246, List I, 7th Schedule of the Constitution of India which speaks on foreign jurisdiction [Article 246(16)] and the issue of entering into treaties and agreements with foreign countries and the implementing of treaties, agreements and conventions with foreign countries [Article 246(14)] as well as citizenship, naturalisation and aliens [Article 246(17)] – the Indian Parliament through due process of law, may make a residuary entry into Central legislations into property related laws and extend their jurisdiction into space.

Also some laws, for example the Hindu Succession Act 1956 or the Special Marriage Act 1954 operates even beyond the geographical boundaries of the country.

Written documentation and conveyancing of deeds and agreements may be in harmonisation with the prevalent provisions of the Transfer of Property Act 1882 which today extends all over India with the exception of the States of Jammu and Kashmir.

Historically, we have seen how the East India Company came to work in India with a Charter from the Queen of England extending authority to the company to carry on trade and commerce. The supreme authority lay vested with the Queen of England in the instant case.

It is today a quintessential truth that the placement of space vehicles and space stations as well as strategic scientific instruments or satellite radio transmitters should be controlled.

Today an international agreement on delimitation of certain restrictive domestic laws must also be practised to elaborate on future developments and justified legal procedures in international space law. This could be the harbinger of future laws on the ambulation of mankind in space.

Otherwise, what are the wherewithals of commercial utilisation of outer space[9]?

Emerging Legal Issues and Concerns

With the not so far away reality of human habitation in space arises the associated issue of space debris and the strong urge to protect the fragile space environment. Why should the pristine space or other celestial bodies become as ravaged as our planet earth? The United Nations should soon develop some practices and recommendations that States must follow. For example, what should be the accepted standard of behaviour of the State?

Also property acquisition on the moon, space or other celestial bodies should not lead to the militarisation of that space. The actions of the Committee on the Peaceful Uses of Outer Space of the United Nations should be charted out more clearly and set a path for all.

Again, *'Bona Vacantia'* means vacant goods and is the name given to ownerless property, which by law passes to the Crown, and in India as per Article 296 of the Constitution of India, to the State. But in the case of space law, which nation can lay its claims on such unclaimed property or materials?

The legal sub-committee of United Nations Committee on the Peaceful Uses of the Outer Space (UNCOPUOS), the Outer Space Treaty, the Moon Agreement, Rescue Agreement, Liability Convention and Registration Convention cancelled the spirit of *res nullis* which would have treated the outer space as "unclaimed territory" available for conquest. Such an agreement would allow nations to peremptorily claim ownership of the celestial bodies if they were the first to reach and preclude access to all others. Rather, outer space is *res communis* where

9 The case of the *S.S. Lotus* (*France* v *Turkey*), Permanent Court of International Justice, PCIJ Ser A. No. 10, 2, Hudson, World Ct Rep. 20 (1927).

all entities, individual or corporate, and nations have common or open access to the natural resources contained within and are precluded from making any claims of ownership. The non-national appropriation of outer space and *res communis omnium* are just like faded daguerreotypes today.

It is also being argued by some dissidents that the exploitation of resources of the moon or other celestial bodies has not begun as yet due to the lack of specific rules establishing how such exploitation will take place and what are the rights and duties of the parties involved.[10]

But sovereignty and property belong to different branches of law.[11]

Article II of the Outer Space Treaty in express terms bans any national appropriation or claim of sovereignty, use or occupation by any country for personal gain. But it says nothing about private ownership of celestial bodies. The Moon Agreement opposes any kind of privatization of the moon and other celestial bodies by even an individual under Article 11. But only a few UN Members ratified it.

Again, the International Law Association (ILA) during its 49th Conference adopted a resolution which stated, *inter alia* about the legal regime in outer space, "Outer space and celestial bodies should be utilised only for practical purposes to the greatest common profit of all mankind in accordance with the principles of the United Nations Charter". It also significantly stated: "Outer space may not be subject to the sovereignty or other exclusive rights of any State."

Conclusion

At present, we have two Acts – the Aircraft Act 1934 to be read with the Aircraft (Amendment) Act 2007 (44 of 2007) and the Carriage by Air Act 1972 which do not say anything about legal

10 Fabio Tronchetti, *The Exploitation of Natural Resources of the Moon and Other Celestial Bodies – A Proposal for a Legal Regime*, 2009, p. 3 (Leiden: Martinus Nijhoff).

11 *Ibid.*

principles governing the space area of the Indian territory. Thence, we require a separate legislation demarcating the extreme boundary limits from the skyline into space covering space travel issues. Concomitant to the above developments, a suitable Insurance Act for the travellers to the moon or mars should be brought into being.

Again, if any portion of moon or mars is occupied by the Indians there should be a law regarding the vesting of the property and the right of extraction or exploitation of the valuable substances like rich uranium and thorium which are said to be available on the moon. Mythologically, 'Chandrajal' or 'moon-water' is available and blessed with nectar-like qualities. But scientifically it is yet to be discovered. Similarly the area of mars or moon or any other planet which shall be touched and occupied by Indian vehicles or any Indian–this should be the vested property of the Indian Government and not any private individual.

Since the establishment of the Committee on the Peaceful Use of Outer Space, the United Nation has become the centrifugal force for the development of space law and its principles through a consensual process of laws and principles. It has collated an international force of leading technical experts on space law and diplomats, and legal scholars to device an acceptable legal framework for space activities. Its membership has increased exponentially. In fact it has been now accepted that law making should focus upon specific areas of space applications and space technology rather than just some principles of public international law or *jus cogens* analogies from international maritime law.

There should also be a vesting of the property which would be acquired through expeditions to the moon and mars. Primarily, such property should be made government property and thereafter suitable legislations like the Transfer of Property Act should be made for allotment and distribution of this valuable property to the Indian people.

Following the model of the Transfer of Property Act, in the legislation there shall be suitable provisions for making compulsory instruments for transfer of interest in the property concerned. Any instrument thereof should be made compulsorily registrable by appropriate registration laws like the Indian Registration Act 1908. Automatically, if these properties in space are made transferable, mortgage sale hypothecation and charge lease lien issues will also follow. And these should be treated to be an attachable property in the Court of Law.

Also, it would be quite helpful if the Secretary-General of the United Nations maintains a register of scientific efforts by nations towards extraterrestrial habitation and monitors the same closely. The degree of liability in case any damage occurs due to such efforts by a nation or group of nations should also be noted.

As scientific and technological advancements lead to a genesis of new opportunities, policy and law should follow suit as new developments in civilian space programs occur.

But with new affordable spaceflight technologies on the rise, extensive private activity in space, space commercialisation and space tourism may be expected to become new benchmarks of space law in near future. The United Nations Committee on Peaceful Uses of Outer Space (COPUOS) also ratified this mandate.[12]

And ultimately, the goal is to reduce friction internationally and nationally with a multidisciplinary understanding. It is also a home truth that the enactment of specific legislation for space-related activities is concomitant upon legal requirements which may vary and not necessarily be proportionate to the space programmes of different nations. Any hypothesis on the future of space law should also not omit municipal laws. Finally, agreements for sharing the astronomical costs between countries in the context of the topic may not be too uncommon.

In fact this was the common resolution of the International Space Year (ISY)-1992 which resolved to dilute sepia perspectives. Why not once more we ask?

12 D. Goedhuis, *Some Trends in the Political and Legal Thinking on the Conquest of Space*, Netherlands International Law Review, 1962, vol. 9, Issue 2, pp. 113–136.

Chapter 4

Regulatory Mechanism for the Exploitation of Natural Resources in Outer Space and Celestial Bodies

ARINDRAJIT BASU*

Introduction

The alluring prospects of outer space together with unforeseen technological developments indicate clearly that the twenty-first century will undoubtedly witness the widespread commercial utilization of outer space. While there has been scientific and strategic interest in the utilization of outer space for the past five decades, we are now at a juncture where large-scale exploration may be possible within the next five years. This increasingly probable prospect compels the international community to arrive at a prevailing consensus on the laws and regulations that will govern the equitable use of outer space once this exploitation becomes a reality. In the absence of a robust, clear and comprehensive international mechanism, developed space-faring nations may be able to impose their writ on this shared space to the detriment of developing countries who do not share similar space-faring capacities.

* Final Year, BA, LLB (Hons), The West Bengal National University of Juridical Sciences, Salt Lake, Kolkata.

Indeed, when the Outer Space Treaty[1] came into force in 1967, space exploration was in its infancy. Technological advancements in the years since have prompted calls for an amendment to the Treaty to respond this altered reality.[2] Further, ambiguity in the drafting of the provisions of the Outer Space Treaty which this chapter attempts to clarify has facilitated the abrogation of its core tenets. While international law does not exist in a vacuum and must respond to geo-political developments, the core principles making up the edifice of a body of law cannot be completely altered or significantly compromised. The overarching goal of the Outer Space Treaty remains the unfettered exploration and use by all States of outer space, including the moon and other celestial bodies, as the 'common heritage of mankind'. Keeping this core principle in mind, this chapter seeks to develop legal mechanism that does justice to the intention of the drafters of the treaty while adapting a functional interpretation that does not unduly threaten the exploitation of outer space.

This chapter is divided into four parts. The first part provides a brief primer on the recent legal and technological developments in outer space. These developments lay the foundations for the legal and regulatory framework detailed in the other sections of the chapter. The second part looks at how, in response to these developments, the ambiguous wording of certain provisions of the Outer Space Treaty has been used to contradict its key tenets. This section deconstructs the arbitrary physical classification of space resources and advocates a uniform functional interpretation that is in line with the core principles espoused in the Preamble of the Treaty. The third part considers the extension of property rights to outer space as a possibility

1 Treaty on Principles Governing the Activities of States in the Exploration and Usage of Outer Space, Including the Moon and Other Celestial Bodies, 1967 [hereinafter the Outer Space Treaty].

2 Brandon C. Gruner, *A New Hope for International Space Law: Incorporating Nineteenth Century First Possession Principles into the 1967 Space Treaty for the Colonization of Outer Space in the Twenty-first Century*, Seton Hall Law Review, 2004, vol. 35, No. 1, p. 299.

in light of increasing technological exploration and concludes that ownership should be confined to infrastructure constructed in outer space. The last part proposes a regulatory framework that uses the theoretical constructions laid down previously in this chapter. The said mechanism has three interlinked components, all of which are integral to the sustaining of the overall mechanism. These components include (1) an Inter-Governmental Authority akin to the International Seabed Authority; (2) a credit-trading system for the allocation of resource appropriation rights and (3) vesting of limited property rights as per the International Space Model. The model seeks to facilitate the exploration of outer space while paying deference to the core tenets of its fair and equitable use.

Recent Developments in the Commercial Space Sector

Recent studies have proved the presence of a variety of lucrative natural resources in outer space.[3] Helium-3 (He-3), found in abundance on the moon is one example as a substance that has more potential for providing clean, efficient energy than any substance available on earth.[4] A single space shuttle load of He-3 could supply the energy reserves required for the United States for one year.[5] Further research done by NASA has found that 1,500 asteroids are within easy reach of earth. A house-sized asteroid may contain metals that worth millions of dollars.[6] It is therefore no surprise, that both government and private companies are in a bid to hastily enter the race for these resources.[7]

3 Harrison Schmitt, *Return to the Moon: Exploration, Enterprise and Energy in the Human Settlement of Space*, Ed. 2006, pp. 44 (New York: Copernicus).

4 Mark Williams, *Mining the Moon*, available at <http://www.technologyreview.com/Energy/19296> last visited 6 May 2016.

5 Kelly M. Zullo, *The Need to Clarify the Status of Property Rights in International Space Law*, Geo L, 2002, vol. 90, pp. 2413 at p. 2434.

6 NASA, "Study: Asteroids Provide Sustainable Resource", available at <https://www.nasa.gov/mission_pages/asteroids/news/asteroidmining.html#.Vy3dQIR97IU> last visited 6 May 2016.

7 Bryon C. Brittingham, *Does the World Really Need New Space Law,* Oregon Review of International Law, vol. 12, pp. 31–53.

Recently, Luxembourg has partnered with Deep Space Industries owned by billionaire entrepreneur. Paul Diamand is to mine highly valuable asteroids.[8] This project, known as Prospector-X is expected to become operational by 2020.[9] Several corporations such as Virgin Galactic, Space Exploration Technologies and Bigelow Aerospace have the technical and financial clout to commercially exploit space soon.[10] Since its inception, space entrepreneurship has received the endorsement of both the government and the public sector.[11] The Obama Administration in the United States has actively supported the development of a burgeoning commercial space sector, as reflected in the 2010 National Space Policy.[12]

Such commercial developments require the evolution of international law that is receptive to these changes. In the absence of a regulatory mechanism, nations may seek to abrogate key tenets of the Outer Space Treaty while devising their space policy or municipal legislation. A recent example of such legislation is the Spurring Private Aerospace Competitiveness and Entrepreneurship Act, which was passed by the U.S. Congress in November 2015 (SPACE Act 2015).[13] The Act explicitly permits the States to engage in the exploitation of

8 Clive Cookson, *Luxembourg Boldly goes into Asteroid Mining,* available at <https://next.ft.com/content/e8e95cf8-12a6-11e6-91da-096d89bd2173> last visited 6 May 2016.

9 Charles Poladian, *Asteroid Mining News: Luxembourg Partners with Deep Space Industries for Prospector-X Mission,* available at <http://www.ibtimes.com/asteroid-mining-news-luxembourg-partners-deep-space-industries-prospector-x-mission-2364780> last visited 6 May 2016.

10 Jack Duffy, *New Mission for American Aerospace Giants,* available at <http://www.nytimes.com/2010/07/19/business/global/19iht-ravspace.html> last visited 6 May 2016.

11 Arindrajit Basu and Arthad Kurlekar, *Highway to the Danger Zone: United States Legislative Framework Regulating the Commercial Space Sector,* Astropolitics, 2016, vol. 14(1), p. 44 at p. 60.

12 Executive Office of the President, National Space Policy of the United States of America, 2010, available at <http://www.whitehouse.gov/sites/default/files/national_space_policy_6-28-10.pdf> last visited 6 May 2016.

13 Space Resource Exploration and Utilization Act 2015, USC §51301.

outer space. Section 51303 (*a*) of the Space Resource Exploration and Utilization Act 2015 controversially states that "any asteroid resources obtained in outer space are the property of the entity that obtained such resources, which shall be entitled to all property rights thereto, consistent with the applicable provisions of Federal Law and existing international obligations."[14] Read together the two provisions clearly violate the non-appropriation principle enmeshed in Article II of the Outer Space Treaty 1967. Still, a lack of clarity in the Treaty prevents the legislation from being rendered entirely in violation of international law. The passage of such a legislation in the country with the world's most robust commercial space industry calls out the need for a clear analysis of the core principles contained in the Outer Space Treaty and a comprehensive legal regime.

Theoretical Analysis of the Existing Legal Regime on Non-Appropriation

Primer on Existing Legal Regime

The existing international law framework preventing the appropriation of outer space is largely provided for in provisions of the Outer Space Treaty 1967 and the Moon Agreement.[15] The Outer Space Treaty, negotiated in 1967 serves as the edifice for all development in space law and policy.[16] Fittingly, it has been described as the *Magna Carta* of Space.[17] It comprises of seventeen articles which deals with issues of sovereignty, liability, safety, information disclosure, cooperation, exploration, use and militarization on outer space[18] and celestial bodies.[19] The Treaty

14 Space Resource Exploration and Utilization Act 2015, USC §51303 (*a*).

15 Agreement Governing the Activities of States on the Moon and Other Celestial Bodies, 1979, [hereinafter the Moon Agreement].

16 Robert A. Ramey, *Armed Conflict on the Final Frontier: The Law of War in Space,* Air Force Law Review, 2000, vol. 48, No. 1, pp. 74, Ramey calls the OST the "Constitution of Outer Space".

17 Francis Lyall and Paul Larsen, *Space Law: A Treatise,* 2009 (Ashgate).

18 Adam G. Quinn, *The New Age of Space Law: The Outer Space Treaty and the Weaponization of Space,* Minnesota Journal of International Law, 2008, vol. 17, p. 475 at p. 482.

19 Michael N. Schmitt, *International Law and Military Operations in Space,* Max Planck Yearbook of International Law, 2006, vol. 10, No. 1, p. 90.

has been widely accepted by the international community and at present has 103 signatories.[20] The Preamble of the Treaty highlights the 'prospects' and the 'common interest of mankind' while simultaneously stressing on the equitable exploration and use of outer space by all nations irrespective of their economic capabilities.[21] Article I re-affirms the objectives stated in the Preamble by stating that "The exploration and use of outer space, including the Moon and other celestial bodies, shall be carried out for the benefit and in the interests of all countries, irrespective of the degree of economic or scientific development, and shall be the province of all mankind."[22] Paragraph 2 of the Article I goes on to state that "Outer Space, including the Moon and other celestial bodies shall be free for exploration and use by all States [...] on a basis of equality [...] and there shall be free access to all areas of celestial bodies." Article II embodies the non-appropriation principle and states that "Outer space, including the Moon and other celestial bodies, is not subject to national appropriation by claim of sovereignty, by means of use or occupation, or by any other means." Essentially, the non-appropriation principle disallows any nation from claiming by any means any part of space or celestial body as their own. Article IX embodies a nuisance provision and provides that "In the exploration and use of outer space, including the Moon and other celestial bodies, States [...] shall be guided by the principle of co-operation and mutual assistance and shall conduct all their activities [...] with due regard to the corresponding interests of all other State Parties to the Treaty..."

In stark contrast to the widely accepted Outer Space Treaty, the Moon Agreement has been recognised only by 16 States.[23]

20 United Nations Office for Disarmament Affairs, "Treaty on Principles Governing the Activities of States in the Exploration and Use of Outer Space, including the Moon and other Celestial Bodies", available at <http://disarmament.un.org/treaties/t/outer_space> last visited 6 May 2016.

21 *See* Bin Cheng, *Studies in International Space Law,* 1997 (Clarendon Press).

22 The Outer Space Treaty, Article I.

23 United Nations Office for Disarmament Affairs, available at <http://disarmament.un.org/treaties/t/outer_space> last visited 6 May 2016.

Envisaged as an addition to the principles encapsulated by the Outer Space Treaty, the Moon Agreement was an attempt to re-enforce the concept of 'common heritage of mankind' with regards to space exploitation and exploration and hence cannot be appropriated by one State.[24] The lack of acceptance could be attributed to it being repetitive of the Outer Space Treaty or prevailing disagreement with the concept of 'common heritage of mankind,' an issue which this chapter will explore.

Article 11 of the Moon Agreement 1979 begins with the declaration that "(t)he Moon and its natural resources are the common heritage of mankind..." It goes on to state that "Neither the surface nor the subsurface of the Moon, nor any part thereof or natural resources in place, shall become property of any State, international, intergovernmental or non-governmental organization, national organization or non-governmental entity or of any natural person.......". Article 11 also reaffirms the prohibition of national appropriation both on the moon and other celestial bodies.

Interpretation of Ambiguous Terms

It follows from the use of the term 'Outer space, including the Moon and other celestial bodies' in Article II of the Outer Space Treaty that the provisions in question apply to the moon as well as other celestial bodies, which form a sub-set of 'Outer Space.' This has been a repeated verbatim in Article 11 of the Moon Agreement. The material scope of the principle as applying to both outer space *sensu stricto* and celestial bodies has never been specifically challenged.[25] However, certain scholars have argued that by restricting the notion of 'celestial body' to a subcategory of phenomena in outer space, the Treaty envisages a third physical category of phenomena that conforms to the

24 Jeremy L. Zell, Note, *Putting a Mine on the Moon: Creating an International Authority to Regulate Mining Rights in Outer Space*, Minnesota Journal of International Law, 2006, vol. 15, p. 489 at pp. 505–506.

25 Philip De Man, *The Exploitation of Outer Space and Celestial Bodies: A Functional Solution to the Natural Resource Challenge*, Dissertation, Leuven Centre for Global Governance Studies, 2010, p. 5.

description of neither 'outer space' nor 'celestial body.'[26] This third category would include phenomena, whose material manifestations are not significant enough to fit into either of the two categories and therefore remain unfettered by the principle of non-appropriation. Virgiliu Pop has argued therefore, that the possibility of a third category has made it imperative to define the notion of a 'celestial body' by distinguishing it from other phenomena.[27] This physical differentiation may lead to objects such as asteroids and meteoroids being made subject to claims of appropriation by States.[28]

Here are three crucial responses to the above-mentioned claims. First, the construction of a third category of phenomena clearly defies the language of Article II of the Outer Space Treaty, which envisages outer space as an overarching and inclusive term that includes the moon, celestial bodies and any other sort of phenomena that may exist. Second, such an interpretation contradicts the intention of the drafters, which was to have a comprehensive legal regime that applied uniformly to the various components of outer space. In the years building up to the negotiation of the Outer Space Treaty, it had been constantly argued that the need to define a 'celestial body' arose from the fact that celestial bodies needed to be distinguished from their void surroundings and therefore needed be regulated by a separate legal regime.[29] Indeed, many General Assembly Resolutions passed during the time period underscored this contention by referring to 'outer space and celestial bodies' when delineating the scope of their provisions, thereby opening the possibility of the establishment of two separate legal

26 S.M. Williams, *Utilization of Meteorites and Celestial Products*, IISL Proceedings, 1969, vol. 12, p. 180.

27 Virgiliu Pop, *Who Owns the Moon: Extra-terrestrial Aspects of Land and Mineral Resources Ownership*, 2009, pp. 47–58 (Berlin: Springer).

28 *Ibid*, p. 55.

29 "Reports of the Working Group III of the International Institute of Space Law (hereinafter: IISL) on the legal status of celestial bodies," IISL Proceedings of the colloquium on the law of outer space, 1962–1966, vol. 1.

regimes.[30] The drafters of the Outer Space Treaty chose not to resolve this quandary for fear of rendering the definition obsolete in light of future scientific or technological developments.[31] Hence, by using the term 'outer space including the Moon and other celestial bodies', the drafters felt no need to define the component parts of space separately.

Third, even if the Treaty were to allow such a creative interpretation, it is problematic to discern physical characteristics that differentiate celestial bodies from other objects.[32] Indeed, a scientific delineation for the definition of a legal concept is untenable as law is required for the regulation of acts undertaken by human beings. Therefore, mere physical differences in isolation of functional realities make for arbitrary classifications. There has to be a reason why celestial bodies should be subjected to different rules and regulations with regard to human exploitation. Scientific taxonomy fails to provide a valid justification. Further, scientific taxonomy itself is subject to constant revision. The re-classification by the International Astronomical Union of Pluto is a case in point.[33] Using a permanent classification of celestial bodies for the creation of separate legal regimes opens the floodgates for the legal status of these bodies changing with re-classification, thereby causing uncertainty with respect to appropriation claims and providing little legal security. Finally, scientists themselves admit that arriving at physical parameters to differentiate between celestial bodies and other objects with any degree of certainty may not be possible.[34] Scientists who have attempted this classification

30 For example, UNGA Res. 1962 (XVIII) of 13 December 1963; UNGA Res. 1721 (XVI) of 20 December 1961.

31 Philip De Man, *The Exploitation of Outer Space and Celestial Bodies: A Functional Solution to the Natural Resource Challenge,* Dissertation, Leuven Centre for Global Governance Studies, 2010, p. 4.

32 *Ibid,* p. 5.

33 IAU General Assembly Resolutions B5 and B6 of 24 August 2006, available at <http://www.iau.org/static/resolutions/Resolution_GA26-5-6.pdf> last visited 6 May 2016.

34 G.P. Zhukov, *The Problem of the Definition of Outer Space,* IISL Proceedings, 1967, vol. 10.

have largely come up short. For example, Fasan argues that celestial bodies are all material objects that can be transported entirely through outer space.[35] This definition was echoed in the findings of Working Group III at the International Institute of Space Law which defined celestial bodies as all "natural objects in outer space including their eventual gaseous corona which cannot be artificially moved from their natural orbits."[36] This metric, however, negates the possibility of future technological advancements that may allow for the displacement of these objects, thereby rendering this distinguishing criterion futile.

Appropriation of Natural Resources

Another term that lacks a watertight definition in the legal framework is the concept of 'natural resources' itself. Most scholars rely on a functional definition of resources by requiring that a particular phenomenon in space must produce an economic value upon human transformation in order to be considered a natural resource.[37] This is in sync with the definition of natural resources in Black's *Law Dictionary*, which defines it as 'any material from nature having potential economic value or providing for the sustenance of life...'.[38]

Although the functional interpretation, based on transformative potential has been widely accepted,[39] there has been much argumentation over the ambit of applicability of the non-appropriation principle to natural resources. The first school of scholars argue categorically that no State has a right to

35 E. Fasan, Weltraumrecht, Mainz, Krausskopf, 1965, 113, cited in Philip De Man, *The Exploitation of Outer Space and Celestial Bodies: A Functional Solution to the Natural Resource Challenge*, Dissertation, Leuven Centre for Global Governance Studies, 2010, p. 6.

36 Article 1 of the Draft Resolution of the Working Group III 1965, IISL Proceedings, p. 352.

37 Stephen Gorove, *Limitations on the Principle of Freedom of Exploration and use in the Outer Space Treaty: Benefits and interests*, IISL Proceedings, 1970, vol. 13.

38 Black's *Law Dictionary*, 10th Ed.

39 Philip De Man, *The Exploitation of Outer Space and Celestial Bodies: A Functional Solution to the Natural Resource Challenge*, Dissertation, Leuven Centre for Global Governance Studies, 2010, p. 19.

appropriate any form of space resources from outer space or celestial bodies.[40] A second school of scholars believe that the applicability of the non-appropriation principle is dependent on the type of resource in question.[41] This again brings us back to the supposed need for a distinction between celestial bodies and other objects. Pritzsche argues that the natural resources emanating from outer space *sensu stricto*, such as orbits and the mineral reserves on celestial bodies are encumbered by the non-appropriation principle while a third category of resources such as solar energy can be appropriated as they are removed from celestial bodies.[42]

However, the international community has raised staunch opposition to the granting of any rights on natural resources that originate from outer space but not from celestial bodies.[43] Significantly, the property claims made by the equatorial countries in the 1976 Bogota Declaration to the sections of the Geostationary Satellite Orbit (GSO) above their territories received widespread opposition as a blatant violation of Article II of the Outer Space Treaty.[44] Given that Article II does not differentiate between objects in outer space and other celestial bodies, Pritzsche's suggestion acts as a dichotomy that cannot be sustained.

Even though classification of natural resources based on their origin is untenable, the existing legal regime does allow for appropriation of natural resources with some riders. There is overwhelming consensus on the notion that the non-

40 E. Brooks, *Control and Use of Planetary Resources*, IISL Proceedings, 1968, vol. 11, p. 342.

41 M. Will, *Solar Power Satellites und Völkerrecht*, 2000, pp. 142–143, (Stuttgart: Boorberg).

42 K.U. Pritzsche, *NatürlicheRessourcenimWeltraum – das Rechtihrer wirtschaftlichenNutzung*, Frankfurt am Main, Peter Lang, 1989, pp. 89–91; quoted in Philip De Man, *The Exploitation of Outer Space and Celestial Bodies: A Functional Solution to the Natural Resource Challenge*, 2010, Dissertation, Leuven Centre for Global Governance Studies.

43 Stephen Gorove, *The Geostationary Orbit: Issues of Law and Policy*, American Journal of International Law, 1979, vol. 73, pp. 452–453.

44 Declaration of 3 December 1976 of the first meeting of equatorial countries, ITU Doc. WARC-BS (1977) 81-E.

appropriation principle has been included in the space law regime to avoid territorial conflicts in outer space and thereby guarantee the unfettered use and exploration thereof.[45] Therefore, it may be argued that the non-appropriation principle extends only to the establishment of titles over territories in outer space and celestial bodies.[46] Article II of the Outer Space Treaty does not explicitly mention natural resources emanating from outer space as being encumbered by the non-appropriation principle. This idea was further re-enforced by the discussions building up to the negotiation of the Moon Agreement.[47]

Article 11(3) of the Moon Agreement explicitly states that natural resources of the moon and other celestial bodies may be appropriated once they are removed. Due to the non-discrimination principle of Article II of the Outer Space Treaty, it may be argued that all natural resources are *per se* appropriable. It has been universally agreed, however that the moon and its resources would constitute the 'common heritage of mankind', which means that appropriation of natural resources must be undertaken keeping the confines placed by this doctrine in mind. The 'common heritage of mankind' doctrine in the modern day can be said to encompass five requirements: (1) the area in question cannot be subjected to national appropriation; (2) all States bear the burden of managing the area; (3) all benefits derived from the exploitation of resources in the area must be equitably distributed among all States regardless of the level of participation; (4) the area must be used only for peaceful purposes and (5) must be preserved for the equitable use of future generations. The most contentious issue among States has been the third element which requires the equitable distribution of benefits.[48] This has been problematic for

45 C.W. Jenks, *Space Law,* 1965, p. 275 (London: Stevens).

46 Philip De Man, *The Exploitation of Outer Space and Celestial Bodies: A Functional Solution to the Natural Resource Challenge,* Dissertation, Leuven Centre for Global Governance Studies, 2010, p. 20.

47 R.V. Dekanosov, *Juridical Nature and Status of the Resources of the Moon and Other Celestial Bodies,* IISL Proceedings, 1980, vol. 23.

48 Lynn M. Fountain, *Creating Momentum in Space: Ending the Paralysis Produced by the Common Heritage of Mankind Doctrine,* Connecticut Law Review, 2003, vol. 35, p. 1753 at p. 1759.

developed space-faring nations who spend money developing their space programs and also bear the enormous risk of liability in case of damage.[49] The developed nations argue, therefore that these resources may be made available to developing nations at a fair market price, thereby ensuring that mankind benefits but not at the same time or in exactly the same way.[50]

Crucially, the 'common heritage of mankind' doctrine stipulates that appropriation claims on resources independent of their exploitation are not legitimate as doing so would amount to obtaining property rights in the areas from which the resources are being appropriated.[51] Engaging in the act that caused the resource in question to be extracted from the original celestial body is crucial for vesting rights in the resources. This claim enables us to develop a regulatory framework that is in line with the overarching objectives of the Outer Space Treaty.

As the edifice of the 'common heritage of mankind' and the Preamble of the Outer Space Treaty require the fair and equitable use of outer space, the extent to which a resource may be exploited should depend on (1) relative scarcity of each resource and (2) the relative economic and strategic value. State practice already supports this contention. The orbit-frequency spectrum has been used by States on a daily basis and radio frequencies continue to be auctioned in various countries.[52] This practice indicates the emergence of a customary norm that supports the appropriation of inexhaustible natural resources regardless of their origin.

49 Carol R. Buxton, *Property in Outer Space: The Common Heritage of Mankind Principle versus the "First in Time, First in Right" Rule of Property Law*, Journal of Air Law and Commerce, 2004, vol. 69, p. 689 at p. 692.

50 Daniel A. Porras, Comment, *The Common Heritage of Outer Space: Equal Benefits for Most of Mankind Case*, Western Reserve, International Law Journal, 2007, vol. 37, p. 143.

51 Philip De Man, *The Exploitation of Outer Space and Celestial Bodies: A Functional Solution to the Natural Resource Challenge*, Dissertation, Leuven Centre for Global Governance Studies, 2010, p. 16.

52 Francis Lyall and Paul Larsen, *Space Law: A Treatise*, 2009, p. 199 (Ashgate).

Now, that we have established that appropriation of natural resources from outer space is legal, we must look towards developing a framework that incentivizes space exploitation while ensuring that resources are not over-utilized by one State or entity.

Property Rights

Since technological advancements made space exploration possible, scholars have argued for an amendment to the legal regime and thereby vesting property rights to outer space territory in States.[53] They support their contentions at two levels. First, they argue that the vesting of property rights along with the powers of alienation would be the most efficient solution to over-exploitation of space resources as a 'tragedy of the commons.'[54] Second, it would reduce wasteful usage of the land as there would be greater incentive to use the resources in an efficient manner if a State owns the land they are exploiting. In the absence of property rights, expeditions would seek to extract whatever they needed while potentially destroying other natural resources.[55] Assigning property rights would mean that it would be used more cautiously to maximize the investment and possibly make it attractive to future buyers that the land may be sold to.

Here are counter-arguments at both levels. First, liability for damage caused in outer space by both governmental and private actors launching from the territory of a State has been ascribed to the launching State through the 1972 Liability Convention.[56]

53 Taylor. R. Dalton, *Developing the Final Frontier: Defining Private Property Rights on Celestial Bodies for the Benefit of All Mankind,* 16 August 2010, Cornell Law School Graduate Student Papers, Paper 25, p. 5.

54 The 'tragedy of the commons' is an economic theory which stipulates that when exploiting global commons, actors will act in rational self-interest to the detriment of other actors in terms of exploiting the resources available at the commons. See Garrett Hardin, *The Tragedy of the Commons, Science,* 1968, Col. 162, p. 1243.

55 Taylor. R. Dalton, *Developing the Final Frontier: Defining Private Property Rights on Celestial Bodies for the Benefit of All Mankind,* 16 August 2010, Cornell Law School Graduate Student Papers, Paper 25, p. 5.

56 Thomas Gangale, *The Development of Outer Space: Sovereignty and Property Rights in International Space Law,* 2009, p. 33 (Praguer).

Such liability has been imposed without any prejudice to the principle of non-appropriation or the fair and equitable use of outer space. While the second level of argumentation on incentives is valid, the vesting of property rights in States, however, will ensure that space no longer remains a common resource for mankind but instead gets converted into a playground for the economically and technologically advanced nations that can afford space programs.

An alternate school of thought has supported the vesting of private property rights in individuals or organizations regardless of appropriation by the sovereign. This argument was raised by in the Nevada Federal Court by Plaintiff George Nemitz.[57] He claimed ownership over asteroid 433 known as 'Eros' and argued for the validity of this claim based on its registration on the Archimedes Institute website[58] and his use of the asteroid as a collateral when he filed a security interest in California. After the National Aeronautics and Space Administration (NASA) landed a spacecraft on Eros, Nemitz claimed that the spacecraft infringed his property rights and that he was entitled to 'parking' fees of twenty cents every year. The Court found in favour of NASA's motion to dismiss by claiming that Nemitz's individual claims of appropriation had no foundations in law and was contrary to the non-appropriation principle.

While the ruling in the *Nemitz*[59] case has not been disputed, a group of scholars have argued for the granting of unlimited

57 *Gregor William Nemitz* v *The United States of America, et al.* no. CV-N-0300599-HDM (RAM), reported in Westlaw as 2003 WL 24268455 (D. Nev.) 6 November 2003; WL 3703798 (D. Nev.) 28 January 2004, WL 3703805, 11 February 2004; 2004, WL 3167042, 26 Ap 2004. Affirmed 126 Fed Appx 343; 2005 US App LEXIS 2350 (9th Circular, 7 February 2005).

58 Virgiliu Pop, *Who Owns the Moon: Extraterrestrial Aspects of Land and Mineral Resources Ownership*, 2009, p. 42 at p. 43 (Berlin: Springer).

59 *Gregor William Nemitz* v *The United States of America et al.* no. CV-N-0300599-HDM (RAM), reported in Westlaw as 2003 WL 24268455 (D. Nev.) 6 November 2003; WL 3703798 (D. Nev.) 28 January 2004, WL 3703805, 11 February 2004; 2004, WL 3167042, 26 Ap. 2004. Affirmed 126 Fed Appx 343; 2005 US App. LEXIS 2350 (9th Circular, 7 February 2005).

private property rights in outer space.[60] Alan Wasser, Chairman of the Space Settlement Initiative, argues that private property is not explicitly excluded by the Outer Space Treaty.[61] Therefore, according to the legal doctrine of *expressio unic est exclusion alterius* one should presume that provisions not mentioned were excluded by deliberate choice, not mistake. He argues that the exclusion of private property rights from the ambit of Article II of the Outer Space Treaty serves as a justification of its validity. He relies on Lockean analysis of property rights that are independent of any sovereign.[62] Wasser's argument has precedence in a civil law approach to real property rather than a common law one. Under common law, theoretically the sovereign obtains control of a certain property and then conveys property to the individual. Under civil law, as per the doctrine of *res nullius*, an individual takes possession of the land to claim ownership and by transforming it through their labour are entitled to be recognized by the sovereign.[63]

While theoretically, private claims independent of sovereign backing may be tenable, practically; such a conception of property rights cannot be realized because of lack of enforceability. In the absence of sovereign safeguarding an individual's right to private property, an individual has little means of enforcing their right, short of employing private militia.[64] Unless the international community recognizes an individual's claims to private property in space, there is no point in staking claim to a right in the first place. Wasser has failed to analyse why the international community would encourage private appropriation of outer space.

60 Alan Wasser & Douglas Jobes, *Space Settlements, Property Rights, and International Law: Could a Lunar Settlement Claim the Lunar Real Estate It Needs to Survive,* Journal of Air Law and Commerce, 2008, vol. 73, p. 37.
61 *Ibid.*
62 *Ibid*, pp. 36–38.
63 Alan Wasser & Douglas Jobes, *Space Settlements, Property Rights, and International Law: Could a Lunar Settlement Claim the Lunar Real Estate It Needs to Survive,* Journal of Air Law and Commerce, 2008, vol. 73.
64 Bryon C. Bittingham, *Does the World Really Need New Space law?*, Oregon Review of International Law, 2010, vol. 12, p. 44.

Still, a complete lack of property rights would mean that any infrastructure built on outer space would necessarily need to be opened up to all nations, regardless of the level of investment of each nation. Such a strict adherence to the 'common heritage of mankind' doctrine acts as a disincentive for nations and entrepreneurs seeking to develop their space programs.[65] Wayne N. White therefore attempted to remedy this gap by advocating a form of 'functional sovereignty' that would assign limited property rights in an area to be determined by occupation and use of that area by the concerned State.[66] This would mean that States may exercise jurisdiction and control over an area of land that has chattel fixed to it for the purpose of appropriating resources within that zone.

White's approach, however, is problematic for two reasons. First, it is in conflict with the non-appropriation principle which prevents the granting of any form of rights in outer space or celestial bodies. This is because functional sovereignty in zones of outer space essentially means that the area can be exploited by one nation to the exclusion of all other nations. Therefore while a State may retain jurisdiction and control over the infrastructure created in outer space, extending this right to areas beyond the space object is illegal. Second, 'functional or limited' sovereignty is not a valid concept in international law.[67] A State's territory and property are two distinct rights. The State's territory is the physical space over which the State exercises sovereignty.[68] The State's property on the other hand

65 Lynn M. Fountain, *Creating Momentum in Space: Ending the Paralysis Produced by the "Common Heritage of Mankind Doctrine"*, Connecticut Law Review, 2003, vol. 35, p. 1758.

66 Wayne N. White, *Real Property Rights in Outer Space*, Proceeding, 40th Colloquium on the Law of Outer Space, 1998, American Institute of Aeronautics and Astronautics, available at <http://www.spacefuture.com/archive real_property_rights_in_outer_space.shtml.> last visited 6 May 2016.

67 Peter Tzeng, *The Right to Property in International Law*, Yale LJ, 2016, vol. 125, No. 6, p. 1548; *Timor-Leste* v *Australia Verbatim Record*, 11-12, 24 (21 January 2014, 10:00 AM), see <http://www.icj-cij.org/docket/files/156/17920.pdf> [<http://perma.cc/XS5Y-66J6>].

68 *Island of Palmas* (*Netherlands* v *United States*) 2 RIAA 829, 838 (Perm Ct Arb 1928).

includes the tangible and intangible objects over which the State exercises ownership. The general right to territory essentially means that any interference with the territory becomes an internationally wrongful act and therefore gives rise to a cause of action under international law. The right to territory is perpetual not ephemeral. Wayne N. White fails to specify the extent of the cluster of rights and obligations and the retention of 'functional sovereignty' over zones of outer space would give rise to both for the appropriating State and the rest of the international community. Under what circumstances would a violation of that territory give rise to an internationally wrongful act? Would the extension of municipal law to these territories be a right conferred through functional sovereignty? When would the limited sovereignty rights cease to exist and who would decide its cessation? These questions cannot be answered through a model of functional sovereignty as the notion enables each State to carve out the extent of its territory and sovereignty in areas that are recognized as the province of mankind. In the absence of these answers, therefore, White's model is ambiguous and dangerously close to an abrogation of the Outer Space Treaty.

Instead, the granting of property rights in the infrastructure itself could be used to safeguard the interests of space-faring nations that have built the said infrastructure. Article VIII of the Outer Space Treaty provides that "...Ownership of objects launched into outer space, including objects landed or constructed on a celestial body and their component parts, is not affected by their presence in outer space or on a celestial body or by their return to the Earth." Therefore, any nation may obtain ownership rights on structures in any celestial body, built either by government or non-government agencies, even in the absence of territorial sovereignty. This model protects the interests of the States who construct this infrastructure as other States would require their permission to use it. Instead of using Wayne White's ambiguous model of functional sovereignty, it is prudent to continue with the existing legal regime that protects the interests of space-faring nations without endangering sacrosanct tenets of space law.

Regulatory Mechanisms

After a survey of existing proposals[69] for the devising of a regulatory mechanism, a hybrid framework is suggested in this chapter that would involve a combination of three existing proposals. First, an Intergovernmental Authority such as the International Seabed Authority needs to be set up that allocates the rights to appropriation of resources and resolves disputes as and when they arise. The mode of allocation should be based on a credit-trading system akin to the emissions trading system envisaged by the Kyoto Protocol.[70] Finally, in order to incentivise space exploration, it confers limited property rights and jurisdiction over fixtures built in outer space for the exploitation of space resources based on the International Space Station Model.

The UNCLOS Framework and an Inter Governmental Agency such as the International Seabed Authority

The legal regime of the law of the seas may act as an appropriate model for developing a framework for the regulation of outer space. Like space, the open oceans are so vast that it is impractical for any one State to state its claim over it. Further, Part XI of United Nations Convention on the Law of the Sea (UNCLOS) recognizes the deep seabed as a 'common heritage of mankind' thereby disallowing any sovereign rights or the appropriation by any national or juridical persons.[71]

The Law of the Sea Convention uses the doctrine of 'common heritage of mankind' in much the same way as the 'province of all mankind' as used in the Outer Space Treaty.[72] Essentially,

69 Sarah Coffey, *Establishing a Legal Framework for Property Rights to Natural Resources in Outer Space,* Case Western Reserve International Law Journal, 2009, vol. 41, p. 119.

70 Kyoto Protocol to the United Nations Framework Convention on Climate Change, 1998.

71 United Nations Convention on the Law of the Sea, opened for signature, 10 December 1982, 1833, UNTS 397 [hereinafter UNCLOS].

72 Rudiger Wolfrum, *The Principle of the Common Heritage of Mankind, Max Planck Encyclopedia of Public International Law,*1983; John E. Noyes, *The Common Heritage of Mankind: Past, Present and Future,* Denver Journal of International Law and Policy, 2011, vol. 40, p. 447.

it stipulates that the rights in the resources of the deep seabed are vested in all of mankind on whose behalf the Authority shall act. The UNCLOS describes in detail how a State may obtain exclusive rights on the ocean's floor and designates the International Seabed Authority (ISA) as a trustee for these resources.[73] It has the power to grant exclusive rights to States that meet the necessary technical and financial criteria and also provides appropriate detail on the location of the resources and the amount of resources to be mined.

An intergovernmental space authority that follows the ISA model may be divided into three bodies. The first body termed the 'Assembly' would be open to all States regardless of their space-faring capabilities. The second body, known as the Council would be reserved for countries that have space-faring capacities. The Council would be responsible for setting up Boards and Working Groups that would regulate and monitor missions to space and the exploitation of resources. The ISA model allows for representation by some developing countries in the Council.[74] However, it may be presumed that developed nations may only accept this model if such seats are kept to a minimum. There is already enough discord among the space-faring nations with respcct to their obligation to share the benefits extracted from outer space equitably. The second challenge now lies in prescribing a mechanism that ensures the fair and equitable appropriation of natural resources. The final body within the ISA would be a dispute resolution body that should adjudicate disputes regarding the activities of States. Like all other international dispute resolution bodies, the ISA should use conciliatory mechanisms such as negotiation, mediation or arbitration should be encouraged before the pursuit of full-fledged litigation.

A Credit Trading System

The exclusive rights granted by the ISA do not last forever but exist only within a certain time frame for the mining of these

73 Part XI, section 2, Article 137 of UNCLOS.

74 International Seabed Authority, "About Us" available at <http://www.isa.org/jm/en/about> last visited 6 May 2016.

resources.[75] Once the government or entity fails to exploit the resources in a given time period, they lose these rights. This is similar to the working of the International Telecommunication Union in the granting of GEO positions where without conferring ownership, a temporary license is granted to a certain nation.[76] The problem with adopting this mechanism for the extraction of mineral resources in outer space lies in the fact that it pays no heed to the relative scarcity of each resource which has been discussed. Merely placing time limits on the appropriation does not set any quantitative limits on the exploitation of these resources.

A credit trading system administered by the international body helps avoid these problems. Under the emissions trading system envisaged by the Montreal[77] and Kyoto[78] Protocols, State Parties look to reduce the overall global emissions of substances that lead to a depletion of the ozone layer or pose other threats to the global environment.[79] The *modus operandi* of this trading system lies in assigning each party a designated amount of emissions per time period. The regimes also enable parties to purchase emission allowances from other parties such that if one nation desires to utilize the resource in excess of its allotted credits, it may purchase the right to do so from another State. In doing so, the overall level of emissions stays the same even if one State exceeds its initially granted quota.[80]

75 Annex § 1, 9 of the United Nations Convention on the Law of the Sea, opened for signature, 10 December 1982, 1833 UNTS 397 [hereinafter UNCLOS].

76 Bryon C. Bittingham, *Does the World Really Need New Space law?*, Oregon Review of International Law, 2010, vol. 12, p. 52.

77 The Montreal Protocol on Substances that Deplete the Ozone Layer, 1 January 1989, 26 ILM 1550 [hereinafter Montreal Protocol].

78 Kyoto Protocol to the United Nations Framework Convention on Climate Change, 10 December 1997, 37 ILM 22 [hereinafter Kyoto Protocol].

79 David B. Sandalow, *Emissions Trading is Kyoto's Success Story*, available at <http://www.iht.com/articles/2005/02/16/opinion/edsa ndalow.php>.

80 Sarah Coffey, *Establishing a Legal Framework for Property Rights to Natural Resources in Outer Space*, Case Western Reserve International Law Journal, 2009, vol. 41, p. 137.

Paxson first suggested the application of the credit trading system under the Montreal Protocol to space mining.[81] Credit trading systems have also been successfully applied as mechanisms governing the extraction of natural resources including fisheries and water resources[82] and land control.[83] If this model is applied to resource in outer space, all space-faring nations would be allotted a certain number of 'resource exploitation credits' that would allow both governmental and private space-faring entities from the State to exploit a certain quantity of each natural resource. It is crucial that the credits be allocated per natural resource rather than cumulatively for all natural resources. This is to ensure that the numbers of credits for resources that are relatively scarce and have greater strategic value across all States are cumulatively less than resources which are comparatively less valuable. Trading credits between resources should also not be allowed for the same reason. The purpose of this trading scheme is to ensure that the utilization of each resource is kept under check.

For example, let us assume that USA was granted 5 credits to exploit a certain resource and India was granted 3 credits based on the initial allocation calculations. USA uses up its 5 credits but has the capacity and desire to exploit more of the same resource. India, on the other hand has used up only 2 of its 3 credits. Using the credit trading system, USA could buy the residuary credit initially allotted to India through payment of a pre-determined sum. Using this model, the total quantity of the resource exploited remains the same even though nations are able to allocate credits among themselves in order to enable them to exploit to their capacity.

81 Edwin Paxson, *Sharing the Benefits of Outer Space Exploration*, Michigan Journal of International Law, 1993, vol. 14, p. 487.

82 Tom Tietenberg, *The Tradable Permits Approach to Protecting the Commons: Lessons for Climate Change*, Oxford Review of Economic Policy, 2003, vol. 19, No. 3, p. 400.

83 The United Kingdom has enforced a credit trading system through which land authorities may add garbage to landfill sites. See Friends of the Earth, "U.K. Landfill Allowance Trading Scheme Briefing", September 2007, available at <http://www.foe.co.uk/resource/briefings/lats.pd>.

The allocation of credits would be done with due regard to the technological and economic space-faring capacities of a country, which would include developments both in the government and private sector. The tradable nature of the credits could enable developing nations to benefit from the exploration and use of outer space monetarily even though they do not have the capability to exploit the natural resources. This credit trading system is certainly in sync with the non-appropriation principle as it is not vesting property rights on celestial bodies but merely allocating the rights to appropriate a certain quantity of natural resources over a set time period.

Applying the ISS Model

The final issue that needs to be resolved is regarding the jurisdiction and control over infrastructure constructed in outer space by nations for the purposes of exploiting natural resources in outer space. Instead of creating a new legal regime for governing the International Space Station (ISS), this model envisages extending national terrestrial law to its station in outer space.[84] Each member registers the components it has supplied to the ISS and retains jurisdiction over them. Hence, U.S. law govern the modules that USA has supplied while the Russian modules will be governed by Russian Law.[85]

The rights and obligations of each party are detailed in a series of instruments governing the ISS-including Intergovernmental Arrangements (IGAs), Memoranda of Understanding (MOUs) and implementing agreements.[86] The IGAs carve out broad principles for the launching of the cooperative effort including the regulation of various parties' actions in outer space. Under these obligations, Member States own portions of the space station in relation to their contribution of technology and finances. The individual MOUs are signed by the heads of the space agency of the State parties and set out

84 Andre Farand, *Legal Environment for the Exploitation of the International Space Station (ISS)*, in Proceedings of Forty-second Colloquium on Outer Space, 1999, vol. 8.

85 *Ibid.*

86 *Ibid.*

detailed regulations regarding the design, development and operations of the ISS. The implementing agreements set out how the parties' rights and obligations carved out by the MOUs may be implemented. The MOUs would also regulate transactions between nations which would allow one nation to use the facilities (fixtures) constructed by another nation for the exploitation of resources.

A disadvantage of adopting this mechanism lies in the fact that only space-faring nations have a say in the assignment of property rights, which should ideally be done through a universally acceptable framework.[87] It could be argued that this model allows a few space-faring nations to dictate obligations to the rest of the international community. When these developing nations do eventually participate in outer space exploration, they will find themselves bound by customary international law that they have not consented to. In order to avert this problem, all MOUs and IGAs agreed to by space-faring nations must be passed by a majority vote in the Assembly of the space authority.

With respect to infrastructure constructed for the purposes of mining in outer space, this mechanism may help in assigning property rights and jurisdiction over said infrastructure purely for the purpose of exploiting resources. Such a construct would incentivise States to appropriate the resources to the extent allowed for through the credit trading system but also obtain some return on investment for the infrastructure created for that purpose.

Conclusion

The goal of this chapter is to devise a mechanism that could equitably regulate resource appropriation in outer space once exploitation became a technical possibility. This chapter argued that natural resources in outer space may be appropriated by State actors with certain conditions. Rather than basing on the

87 Sarah Coffey, *Establishing a Legal Framework for Property Rights to Natural Resources in Outer Space,* Case Western Reserve International Law Journal, 2009, vol. 41, p. 142.

physical characteristics of the resource itself or that of its origin, it recommended a functional approach in determining the extent of appropriation of a natural resource in relation to both its relative scarcity and strategic value. In doing so, it preserves the essence of the notion of space being a province of all mankind.

This chapter advocated balancing the need to incentivise space programs with well-recognised principles of space law that ensure the equitable exploitation of outer space. It argued against the vesting of complete property rights in States as this would deter other States benefitting from the global commons. Further, while theoretically agreeing to the possibility of vesting property rights in non-state actors, pragmatically, it is clear that such a regime would not survive short of enforcement by the sovereign. It therefore recommended the continuation of *status quo* where States have property rights in the infrastructure constructed in space rather than on swathes of territory.

Building on the theoretical constructs set out in the above-mentioned parts, the chapter recommended a three-pronged model that could adequately regulate resource appropriation in outer space. Under the aegis of an intergovernmental authority, nations would be able to exploit resources according to a credit trading system, which would allocate a certain number of credits to each State. The States would be allowed to trade their credits in resources or buy credits from other States in case they wanted to utilize more than their allotted share. Finally, in order to regulate the assignment of limited property rights in the fixtures created in outer space, a regime akin to the existing ISS regime was advocated. Through IGAs and MOUs, this mechanism will enable space-faring nations to arrive at an agreeable framework that would be regulated by the space authority.

In the absence of pragmatic enforcement that is in sync with the prevailing geo-political realities of a certain day and age, the principles of international law come close to being rendered obsolete. By devising a framework that echoes these principles but still reflects the altered realities of the 21st century, this chapter sought to prevent such redundancy eclipsing the crucial tenets of Outer Space Law.

Chapter 5

Legal Protection to the Entrepreneurial Interest of the Private Players in the Commercial Mining of the Lunar Resources

AMRISHA TRIPATHI*

Introduction

The pace of development in outer space technology has taken humanity a step closer to the moon. The exploding human population on earth has made it inevitable to step out of our planet and look for alternatives of the exhaustible energy resources that would help the humanity last a little longer. In the recent years, the increasing pressure on the governments and various space agencies across the world, to design a framework to regulate the exploration and use of such resources is indicative of the fact that the anticipated phenomenon is around the corner. The logical progression of human development makes the exploitation of the mineral resources of the moon and other celestial bodies a necessity.[1] The economic conditions for exploitation of minerals in outer space, which presently seem not feasible, are going to eventuate from the continuous depletion of natural resources on earth. The current

* Research Assistant, The West Bengal National University of Juridical Sciences, Salt Lake, Kolkata.

1 R.J. Lee, *Law and Regulation of Commercial Mining of Minerals in Outer Space*, 2012, p. 1 (Springer).

system of outer space treaties does not provide a regulatory legal framework for mining operations and defies the three fundamentals of outer space—freedom of exploration and use, the principle of non-appropriation and the principle of common heritage of mankind.

Space Mining Operation

A relatively new phenomenon, mining of minerals on the moon and other celestial bodies cannot happen under legal uncertainty. It would be imprudent and risky on the part of the investors to invest into something that has no regulatory framework. When the reality eventuates, a commercial mining venture in outer space will have to confront the legal issues based on the present body of international and domestic space law.[2] Thus, it is cogent to prepare a legal framework adaptable to the existing body of international law. Space mining operation can be segmented as under:[3]

1. *Planning segment* which involves the study of technical feasibility of the operation.
2. *Exploration segment* which involves the use of spacecraft to collect and analyse the samples and assess their viability.
3. *Launch segment* which involves the launching of the mining spacecraft.
4. *Transit segment* which involves the arrival of the mining craft to the target celestial body.
5. *Extraction segment* which begins with the landing of the mining craft on the celestial body to the complete recovery of mined ores.
6. *Return segment* which involves the return of the mined ores to the earth either through *in situ* processing or placing a huge portion of such celestial body into the orbit of earth or lunar orbit.

2 R.J. Lee, *Law and Regulation of Commercial Mining of Minerals in Outer Space*, 2012, p. 10 (Springer).

3 *Ibid.*

7. *Exploitation segment* which involves the commercially profitable use of the mined ores.

The applicable legal issues in the course of execution of the above-mentioned, are similar to any commercial payload launch and can be under laws, both international and domestic.[4] Some of the international issues that could arise by the operation of international law are the vaguely defined limits of airspace and outer space, liabilities of the foreign third parties and the use of flyovers of the foreign territories as trajectories. On the other hand, domestic legal framework could raise issues concerning export control. Also, operations involving movement of the celestial bodies from their natural orbit to the lunar orbit or the orbit of earth may invoke legal principles pertaining to appropriation of celestial bodies.[5] The fundamental principles of space law also stand in contradiction to the launch and transit segments of outer space mining ventures. Again, the outer space treaties do not clearly define important terms like "launching State", "appropriate State", "space object" which could have important international ramifications. The space treaties, particularly the Liability Convention[6] still does not answer to the dilemma of liability in cases where more than one State is involved in the launching of an outer space mission.

Unstable Legal Framework

Article I(*c*) of the Liability Convention attributes the status of a space object of a "launching State" upon two categories of States – those who launch or procure the launch and those who assist the former with their facilities to effectuate the launch. However, if there is more than one launching State in the sense that States provide assistance beyond their facilities for launch and have major contribution in the assembly of the space object, who shall bear the liability of default or who shall have a rightful

4 R.J. Lee, *Law and Regulation of Commercial Mining of Minerals in Outer Space*, 2012, p. 10 (Springer).

5 *Ibid.*

6 Convention on International Liability for Damage Caused by the Space Objects was opened for signature on 29 March 1972, 961 UST 2389, TIAS 7762; 1975 ATS 5 (entered into force on 1 September 1972).

claim over the space object. In such a case, the States can both admit and evade their responsibility. The aforementioned scenario could cause substantial damage to the future space ventures when multinational endeavours shall be at peak. Also, the myopic vision of the drafters has led to the absence of a specialized dispute settlement mechanisms between States and between commercial entities.[7] The Liability Convention[8] remains silent in this regard in the context of private or commercial space financing. The problems associated with executing and recovering security interests over satellites and other space-based assets have already been highlighted following the recent collapse of some high-profile satellite telecommunication ventures, though some measures have been taken outside the arena of intergovernmental organizations to provide some international legal rules for such matters.[9] Technology exists to retrieve mineral resources on the moon,[10] but mining will require the adaptation of conventional equipment for use on the lunar surface[11], substantial private investment, and a system to develop these resources.[12] Some experts contend that mining on the moon could be easier than mining Antarctica or the deep seabed.[13] However, the unstable

7 R.J. Lee, *Law and Regulation of Commercial Mining of Minerals in Outer Space*, 2012, p. 12 (Springer).

8 Article I of the Liability Convention.

9 Martin Stanford, *The Cape Town Convention and the Preliminary Draft Space Protocol: An Update*, paper presented at the ISRO-IISL, Space Law Conference 2005, Bangalore, India.

10 G.C. Raclin, *From Ice to Ether: The Adoption of a Regime to Govern Resource Exploitation in Outer Space*, Northwestern Journal of International Law and Business, 1986, vol. 7, Issue 4, pp. 727–761 at p. 729.

11 Anthony R. Filiato, *The Commercial Space Launch Act: America's Response to the Moon Treaty*, Fordham International Law Journal, 1986, vol. 10, Issue 4, pp. 763–781 at p. 763.

12 Possible definitions of the common heritage principle range from requiring profit sharing, to international control of resources for redistributing wealth and technology among nations, to the opinion that the term merely denotes access to land for mineral exploitation. See *supra* note 9, pp. 738 & 739.

13 Martin Stanford, *The Cape Town Convention and the Preliminary Draft Space Protocol: An Update*, paper presented at the ISRO-IISL, Space Law Conference 2005, Bangalore, India.

legal environment has discouraged the various enterprises from investing huge sums into outer space mining ventures. Lee says that mere legal framework would not facilitate order to the outer space mining activities.[14] Practical issues need to be looked into in order to ensure effective implementation of such a framework. He suggests the formation of a separate intergovernmental organization like (hypothetically) an International Space Development Authority (hereinafter the "Authority") which should consist of organs like—

1. A quasi-judicial legislative body;
2. An administrative secretariat; and
3. Judicial mechanism(s) for dispute settlement.

Mining of celestial bodies is both, technologically and scientifically, a hefty affair. A close monitoring of such operations would be possible only through the establishment of a separate governing body. The composition, powers, functions and structure of this body shall have a significant role to play considering the bright prospects of outer space mining ventures.

Economic and Technological Prospects of Mining

The depleting natural resources of earth and the recent developments in the outer space technology have increased the possibility of exploration and use of minerals on moon and other celestial bodies. In any market economy the price of an exhaustive mineral resource would inevitably rise. Not only would this discourage the producers to invest in production cost but also encourage the consumers to resort to alternatives like opting for cheaper substitutes and going for conservation methods like recycling or reducing the consumption of the scarce mineral. Also, a rise in the demand of the substitute resources would encourage technological developments increasing the production and decreasing the cost of such energy efficient substitutes.[15]

14 R.J. Lee, *Law and Regulation of Commercial Mining of Minerals in Outer Space*, 2012, p. 1 (Springer).

15 *Ibid*, p. 35.

Rees[16] says in the context of minerals that substitution can take place at three levels: the primary extraction level, secondary production level and the tertiary end-use level. At the primary level of extraction, the diminishing mineral resources may give rise to the developments of extraction of alternative ores. For example, a decline in the availability of bauxite and aluminium oxide has resulted into extraction of aluminium from kaolin clays, carbonaceous shales, nemeline and nephelite.[17] At secondary level of production, one metal may completely replace another based on its use by the consumers. For example, aluminium has replaced copper in high-voltage transmission lines and stainless steel has replaced copper in kitchen wares. There have been views suggesting that there are substitutes available for almost all scarce minerals on earth thereby diminishing the issue of their scarcity.[18]

Substitution can also take place at the end-use level where demand of a particular mineral may reduce due to the use of a different technology, for example, copper which was mainly used in underwater transmission cables is replaced by a significant rise in the demand of microwave transmission technologies and communication satellite constellations.[19] Another example of this is the reduced use of metallic silver in photographic films due to the use of digital cameras.[20]

However, this optimistic view on replacement of scarce minerals with their substitutes is nearly idealistic. It relies on a perfect market force, where the predictions on the ratio of demand, supply and the price levels shall always be accurate and all the economic units shall always function in a perfectly

16 Judith Anne Rees, *Natural Resources: Allocation, Economics and Policy*, 1990, p. 39 (London: Routledge).

17 *Ibid.*

18 Gerald Manners, *Three Issues of Mineral Policy*, Journal of the Royal Society of Arts, 1977, vol. 125, No. 5251, pp. 386–401 at pp. 390–393.

19 Raymond F. Mikesell, *The World Copper Industry: Structure and Economic Analysis*, 2011 (New York: RFF Press).

20 R.J. Lee, *Law and Regulation of Commercial Mining of Minerals in Outer Space*, 2012, p. 38 (Springer).

rational way. The possibilities and suggestions by various economists and technocrats are overly optimistic and have failed to take into account the negative factors like monopolistic policies of major market players, their over-exploitative measures and volatile market conditions.

Launching of materials on the moon requires high escape velocity due to its deep gravity well. The moon is one-fourth the size of the earth and thus has lesser gravitational pull. However, this pull is directly proportional to the mass of the object on the moon.[21] This gravitational phenomenon of the moon makes civil engineering of the launch missions much similar to that of the earth.[22] This implies that large scale mining operations are easier to conduct on moon. One of the reasons of feasibility of mining of the lunar resources is its proximity to the earth. This makes the moon accessible for such operations and makes communications virtually instantaneous, thereby allowing for real-time remote control of robotic mining operators from the earth.[23] The discovery of water resources on the moon in the 1990s has made it a potential location for establishment of permanent lunar bases on its surfaces. This could facilitate the *in situ* production of hydrogen and oxygen, which are basically used as propellant fuels, provided that, a source to replenish such water resources are found.[24] Low gravity, a vacuum environment and seismic stability makes the moon a perfect platform for conducting unique experiments which are not possible to conduct on earth.

Near-Earth Asteroids as Alternatives to the Moon

The moon is the most sought after outer space entity for the exploration and use of diminishing mineral resources on earth. However, mining the moon has some serious environmental

21 R.J. Lee, *Law and Regulation of Commercial Mining of Minerals in Outer Space*, 2012, p. 38 (Springer).

22 *Ibid.*

23 *Ibid.*

24 Dennis Wingo, *Moon Rush: Improving Life on Earth with Moon's Resources*, 2004, pp. 204 & 205 (Burlington: Apogee Books).

concerns. While the earth takes a significantly long time to rejuvenate, the time of the moon is 1,000,000 years more than that of the earth. On the moon, micro-meteoritic action turns over the top 3 mm of the lunar surface every 10 million years. In this time span, the lunar surface is destroyed, recreated, and shaped.[25] However, this does not eclipse the prospects of exploiting mineral resources in the outer space. Near-Earth Asteroids (hereinafter as the "NEAs") are one of the most reliable sources for extraction of such minerals which are diminishing on earth. Some group of asteroids such as Apollo, Amor and Aten are categorized as NEAs. Just like the moon, the proximity of the NEAs is their advantage. When compared to the moon or even the other celestial bodies like mars, they are easier to reach and return from due to the low thrust required to depart from the LEOs and soft landings on asteroids, as well as departing back on the return trajectory from the asteroid to the earth.[26] The technology needed to avert the potential disasters due to comets and asteroids is the same as the technology needed to harness their mineral resources. Thus, developing this, one kind of technology would not only prevent the probable calamities from asteroids and comets but would also help realize the objective of harnessing the benefits of extraterrestrial mineral resources.[27] Outer space consists of various natural resources like volatile elements including water, methane, carbon-dioxide and ammonia. It also contains metallic elements like silicates, hydrated minerals, nickel-iron alloys, etc. Spectral studies have shown that while some of the asteroids contain regoliths and concentration of free metals higher than

25 Donald E. Gault, *et al.*, *Some Comparisons of Impact Craters on Mercury and Moon*, Journal of Geophysical Research, 1975, vol. 80, No. 17, pp. 2444–2460.

26 Reinhold Bertrand and J. Foliard, *Low-Thrust Optimal Trajectories for Rendezvous with Near Earth Asteroids*, paper presented at the 18th International Symposium on Space Flight Dynamics, 11–15 October 2004, Munich, Germany, pp. 2 & 3.

27 M.J. Sonter, *The Technical and Economic Feasibility of Mining the Near-Earth Asteroids*, available at <http://www.nss.org/settlement/asteroids/MiningNearEarthAsteroids(Sonter).pdf> last visited 1 July 2015.

the lunar surface, 20% of the NEAs are rich sources of the volatiles and all the asteroids are rich in metallic compounds.[28] The industrial development operations in outer space, which are likely to use a thousand tonnes of propellants or structural mass every year, shall inevitably focus on these resources as ores.[29] Determination of the mineralogy of the potential asteroids for mining can only be done through unmanned spacecrafts.

Mining of NEAs has various benefits over mining earth for mineral resources—

1. It creates prospects for various asteroids which could be the potential targets for exploitation of mineral resources.
2. The processing of ores is easier due to uncomplicated metallurgy of ores on asteroids.
3. It takes lesser time to create mine sites on asteroids since issues of protection of habitation and nature do not arise there. Consequently, the surface could be mined easily using equipment that can be relatively less expensive.
4. Equipment which is produced to mine the asteroid can either be discarded or can be relocated to other asteroids for further use.
5. Besides the technical advantages, it would be free of various legal issues which otherwise occur at domestic level on earth. This includes benefits from absence of landowner's rights or acquiring of mining rights.
6. Mining on asteroids has no constraints arising from environmental issues and disposal of the resultant waste.

28 A.S. Rivkin, *et al.*, *Diversity of Types of Hydrated Minerals on C-Class Asteroids*, Lunar Planetary Science XXXV, 2004, available at <http://www.lpi.usra.edu/meetings/lpsc2004/pdf/1646.pdf> last visited 1 July 2015.

29 *Ibid.*

Nevertheless, the above-mentioned advantages are feasible in case of absence of legal loopholes and presence of a regulatory framework at international level. Since many of the above benefits are not in conformity with the existing international space law, their realization is impracticable in the near future.

State Responsibility for Commercial Mining in Outer Space

The legal framework governing mining operations in outer space needs to resolve the existing legal issues arising out of space commercialization. Thus far, the current commercial activities have not been hindered by the existing ambiguities in the international space law but it is notable that activities like mining of natural resources of celestial bodies would require a much greater investment than normal deployment of space missions. Thus, eventually, there will be conflicts arising between the existing provisions and the upcoming activities in outer space.[30] The value of a typical asteroid mission in the year 1996 was estimated to be US $100 billion while the cost of deployment of an Iridium communication satellite was estimated to be US $7 billion. Such a huge investment today requires a strong legal foundation on which they could rely for a mission.[31]

During the deliberations and formulation of the legal principles governing activities in outer space, the framers did not envisage private enterprises or individual investments in space activities.[32] States and their authorized agents were the only players that were anticipated in the space-race. Therefore, the norms on jurisdiction and State responsibility were restricted to the States only. However, this stereotype broke with adoption of General Assembly Resolution 1962 (VIII) which gave definitive principles on international space law.[33]

30 R.J. Lee, *Law and Regulation of Commercial Mining of Minerals in Outer Space*, 2012, p. 95 (Springer).

31 *Ibid*, p. 96.

32 *Ibid.*

33 General Assembly Resolution 1962 (VIII), U.N. Doc A/5415/Rev.1. (13 December 1963).

Endeavours like International Space Station involve various nations; however, it is not entirely an intergovernmental effort. It involves various contractors hired for constructing vital components.[34] The absence of a definitive legal framework governing duties and liabilities of the governments and private contractors *inter se* has compelled them to resort to private contracts. It is through these contracts that the parties prescribe, clarify and limit their liabilities towards each other.[35]

With regard to the States whose private players are engaged in major space ventures, Article VI of the Outer Space Treaty is of great importance. It obliges the States—

1. To bear responsibility for their national actions in outer space regardless of their public or private nature.
2. To assure that all the space activities conform to the principles of Outer Space Treaty and with international law in general.
3. To supervise the activities of non-governmental organizations.
4. To share responsibility in international organization to which the States are party.

The first issue which needs to be determined here is the nature of responsibility of State. Some commentators have been of the view that "responsibility" under Article VI is akin to "liability" under Article VII of the Outer Space Treaty. The rules of interpretation of treaty in different languages under Article 33 of the Vienna Convention on the Law of Treaties 1969 (hereinafter as the "VCLT") states that the terms of a treaty are presumed to have the same meaning across the texts

34 The International Space Station is an outcome of an agreement between the governments of Japan, Canada, USA and Russia with the Member States of the European Space Agency namely Austria, Belgium, France, Finland, Germany, Denmark, the Netherlands, Ireland, Italy, Greece, Luxembourg, Portugal, Sweden, Switzerland, Norway, Spain and the United Kingdom.

35 R.J. Lee, *Law and Regulation of Commercial Mining of Minerals in Outer Space*, 2012, p. 97 (Springer).

authenticated in two or more languages. Thus, if the French use the *"responsibilite internationals"* to mean both responsibility and liability and so do Spanish, Russians and Chinese (in their respective languages), it implies that across the various authentic texts, the terms "international responsibility" and "international liability" are used in the same context. Consequently, Article VI of the Outer Space Treaty is exposed to ambiguity. While one interpretation can be that it is a mere regulatory measure on States to carry out their international responsibility without incurring any liability, the other can be a sharp antagonism of this. However, since any treaty needs to conform to the peremptory norms of international law, which in this case are the customary norms of State responsibility, a breach of these norms involves obligations to make reparations.[36] Thus, the provision should veritably be looked at as the one imposing liability for outer space activities attributable to the State.[37]

Article VI of the Outer Space Treaty imposes international responsibility on States for outer space activities by both, public and private bodies. While the acts by the public entities can be attributed to the State, it is not so in the case of private bodies. The contention here is whether Article VI reiterates the existing principles of State responsibility or has a wider ambit. Activities of a private entity can be attributed to the State only when involvement, influence or interest of the State in the operation can be objectively determined.[38] However, the use of the term

36 *Chorzow Factory (Indemnity) (Merits)* Case (1928) PCIJ REP., Ser. A, No. 17 at 29. The Court, in this case, held that both, by the general conceptions of law and by the established principles of international law, "...reparation is the indispensable complement of a failure to apply a convention, and there is no necessity for this to be stated in the convention itself." emphasis added.

37 R.J. Lee, *Law and Regulation of Commercial Mining of Minerals in Outer Space*, 2012, p. 130 (Springer).

38 *Flexi-Van Leasing Inc.* v *Iran* [1986] 12 Iran-USCTR 335. The Court held that even if an entity was under the control of the State, there must be an evident influential or directory conduct of the State, for the act to be imputable to it.

"national activities" in the provision qualifies the international responsibility of the States to the activities which are carried out under the direction or influence of the State regardless of them being public or private. Nevertheless, Article VI also mentions the role of "appropriate State" in control and supervision of the activities of the private parties, a term which has no qualifications attached to it. Consequently, this obligation creates a certain authority of State over private entities turning it into a national affair. The cumulative effect of this provision is that all the activities in outer space by public and private organizations come under the scrutiny of the State under both junctures— when it is exercising a direct control over such activities and when it is acting in the capacity of the appropriate State.

A glaring example of State responsibility is the ASTEROIDS Act of 2014[39] (hereinafter referred to as "the Act") passed by the USA to promote commercial utility of natural resources of asteroids. The Act purports to confer property rights on the natural resources from asteroids on any entity which extracts them *first-in-time.* On 10 July 2014, two Congressmen– Bill Posey and Derek Kilmer introduced the Act whose objective was to facilitate commercial exploration and utilization of natural resources of asteroids to *meet national needs* and to promote the rights of the commercial entities to explore and utilize these resources, within the international obligations of the US. The Act applies on all the persons and companies who are either organized under the US law or subject to its jurisdiction. Through this Act the US has brought the space operations conducted by both public and private entities under the State's supervision. In addition to this, it has also entitled them to property rights in the resources which they procure from the asteroids. This provision is in strong conflict with the most important fundamental of *non-appropriation of outer space* purported under both, the Outer Space Treaty and the Moon

39 American Space Technology for Exploring Resource Opportunities in Deep Space Act 2014 (ASTEROIDS Act) was referred to the Committee on Space on 10 July 2014 and has been enacted subsequently.

Agreement. Not much can be said in opposition of this Act owing to the elusive content of Outer Space Treaty and USA's non-ratification to the Moon Agreement. The Outer Space Treaty does say that *outer space including the moon and other celestial bodies* cannot be appropriated but it does not really specify what comes within the purview of "celestial bodies". This major definitional void might probably be one of the reasons why this Act came into existence. Moreover, the Outer Space Treaty is silent on whether the natural resources of the celestial bodies are included within the prohibition clause and whether prohibition on appropriation also includes prohibition of extraction. Considering the text of Article II and also the *traveaux preparatoires* of the Treaty, there never were deliberations on the natural resources of the celestial bodies because such idea was a bit far-fetched at the time of the drafting of the Outer Space Treaty. Also, the Outer Space Treaty prohibits the appropriation of the celestial bodies but does not say if their extraction is proscribed as well. Hypothetically speaking, if commercial mining of one asteroid consumes it in a way which significantly diminishes its utility and renders it useless for other missions, wouldn't that amount to appropriation of that asteroid by the concerned State?[40] Such questions reflect the inability of the Outer Space Treaty to regulate the commercial activities which are about to commence in the outer space. The need of a new legal regime is inevitable and currently the USA seems to be the only one leading that front. November 2015 was another reason for the US commercial space industry to rejoice since President Barack Obama signed into law the US Commercial Space Launch Competitiveness Act 2015 (CSLCA). The Act has provisions which would remove the impediments in way of more investments, risks and bold experiments with outer space commerce. The objective of the Act is to promote a viable industry in lower earth orbit and beyond and ensure American presence in the areas assigned to it by NASA while the agency

40 Charles Stotler, *The ASTEROIDS Act and Hearing: Some Observations on International Obligations*, available at <http://www.thespacereview.com/article/2604/1> last visited 29 September 2015.

works around its plans on manned missions to mars.[41] The CSLC essentially combines four bills on exploration and commercialization of outer space resources known as Spurring Private Aerospace Competitiveness and Entrepreneurship (SPACE) Act of 2015. The Act, by explicitly allowing the US citizens to engage into exploration and use of outer space resources, creates a pro-growth environment which promotes commercial space industry and establishes a more predictable regime governing private investments in this industry, creating both stability and incentives for the entrepreneurs venturing in this sector.

Conclusion

The exploration and exploitation of natural resources on the moon and other celestial bodies are going to be a necessity owing to their increasing scarcity on earth. The study of technical and economic feasibilities in this chapter has proved that possibilities of such activities either exist or can be easily created in future. While analogies can be drawn from the existing regime on outer space through the five space treaties, the lack of an expressed legal framework discourages investments in commercial ventures in this field. Any common investor would invest in outer space commercial activities only after making a comprehensive assessment of risk of failure and expected return on the investment. Sadly, none of these can be guaranteed in the absence of a specialized legal framework. The existing body of international space law is not as well adapted to the current developments in commercial space industry. This is precisely because at the time of the drafting of the Outer Space Treaty, the *magna carta* of outer space, the drafter did not anticipate the need of mining activities with regard to the moon and other celestial bodies. It was not until the Moon Agreement that the possibility of mining of natural resources in the outer space was considered feasible. Property rights in outer space are

41 Vidya Sagar Reddy, *Spurring Commercial Human Spaceflight to the Moon*, available at <http://www.thespacereview.com/article/2877/1> last visited 12 June 2016.

essential but they cannot be unchecked or arbitrary and subject to the financial and technological ability of the nations. A legal regime regulating such rights would ensure non-concentration of these resources in the hands of major players and make them accessible to developing countries and LDCs through equitable sharing and distribution. The entire burden of cost of space ventures cannot rest upon a State's economy which is where the private players come in. Not only would they invest the requisite amount of money for such missions but also promote such commercialization globally through multinational cooperation.

The Moon Agreement does not outright prohibit the commercialization of outer space and neither imposes an absolute restriction on the ownership and property rights. Article 11(5) of the Moon Agreement speaks about an international legal regime to govern exploitation of natural resources on moon. Once such exploitation becomes feasible, it would include the use of such resources for both scientific and non-scientific purposes. To prevent the chaos this inevitable situation could cause, there needs to be an internationally accepted set of procedures that would ensure a rational management and equitable sharing of benefits derived from these resources. Precisely, the Moon Agreement permits ownership and property rights as long as global interest is given due consideration. The Outer Space Treaty is currently so much drowned into its own rhetoric of "benefit of mankind" and "province of mankind" that its own Member States are challenging its principles. Initially the provisions of the Moon Agreement seem to be clear on the issues in question. It prohibits property rights on the moon and its natural resources in place and says that they can be exploited only after a legal regime regulating such operations comes into force. However, it does fail to resolve the legal glitches which are likely to dent the procedure. First, it permits exploitation of natural resources thereby nodding to the property rights inexplicitly but is does not mention the limitation on such rights. It does not define the extent to which property rights can be acquired over the samples that have been removed from the lunar surface.

Secondly, it talks about the need of legal regime to regulate exploitation of natural resources on the celestial bodies but does not state whether such activities are forbidden before the establishment. Article 11(5) says that the international community must strive to establish a legal regime governing exploitation as it is about to become feasible. The current scenario is evident of the fact that the space-faring nations are close to achieving such technology which would enable them to exploit the resources in outer space.

Article 11(3) the Moon Agreement states that no property rights will be created on the resources in place. However, once such resources are removed from the surface or the sub-surface of the celestial bodies they can be claimed as a matter of right. What really needs to be looked into here is that such property rights on the components of entities which are not only global commons but difficult to reach for nearly half of the world, should not sabotage the interest of the developing and underdeveloped economies. Nevertheless, the use of the term in place is evident of the fact that the framers of the Moon Agreement did intend to create some kind of property rights on outer space resources.

So far the Outer Space Treaty has peacefully regulated the space activities but the era of space commercialization is yet to commence. In this context the Outer Space Treaty has two major problems; first, it is nothing but a set of general principles which are useful in regulating emerging space activities but would entirely fail to address the specific legal issues likely to arise in the upcoming commercial space age. The aspirations of the States and private individuals demand the need of a new legal regime ensuring peaceful execution of commercial operations in outer space. Second, the Outer Space Treaty has failed to explain the precise meaning of the terms used which has left immense scope of ambiguity not only among the legal scholars but also in the space community. Exploitation of space resources is just as legally complex as it is fascinating. The contention is whether an entirely new field (field of commercial activities in outer space) should be left to the governance of a set of discretionary principles? With the controversies that these principles have engendered so far, the need of a supplementary legal regime has become more glaring. This regime would promote an orderly execution of commercial space activities and development of space resources. In order to ensure a peaceful manner of exploitation, the new legal regime would require lying down unambiguous terms and conditions, appropriate limitations and necessary rights and duties for the States to follow. Commercial use of outer space is an expensive venture which would require a joint participation of the States and the private enterprises. The presence of a new legal regime would encourage the private players to invest in the space activities as it would provide them with a stable legal framework securing their financial investments.

Chapter 6

Space Tourism— Some Legal Implications*

G.S. SACHDEVA**

Introduction

Tourism is in vogue globally and space tourism seems just round the corner. Commercial space travel has begun already and paid passengers have travelled to experience the joys of zero-gravity and stay at the International Space Station. More enthusiasts world-wide are keen to undertake the exhilarating journey. Shuttle and other reusable space vehicles are under testing for safety and cost reduction. There is a race among competitors for early introduction of regular space flights. It is thus a prophecy based on logical analysis into developments of the recent past, an assessment of current trends and future potentials of space technology. These inputs have been extrapolated with anticipated entrepreneurial investments as well as market surveys of public interest in experiencing the thrills of space travel and a desire to view the planet earth in cosmic perspective and *lumiere* splendour.

* This chapter is a revised and updated version of a previous publication of the author on the topic. The seminal article titled, Space Tourism: Some Legal Implications was published in *Indian Journal of International Law*, 1999, vol. 39, No. 1.

** Adjunct Professor, NALSAR University of Law, Hyderabad.

Mankind has well nigh reached the threshold of technology where the era of space travel just seems to dawn.[1] The hybrid space shuttle has since undertaken scores of successful missions and its technical competence, safety standards and effective re-usability as an aero-space vehicle of transportation has been proven. On the other hand, enterprising media organizations have carried out extensive market research in the US, Japan and Germany and there is optimism about the imminence of a splurging space tourism industry despite endemic hazards in such an adventurous transport mode. The latest proposal is by Dennis Tito for a 501-day round-trip to fly-by Mars in January 2018.[2]

Any new mode of transportation, when commercialized and declared open to the public as a service, carries with it tort obligations and *vinculum juris* for liability, rights ordained for the users and concomitant regulatory responsibilities. Likewise in aviation, this mutual obligation of space tourism is also beset with multitudinous juristic obstacles and legal implications as well as dilemmas of entrepreneurial decisions due to future business imponderables. The existing legal regime of outer space comprises a few international conventions, a few non-obligatory guidelines, scant national law and a few nascent concepts of space jurisprudence. Its relevance is woefully inadequate for the space transportation industry and rings a bell for radical legal ideation.

The other component of space tourism is hospitality industry. To this end, commercial space stations as floating hotels,

1 Space sojourns are not new to the Indian psyche. Native sages and *rishis* are known to have transported themselves through space by their spiritual feats and yogic skills. Ancient texts and religious scriptures, e.g. *the Vedas* and *Sri Guru Granth Sahib* (the Holy Book of the Sikhs) are replete with references which are not sheer mythology or fantasy but exude actual knowledge of celestial bodies as revealed by modern science; and reflect authenticity from intuitive knowledge and psychical experience. Refer G.S. Sachdeva, *Cosmos in Theological Scriptures*, Astropolitics, 2012, vol. 10, Issue 3, pp. 268-281.

2 Mars Society has announced, and beer lovers are ecstatic, that beer gets bubblier on the surface of the mars and thus more enjoyable.

Woerner's concept of Moon villages,[3] mars colonies or camps and exo-Mars deep-space habitats have been visualised and are under planning on blue-prints. A recent NASA statement of sending humans to the mars appears optimistic and realistic.[4] At the same time, hotels in space and on celestial bodies, for leisure and pleasure, is no crazy idea today and will be achieved sooner than anticipated. Thus space tourism is just on the cusp of substantial pick-up. However, these commercial activities in outer space by private enterprise are not directly permitted in law but legality can be legitimised through jurisprudential interpretation; and their proper governance ensured through regulatory measures at national and international level.

Thus space tourism would cover two major activities—space transportation and space hospitality—and each of these would need specific and *specialis* rules to regulate and govern their operations. Further, the law of outer space has so far reckoned with State-centric operators, whereas private enterprise is very soon going to seize and dominate on commercially lucrative opportunities in space business arena. Of course, private corporations would look for guarantees of realty rights and assurance of sustained operations or provisos for long-term leases, etc. and existing law does not allow of such eventualities and instrumentalities.

Space travel commands safety of the passenger and no regulatory norms exist as yet. The other aspect is standardisation of ticketing format and liability conditions. The early experiences of air passengers have not been pleasant in claims of compensation due to jurisdictional hassles and fine-print clauses contracting out liability under the legal maxims of *volenti non*

3 Peter B. de Selding, *Europe Hits Snooze on Woerner's The Moon Awakens Push*, Space News, 8 January 2016, available at <http://spacenews.com/europe-hit-snooze-on-woerners-the-moon-awakens-push/> last visited 4 February 2017.

4 Statement made by Charles Bolden, Director NASA. See Trent Gillies, *NASA's Bolden: Mars Mission in Closer than Ever* available at <http://www.cnbc.com/2016/04/02/nasas-bolden-mars-mission-is-closer-than-ever.html> last visited 3 February 2017.

fit injuria or *ad impossibilia* or *force majeure* for hazardous transportation and shrugging off the onerous burden of evidentiary proof. The other angle is emigration formalities and health fitness that would need some sort of travel document; as well as the moot issue whether passengers can be treated as astronauts for rescue and return. These and other issues will be discussed later in some detail.

Space hospitality has its own peculiar legal implications. First, hotel or resort would require permission or lease of land to set up shop because proprietary rights on celestial land, deemed common heritage of mankind are prohibited. Then any habitation needs discipline and law and order, more so in cramped places where space is at premium. Food and beverages need purity and hygienic standards. Sanitation needs high level of maintenance. Medical facilities in first-aid and more would be required for guests and hospitality workers. This list is not comprehensive but only illustrative.

In general, the metabolism of space law has been sluggish and has yet to evolve suitable adjuncts to address several specific challenges. A legal regime of space tourism may have to "conventionalise" several aspects like liability in accidents, damage on earth's surface, technical standards of safety, standardization of travel contract, space-worthiness of vehicles, traffic control in space, disposal of space debris, hospitality discipline enjoined on the staff as well as the guests and myriad other implications consequent to space activities.

This chapter therefore, only seeks to draw attention to some such implications and legal obstacles; proffers a few suggestions, apparently radical, to keep abreast with the technological developments in space sciences and exhorts to evolve suitable operational regimes to cope with futuristic developments and anticipable exigencies. Hence, we must shed our narrow focus, discard orthodox legal idioms and be prepared to evolve new juristic paradigm that suitably accommodates the second generation of space law for assuring unhindered commercial growth, affording desired economic fillip, ensuring fullest accruals to beneficiaries and providing equitable distribution of gains for the common benefit of mankind.

There is thus an undoubted need to address these issues appropriately so that we are not overtaken by technology, public zeal for space travel and resultant contingencies. UN, as usual on space issues, may take an initiative through. Committee on the Peaceful Uses of Outer Space (COPUOS). Concurrently, law scholars must also cognise the ensuing developments and be pro-active in legal thought and responsive to treaty initiatives. This is a clarion call and the time is now to cogitate on impending challenges, address them squarely and act decisively.

Transition to Space Tourism

Tourism became the fastest flourishing industry of the twentieth century as the world metaphorically shrunk into a "global village". At this time, people became reasonably cash-rich and developed a desire to venture out for various reasons. The resultant economic multiplier effect as well as employment generation potential played the miracle and some economies boomed and became affluent only on the tourism binge. Such economies exist both in the eastern and the western world.

The fetish of tourism was let loose in the second half of the last century and today, tourism has come to stay; of course, in varied manifestations and for diverse reasons stemming from sheer wander-lust to themed trips. And preferred destinations are the beaches to laze around, culture hubs to appreciate art and architecture, forests to seek relaxation in the midst of nature and study wildlife or health tourism to visit spas for medicinal or aromatic massages or to discover the sheer mystique and spirituality of ancient civilisations. And reasons could be many more.

Of late, land tourism seems to have nearly run out of steam. It is almost hitting the plateau of growth because beaches however exquisite and exclusive, monuments however hoary and informative, mountains however serene and refreshing, by and large offer the same environs, similar attractions, prosaic styles of entertainment and vapid pleasure opportunities. Venues may be different but experiences tend to be repetitive, monotonous and humdrum. Therefore, new pastures which provide novel excitement, different experiences, unexplored domains and unventured excursions have to be constantly discovered or even innovated to nurture sustainable tourism. One such avenue could be under–water tourism or scuba diving at sea and yet another, space tourism, which could offer a new type of romance with adventure, though somewhat ultra-hazardous, yet the breathtaking sights, strangeness of thrill and exclusiveness of experience in zero-gravity space would make such touristic events well worth the risk and expense, at least for the rich, elite and the brave at heart.

The prophecy about space tourism is not new. In fact, earliest practical visions of such travel are already over two decade old. On 22 October 1997, an advertisement appeared on CNN television network offering space rides at US $98,000. An earlier one on 25 May 1997 had announced "Honey mooning in zero gravity – Japanese plan hotel in space". A Reuter release of 31 December 1997 reported, "First tourist to blast off to space in 2001", and it was Dennis Tito. By hindsight today, one can easily concede that even speculative offers were almost dead on the mark.[5]

The historic event of commercial sojourn by a U.S. space tourist, Dennis Anthony Tito, who stayed aboard the spaceship ISS from 28 April 2001 to 6 May 2001, is testimony to this. Dennis Tito, a financial advisor and former NASA engineer, reportedly paid $20 million for an eight day trip.[6] A score of fare-paying passengers from all over the world, including two women, have since enjoyed this experience, some with privilege of stay at the International Space Station (ISS). All fare-paying passengers have travelled in State-owned and State-operated Soviet space shuttles and lived in the Russian Quarters of ISS. Fortunately, they all had safe flight and safe landing; and no implications came in for test.

5 G.S. Sachdeva, *Outer Space: Security and Legal Challenges*, 2010, p. 130, (New Delhi: KW Publishers Pvt. Ltd.).

6 Tito was lifted aboard the Soviet Soyuz TM-32 from Baikonur Cosmodrome in Kazakhistan on 28 April 2001 and returned to earth on 6 May 2001. See <http://www.russianspaceweb.com/iss_soyuztm32.html> last visited 4 February 2017.

The response to one-way ticket to the mars has been stupendous and now Dennis Tito is planning another 501-day mission to mars in 2018. Martin Lockheed has announced a bold plan of humans in mars' orbit by 2020 and a Red Planet Base Camp for human landings by 2028.[7] Other offers of economy space trips, in the future, for extraterrestrial sight-seeing comprise a package of one week consisting of training of faculties, fitting out for space suit, acclimatization to weightlessness, briefing for emergency procedures and the actual blast off with almost 3 hours in an orbit 100 km above the earth. All this clearly shows a popular upsurge of interest in space travel and that enterprising corporations are expectantly looking forward to this highly lucrative and fast expanding business frontier of immense potential. It thus appears certain that space tourism will be the industry of the twenty-first century; its harbingers are already visible and active.

Space Tourism—Vision to Reality

Optimism about the imminence of splurging space tourism industry is based on certain assumptions, which form the bedrock of our shared views of a vision to reality. Some of these are patently logical and grounded in reality of contemporary developments in space technology which is taking rapid strides and evolving useful applications while others are intuitively probable postulants with pragmatic futuristic visions *sans* illusions. Some salient assumptions are:-

(*a*) Technical Feasibility

(*b*) Safety Standards

(*c*) Commercial Viability

(*d*) Public Response

7 Leonard David, *Humans to Mars by 2028? Checkout Lockheed Martin's Red Planet 'Base Camp' Idea,* available at <http://www.space.com/32963-mars-base-camp-lockheed-martin-video.html> last visited 4 February 2017.

Technical Feasibility

The earliest satellite was a Soviet Sputnik-I launched in 1957 and thereafter the achievement of landing the first container on the moon on 13 September 1959. The first manned landing on the moon was by the U.S. Eagle (Apollo 11) in July 1969 and the safe return of the crew with Columbia space shuttle were miracles of science and technology that caused a quantum jump in human understanding of the outer space and celestial bodies. It opened new vistas for use and revealed potential for myriad applications of the budding space technology. The U.S. space shuttles have since undertaken scores of successful missions and have been phased out, too.

The replenishments to ISS are now privatized. Research and development have tempted private enterprise into this arena of ultra-high investments with long gestation period. The Lockheed has financed Venture Star project. The power for this aerospace vehicle has been provided by the X-33 rockets which can enable it attain the speed of Mach 15. It is capable of a vertical takeoff, unpiloted, single-stage-to-orbit (SSTO) launcher with a payload of 59000 lbs. Another project on the anvil with similar ambition is the Delta Clipper, which is a user-friendly spacecraft. Promising reports are emanating from the sponsors. As Prof. U.R. Rao has stated, that as on today, "[i]t is no more the technology, but economics which has become the limiting factor for taking revolutionary strides in the new space frontier".[8]

Today, the monopoly of State ventures into the outer space has been burst credibly. Private enterprise has invaded this field and has tasted success. Scaled Composites of California has launched Space Ship One but have not been successful; further plans for Space Ship Two are under way. Virgin Galactic and Space X are also in this race and are fairly advanced in their efforts and trial demonstrations. The race seems fierce and competitive.

8 U.R. Rao, *Space Technology for Sustainable Development*, 1996, p. 52, (New Delhi: Tata McGraw-Hill).

Safety Standards

There is no denying that space travel is ultra-hazardous, hence achievement of reasonably acceptable standards of safety becomes a cardinal assumption. As of today, the element of disaster risk is rated as 1:100 in shuttle flights. This may be acceptable for government missions for defence research purposes but certainly not for a service offered to the general public. The high risk factor might make space travel an unacceptable and unattractive adventure and dissuade even the die-hard enthusiast. Conceded that space flights shall at all times remain more risk prone than air travel yet steps towards better architecture of spacecraft, continued development of power packs, improvements in certain ancillary equipment and "spaceonic" systems are important and urgent for safer space travel. Developments are taking shape.

Apart from this, major improvements are required in fabrication materials to withstand radiation, be able to counter risks of depressurisation and bear capacity to withstand *uber*-high temperature on re-entry into the atmosphere. However for aerospace vehicles, apart from safety considerations of aviation, additional parameters and norms would have to be established to assure safety from the hazards of space debris. Another additional safety parameter would be intelligent traffic control of space vehicles or space situational awareness at the operational level. All this appears important because a full-fledged space transportation service is likely to be operationally over the next decade.

Commercial Viability

Having convinced of the technical feasibility of space travel, it is important to analyze the prospects of its commercial viability which is primarily dependent on development of advanced reusable launch vehicles. This would make spacecraft almost as mature as airliners of today with capability to engage at least a couple of flights per day and have a reasonable operational life on economic arithmetic. Need for savings in the recurring cost of propellants and development of fail-safe single-stage-to-orbit (SSTO) rockets are essential requirements. Despite economic algorithms, engineering acumen shows that these objectives would require painstaking incremental development over years of in-service evolution rather than an immediate quantum leap in technology.[9]

Therefore, to make this concept commercially lucrative there is need to develop a cost-effective reusable launch vehicle and cheaper fuel substitutes which can bring down the cost per seat by more than 1000 times than that incurred on the space shuttle. Venture Star is one such project being financed by Lockheed. Other private endeavors, like Space Ship One that has now graduated to Space Ship Two, are also in progress and it can be reasonably hoped that full orbital travel might approach the cost level of US $ 25,000 in a decade from now.

Public Response

Public enthusiasm and response to space travel is vindicated by the fact that the first private and paid-for space tourist, Dennis Tito, has already orbited the earth. His safe return and paid space travel by another score of men and women have further boosted public confidence leading to an understanding that space travel is not as risky as generally imagined or publicly feared. The angst, though real, seems exaggerated.

Enterprising organizations have carried out extensive market research in the US, Japan and Germany and have thrown up spectacular results. In the US, there is a sizeable section of people who are willing to pay up to US $ 100,000 for a trip into space. In Japan, a large number of responses revealed an aspiration to make at least one trip in space in one's life time and they are projected to possess capacity to finance such a trip out of their life-time savings and other resources. In Germany also people have expressed similar longings.[10]

9 David M Ashford, *Space Tourism—How Soon will It Happen?*, Proceedings of the 1997 IEEE Aerospace Conference, February 1997, available at <http://www.spacefuture.com/archive/space_tourism_how_soon_will_it_happen.shtml> last visited 4 February 2017.

10 Refer Survey Report from Shimizu Corporation and Obayashi Corporation of Japan. Similar projections have been made by NASA in *NASA Watch Update* dated 7 August 1998. See <http://www.

In the US, particularly, the response appears stupendously exploitable and commercially explosive. Several firms have already started offering spots on future space flights at costs which seem highly affordable, yet eminently realistic though, of course, the dates of flight remain speculative and uncertain. The Civilian Astronaut Corps, based in Houston, has accepted thousands of dollars from members, offering a hope to orbit at more than 60 miles above the earth's surface in weightlessness in the near future, aboard "the Mayflower".

Even the recent offer of one-way ticket to the mars has evoked great interest. Compared to this, planned offer of stay at Woerner's Moon Village[11] or habitat in Mars may elicit still greater interest. Even Tito's planned round trip to fly-by-Mars is a great awakener.[12] In nutshell, conservatively speaking, the public response seems significant at the cost held out by the space corporates and it appears highly probable that within a decade, the space tourism industry may collectively touch a turnover of US $ 10 billion. It can be expected to generate an unprecedented multiplier effect in the global economy as well as in the space commerce.

Legal Implications

Space has not yet been legally considered as an arena for private enterprise nor viewed as a frontier for commercial forays. Space activities, so far, have been undertaken by State-funded agencies like NASA or by the government itself in certain countries. Further, space activities have been strategic in importance and State-centric in objectives. Lately, however, a few giant multi-tech conglomerates and multi-national joint ventures have dared

---

aparchive.com/metadata/JAPAN-COMPANY-PLANS-TO-OFFER-A-WEEK-LONG-HOLIDAY-IN-SPACE/392460e36179dec053d47b6313dc4196> last visited 4 February 2017.

11 Dietrich Johann Woerner is the Director General of European Space Authority.

12 The launch is planned for January 2018. Alex Knapp, *Dennis Tito's 2018* Mars *Fly by is on the Ragged Edge of Feasibility*, available at <http://www.forbes.com/sites/alexknapp/2013/02/27/inspiration-mars-aims-for-2018-flyby-of-the-red-planet/#7ce40869247f> last visited 4 February 2017.

into the space industry and are gradually developing their independent private operations in fields like remote sensing, telecommunication and broadcasting, satellite launches and now on to manned flights.

Some other spheres also no longer remain monopolistic domain of the State alone. Increasing areas of space activity are falling within the ambit of economic viability and commercial feasibility. One such area so identified is space tourism which involves two major players – the space carriers and the space hospitality. Each of these operators needs specific-to-type facilities and rules to regulate their space activities and operations including on the surface of celestial bodies.

The element of hospitality is for pleasure, education and entertainment. This necessitates placement in orbit and operation of space-hotels, entertainment centers as also resorts on the moon and the mars to begin with. These would require considerable capital investment and operational costs. Outlays of such high magnitude for commercial purposes cannot be expected to come from the State exchequer. Therefore private enterprise shall have to address and assess this business opportunity in terms of economic viability and sustained profitability. Entrepreneurial risks are endemic and conscious investment decisions would have to be taken. It can be alluded to, in tandem that private investments would demand guarantees of long-term leases or perpetual usufructuary rights in the realty so utilized or infrastructure created.

Therefore, this restrictive governance of outer space is economically claustrophobic and legally strangulative from the perspective of space tourism industry. There is thus a dire need to liberate the outer space from the shackles of legal catholicity and to cogitate juristic innovations and evolve radical legal idioms to husband the ever-palinating business and industrial potential of outer space and celestial bodies for advantages aimed at the ultimate well-being and common benefit of mankind. Of course, there are some legal implications and challenges posed by space tourism industry which will be briefly discussed in this chapter, separately for space travel and space hospitality.

Commercial Space Travel–Legal Implications

Most of the conventions and agreements governing space activity were drafted to facilitate scientific exploration and peaceful uses by government agencies whereas space carrier is a concept of commercial travel and business operations. In order to exist and grow, it would need a conducive legal environment and permissive governance. Current space regulations, however, recognize space activities by State entities or under State control and accordingly stipulate corresponding State responsibility and liability. Such a regime would appear inhibitive for free commercial activities in space. A few suggestions to improve, improvise, innovate and even to establish altogether new tenets of space jurisprudence and proposed regulatory solutions are discussed in succeeding paragraphs.

Legality of Commercial Activities by Private Enterprise

The space law "conventionalized" so far treats States as parties and as such the only players in the space arena. This was true so long, but commercial activities in space cannot be expected as State ventures from public exchequer and necessarily have to be private corporate initiatives. Space law has made no provisions towards this advent. The only reference to space activities by other than the States and State agencies occurs in Article IX of the Outer Space Treaty 1967.[13] Even this mention of activity or experiment by "its national" has a derogatory slant rather than salutary encouragement.

The relevant provision of Article IX reads that "... If a State Party to the Treaty has reason to believe that an activity or experiment planned by it or its national in outer space, including the Moon and other celestial bodies, would cause potentially harmful interference with activities of other States Parties in the peaceful exploration and use of outer space, including the Moon and other celestial bodies, it shall undertake appropriate international consultations before proceeding with any such

13 The Treaty on Principles Governing the Activities of States in the Exploration and Use of Outer Space including the Moon and Other Celestial Bodies 1967 (in short OST).

activity or experiment....". Nevertheless, if private enterprise is to participate in commercialization of 'new space' and operate space vehicles on the lines of civil aviation of today, then a promotive and permissive legal environment has to be induced.

Determinate Liability and Standard Contract for Passenger Travel

For any mode of transportation, generally, the ticket constitutes the contract to travel. Apart from duties of the common carrier under Tort Law, the carriers tend to contract out their liability in fine print clauses for reason of its specific characteristics or under common law doctrines of *volenti non fit injuria, force majeure, ad impossibilia, abundant cautela,* contributory negligence, etc. these can be confusing to a layman desirous of space travel. Not everyone can hire a battery of lawyers like Dennis Tito to scrutinse the contract. And future space passengers are expected to be from the middle class excited for the exhilarating trip bargained at their life-time savings. The unsuspecting common man needs an assurance of equity and due protection against exploitation.

The contract assumes importance because apart from other conditions, it defines the jurisdictional forums, ceiling on liability, the defence pleas available to the carrier and on whom is the onus of proof. These aspects form the core of the contract. Carriers tend to be iniquitous and self-biased on such clauses while on the contrary, absolute liability may be imposed with feeble defences. The hapless passenger needs protection as consumer of a service; and space travel contracts need to be standardized in information format, liability limits and evidentiary procedures.

In an activity as ultra-hazardous as space travel, accidents, however minimal, are very likely despite state-of-the-art safety measures. Probabilistic studies put the risk of accidents in space 100 times higher than in air operations which is not a desirable safety standard. The recent accident of the US "Challenger" spacecraft in which some lives were lost is still fresh in our mind. Hence a ceiling on quantum of compensation for accidents should be negotiated considering equitable interest of stakeholders. It is a contentious issue but has to be resolved. Needless to mention that as most of the passenger liability in air accidents is borne by insurance companies, a similar practice may evolve in space travel.

Early days of air travel gave harrowing experience to the unwary passenger in claiming compensation for air accidents whether for court jurisdiction, burden of evidence on the complainant or potent contractual defences. Despite improvements in law, like adoption of *res ipsa loquitur*, little has changed. The fate of space passengers is not likely to be any different unless space lines are restrained and regulations put in place. May be, a protocol to Montreal Convention 1999 selectively adapting it to make it applicable to space travel and consequences of space accidents would help all stakeholders.

Safety of Space Travel

In any system of transportation, safety considerations always remain of utmost importance. The same should be equally pertinent to space travel. Apart from considerations of technical safety and aspects of space-worthiness, risk from space debris constitutes a salient element. It is estimated that since the Sputnik of 1957, more than 10,000 launches have taken place and out of these barely 800 are operational spacecraft in orbit at present. Besides the spacecraft, each launch sheds in space upper stages of launch vehicles, spent rocket motors, fuel tanks, shrouds, fairings, clamps, nuts and bolts, peeled paint and mission related objects like the US experiment in copper needles, not to mention that the US Gemini-10 and Soviet Salyut-7 astronauts have, not inadvertently, thrown trash and personal garbage into the space void. Many of the satellite accoutrements abandoned in space further disintegrate for unknown natural causes or because of residual fuel remaining in tanks or it could even be a controlled explosion for national strategies.[14] This

14 The USSR exploded Kosmos 1654, Kosmos 1813 and Kosmos 1906 in space, ostensibly in a controlled manner, to eliminate the possibility of retrieval by another State. See <http://www.friends-partners.org/oldfriends/jgreen/bispaper.html> last visited 4 February 2017. The recent case is of ASAT experiment by China in 2007 followed by the US display of technical capability in 2008. See Gregory Kulacki, *The United States, China, and Anti-Satellite Weapons*, available at <http://allthingsnuclear.org/gkulacki/the-united-states-china-and-anti-satellite-weapons> last visited 4 February 2017.

proliferates detritus and clutters the outer space, not always for *bona fide* operational reasons.

It is estimated that as of today nearly 1,00,000 pieces of size 10 sq. cm. and above, which are trackable, are floating in the space and that particles of submillimeter range are likely to run in millions. And to believe that a few thousands of these pieces are radioactive, only adds to our scare and dismay. Further, all these particles are orbiting at approximate speed of 10km/sec or about 36,000 km per hour. Even the smallest chip will have the impact to pierce through a space station antennas and kill the mission. Even paint peels are known to have dented spacecraft. The scenario comprehends the magnitude and gravity of the problem which is escalating fast. Hence, there is an urgent need for remedial measures.

One such recommendation could be to make it mandatory for the launch State to reserve adequate fuel in the spacecraft to ensure its return to the earth or placement in graveyard orbit. This would reduce the number of dead and defunct objects out there and lessen the risk of their disintegration. It should be possible for the UN and other world fora to exhort and compel the space-faring nations to adopt such palliative and preventive measures as stipulated in Space Debris Mitigation Guidelines of the United Nations Committee on the Peaceful Uses of Outer Space 2007 and thereby making the space traffic safer.

Another measure to cut down clutter, albeit radical in approach, is to recommend a suitable law of scavenging from outer space. Technology for retrieval of waste objects from space, particularly the low-earth-orbit-segment, which is highly congested yet most suitable for space tourism, is almost ready in Switzerland and Japan. Besides, materials used in manufacture of spacecraft are highly expensive and can be recycled for economy and profit. Therefore a minor impetus of commercial returns can activate a system of retrievals from space rather soon. But existing space law does not permit this and treats such reclamations violative of jurisdictional and proprietary rights of States over their objects.

The public scavenging in outer space and charging cess on launches could be effective to provide strong incentive for business to reclaim useful objects. Identifiable proprietary items can be offered to the owner/launch State on reimbursement of cost of retrieval. Unidentifiable scrap material could either be sold or recycled or commercially disposed of as souvenirs, mementos and relics. This prospect appears inspiring.

Tourists are not Astronauts

The Outer Space Treaty under Article V regards astronauts as "envoys of mankind" in outer space and according to accepted connotation any space tourist would also be classified as astronaut. It was laudable to accord a halo of a hero to honour the daring adventure of an astronaut. It was also logical and a valuable ruse for eliciting cooperation between the USA and USSR during the cold war period. But now it makes no business sense and still lesser legal sense. Nor is it any good for the tourists. This clause seems to have already served its purpose and outlived its utility. In fact, the wisdom of this dictum has been questioned and legal basis of this status has been controverted.[15]

'Astronaut' is an oft-used word in space law and legal literature but nowhere have the attributes of an astronaut been described for proper identification of such a persona. Astronaut is a person trained to travel in a spacecraft.[16] One wonders whether only the pilot-navigator or the commander of the spaceship alone is the astronaut or whether his crew involved in control or other allied science experimenters also qualify to be generically called astronaut. And lastly, can the passengers or other spacefarers who travel in the space vehicle, whether for pleasure or business, may also be deemed astronauts. Different languages have different words like Russian language puts them as Kosmonauts and different countries accord different definitions which are neither compatible nor congruent.

15 G.S. Sachdeva, *Outer Space: Security and Legal Challenges*, 2010, pp. 89–102 (New Delhi: KW Publishers Pvt. Ltd).

16 *Concise Oxford English Dictionary*, 12th Ed.

The US and the Soviet definitions of astronaut have been found to be loose, vague and confusing. Commercial passenger in no way qualifies for supra-national status of an astronaut.

An analysis of the Space Treaty and other international agreements including Rescue and Return of Astronauts, reveals an extensive use of the term 'astronaut' which has variously been alluded to indicate different types of spacefarers who have in several texts and contexts been referred to and addressed differently, e.g. astronaut (Article V of Outer Space Treaty and Preamble to the Rescue Agreement), personnel (Article VIII of Outer Space Treaty and Articles 1-4 of the Rescue Agreement), representative (Article XII of Outer Space Treaty), persons on board a space object (Arts. III and IV of the Convention on Liability) or crew (Article 8 of the Russian text of Space Treaty). But no definition of an 'astronaut' has been enshrined in any treaty or agreement which makes legal position of multiple astronauts at ISS as envoys of mankind rather paradoxical.

Be that as it may, it would appear sagacious to designate only the commander of the space vehicle to act as 'Envoy of Mankind' in clear understanding rather than create multiplicity of envoys at any given point in time and space.[17] Therefore, a commercial traveler in space can have no diplomatic status by sheer virtue of such travel and there is need to find other solution to his rescue and return, if such eventuality arises. International community would be well advised to act judiciously and fast in this regard.

Need for Interterrestrial Travel Document

It is pertinent to hint that in due course, not pretty far in future, space travel may offer multiple destinations to the space tourist and experience of outer space may turn into inter-planetary travel and may soon extend to deep-space probes towards inter-stellar travel. Thus a space tourist will have a choice of

17 For a detailed analysis on the subject refer G.S. Sachdeva, *Astronauts: Envoys of Mankind—An Analysis of Legal Basis* in V.S. Mani, *et al.* (eds.), *Recent Trends in International Space Law and Policy,* 1997, pp. 209–217 (Lancer Books).

movement and commute for continued visits in space and on celestial bodies. Even at that stage, would we like to identify a person by global nationality or treat him as Inhabitant of the Planet Earth (IPE)?

As such a situation can soon arise, it becomes important to consider issuance of an earthly identity document to space visitor as IPE on the lines of national passport. This would help trace travel movement of space tourists and hospitality workers in outer space. Incidental to this requirement is the need to keep record of emigration from the earth and return whenever it occurs. This process would seem analogous to global immigration procedures and could find similar purpose.

Space Hospitality–Legal Implications

Space hospitality is a new concept for space scholars and its commercial connotation makes it still stranger. Its parallel is global hotel and entertainment industry on the earth. And comparable concepts are floating space station as casinos and entertainment hubs or zero-gravity motel for honeymooners. There could also be resorts for luxury accommodation or Woerner's Moon Village or habitats on the Mars or transit guest houses for deep-space travellers in due course of time. These envisioned possibilities are likely to have peculiar legal implications. Replenishment problems relating to food stuffs, beverages and drinks, their food standards and quality and space-shelf-life pose different regulatory challenges.

However, such commercial activities in outer space by private enterprise or their impending demand from future tourists are neither explicitly contemplated nor directly permitted under the present legal regime of outer space. Space is common heritage of mankind and thus "*res communis*" and no private proprietary rights can be created or attached under the law. Nevertheless, legality can be contrived through jurisprudential gymnastics and proper superintendence ensured through statutory measures at national and regulatory provisions at international level.

Leases in Outer Space

Article I of the Outer Space Treaty stipulates that "Outer space, including the Moon and other celestial bodies, shall be free for exploration and use by all States without discrimination of any kind, on a basis of equality and in accordance with international law, and there shall be free access to all areas of celestial bodies." It further states that such activities, "shall be carried out for the benefit and in the interests of all countries ..., and shall be the province of all mankind." The provision outlined here can be roughly summed up under the concept of "Common Heritage of Mankind."[18] It is a laudable principle of non-appropriation and non-sovereignty that mandates to retain this medium and celestial bodies therein free from proprietary claims and possessory conflicts so as to assure egalitarian freedom of use by all. The Treaty states that "Outer space, including the Moon and other celestial bodies, is not subject to national appropriation by claim of sovereignty, by means of use or occupation, or by any other means."[19]

A pedagogic interpretation of "common heritage of mankind" could be that outer space and the celestial bodies are "*territorium communis*". It therefore follows that outer space should be treated *extra commercium* and *communes omnium* without necessarily being a *res*.[20] Outer space tends to appear a global resource considered to be as common 'Province of All Mankind.' From the above legal postulates it comes clear that outer space and the land on the celestial bodies including the moon is beyond discrete ownership whether by States, organizations or individuals yet remains universally accessible and usable resource for each generation of mankind. Leases of varying terms could be possibly granted by any UN Space Superintendence Authority obliquely under legal clause of sharing of benefit by all nations.

18 Rega J Rao, *Outer Space: A Part of Common Heritage of Mankind*, in V.S. Mani, *et al* (eds.), *Recent Trends in International Space Law and Policy*, 1997, pp. 191–208 (Lancer Books).

19 Article II, the Outer Space Treaty 1967.

20 For more detailed analysis, refer G.S. Sachdeva, *Sovereignty in the Air—A Legal Perspective*, Indian Journal of International Law, 1982, vol. 22, No. 3 & 4, pp. 397 & 398.

Anyway, hospitality industry would need huge private investments, and would certainly like to be informed of the nature and definition of grant of rights of ownership or usufructuary leasehold or at least an assurance of guaranteed right to operate and free and unfettered use for a reasonably long time and for *bona fide* commercial purposes. Strictly viewed, this demand may not appear legally tenable nor in conformity to the existing regime under the treaty law but implied permissive references can be culled out of existing space law.

This conflict however, could be partly resolved in relation to orbiting hotels, entertainment centers and construction of habitat on a celestial body by invoking Article VIII of the Outer Space Treaty. This Article reads that "A State Party to the Treaty on whose registry an object launched into outer space is carried shall retain jurisdiction and control over such object, and over any personnel thereof, while in outer space, including objects landed or constructed on a celestial body, and of their component parts, is not affected by their presence in outer space or on a celestial body or by their return to the Earth."

Additionally, Article IX of the Outer Space Treaty admits of activities or experiments in outer space by "its nationals" as individual legal entities. While Article VI commands that "States Parties to the Treaty shall bear international responsibility for national activities in outer space, including the Moon and other celestial bodies, whether such activities are carried on by governmental agencies or by non-governmental entities..." It is obligatory that "object launched into Earth orbit or beyond" be registered by the launching State and this information be furnished "to the Secretary-General of the United Nations, as soon as practicable ..."[21]

The foregoing discussion explicates by inference and in conjunction with specific provisions of different treaties and conventions relating to outer space that non-governmental entities including individuals can launch objects into outer space,

21 Articles II, IV & V of the Convention on Registration of Objects Launched into Outer Space 1975.

register the same with the State to retain ownership and control over them subject to State supervision, and of course, use the same for the benefit of mankind. The patch work argument appears ostensibly tenable and legally expedient. Other regulations and supervising organization, as necessary and germane, can be evolved suitably as expedient or with experience.

Of course, absolute ownership rights, as relevant to private property on the earth, are not recommended by any stretch of imagination. But a system of long-term leases with suitable regulatory clauses and safeguards assuring freedom of private enterprise in space with reasonable longevity to amortize capital costs and expect profitable returns on the heavy investments is definitely advocated. The task of regulating leases could be entrusted to a competent and empowered authority on the lines of International Telecommunication Union responsible for allotment of geo-stationary slots or perhaps put directly under the aegis of the United Nations as World Space Organization, which could be evolved into and cherished as a mascot of global cooperation.

Governance and Public Order

Hotels, entertainment hubs, leisure islands, moon village or mar's habitat would all be human settlements, temporary or permanent. And human interaction anywhere needs maintenance of public order. Therefore, security and safety of guests, settlers and workers as well as hospitality infrastructure and corporate properties floating in outer space and immovable assets on celestial bodies constitute another area of concern. Good governance over there cannot be effectively controlled from the earth and the policing resources for ensuring this – whether through human, mechanical, electronic, optical and even futuristic gadgets – would always remain inadequate and woefully short of the incumbent needs. Therefore, the risk of disputes and fights in the queer space environment is not unimaginable. Disruptions may as well be caused by terrorists or behaviourial disorder due to cramped and claustrophobic environs. We, therefore, have to intelligently preempt and obviate any such delinquency and formalize contingency plans and empower a duly constituted authority to obviate crises.

Thus there is need for framing rules for orderly living and affable interaction of tourists in space. Many jurists have not even visualized such exigencies where legal intervention, adjudication and even sanctions may become palpably evident option and circumstantially prudent action. Apropos, for superintendence in spacecraft, it may be meaningful to have regulations analogous to those stipulated as Rights of the Commander of an Aircraft.[22] Adaptations as necessary could be made. However, to maintain public order and peace in residential areas and leisure islands on the moon or mars, specific laws may have to be adapted from the earth and modified as necessary.

Expectations of a Fare-paying Tourist

A fare-paying space tourist who is willing to wager his life-time savings for a one-time experience would surely have certain expectations from the space trip. First, the tourist expects that the fare is not extortionist and would get reasonable value for money. He expects the best and safest travel from space carrier, the best in space hospitality and entertainment and in overall from tourism industry an exhilarating and unique experience of outer space. Delays and goof-ups detract from the anticipated excitement, real enjoyment and true-value of the experience. Hence, scope for resultant disputes.

Howsoever organized be a system, certain slip-ups do occur occasionally to mar the consumer/guest-industry relationship. These are termed service deficiencies on the part of the service provider and at times can be compensated in terms of money to mitigate a partial devaluation of the experience or consequences of an accident. This would require a liability regime which could be a comparable adaptation to one for civil aviation operations, evidentiary procedures and stipulation of

22 Convention on Offenses and Certain Other Acts Committed on Board Aircraft (Tokyo Convention) 1963, Chapter III.

judicial forums to litigate for compensatory relief. For the purpose, a suitable Protocol to Montreal Convention 1999, duly novated to the peculiarities of space tourism could help in the situation.

If disputes are endemic in any commercial activity and can be adjudicated for compensating incurred loss or damage *in restitutio in integrum* then dispute redressal forum and its internal working procedures are necessary. For space travel and hospitality the complication can be inter-planetary or interstellar residence. Or that the cause of action may arise in outer space or on a celestial body other than the earth. It seems almost certain that in such matters international law will be applicable and that such cases will be seized by courts but their jurisdiction needs to be defined or that designated international courts can be constituted for the specific purpose. However, in times of internet and multi-media e-communications, e-litigation could be possible from anywhere provided courts are suitably equipped and are permissive of e-evidence and e-arguments.

Security of space activities and space assets

Terrorism is rife and rampant on the globe. Cultural values have deteriorated and social perceptions have been blurred with biases. Racial groups and ethnic denominations often take to violent methods for perceived grievances and illusory wrongs believed to be perpetrated on them. These outfits most often select soft targets to avenge themselves. It is logical to surmise that once space travel becomes popular, these unsocial elements would not spare this field too. Security is thus critical to space travel and space infrastructure.

In aviation, tightened security measures and anti-hijacking laws were resorted to by international conventions and by complementary national statutes in almost all States. Strict sanctions and eternal vigilance have also paid good dividends. Similar security arrangements and governing laws would be necessary for the protection of the space tourists, spacecrafts, space hotels and moon colonies as well as support infrastructure on the earth, outer space and on other celestial bodies. It would be rather simplistic to recommend enactment of analogous laws like anti-hijacking or suppression of unlawful acts against safety of civil aviation.[23] Each mode of transportation has its own frailties and sensitivities which have to be addressed specifically and imaginatively.

Apart from terrorist acts, minor crimes can also occur in shuttles cramped in space or in floating hotel stations or in habitats on celestial bodies. These need to be handled tactfully yet legally. Conflicts may arise on application of national law or international law and at the same time, the latter may be found wanting to define nature of offences and awardable sanctions. For such contingencies new legal solutions may be necessary; and for enforcement, a new type of suitably equipped police force with necessary legal immunities may be required. New policing techniques, new weapons and action drills may have to be conceptualized and practiced for weightlessness under zero–gravity conditions.

Space Tourism to Operate as Industry

The two components of space tourism must operate in parallel and in harmony as an industry and perform business regulatory duties. This is important because entrepreneurial management and labour workforce have not always enjoyed harmonious relationship. In fact, discord is endemic due to conflict of interests. Therefore, workforce should not be kept hostage in a lonely, inhospitable and hazardous environ of outer space. Management should be humane and benign and welfare-oriented towards hospitality workers and labour force in general.

Conclusion

Man has always been mystified by the outer space and was ever inquisitive to explore it. As he explored, he found this medium highly useful and tended to take greater advantage of the space

23 Tokyo Convention 1963, Convention for the Suppression of Unlawful Seizure of Aircraft (Hague Convention) 1970 and the Convention on the Suppression of Unlawful Acts against the Safety of Civil Aviation (Montreal Convention) 1971.

in floatation in zero-gravity. The repeated technological success of reusable vehicles has reduced costs of space travel and opened up a new vista of tourism as industry. The prospects appear promising and space tourism seems to be a new business frontier that certainly would flourish as industry of the twenty first century. Private enterprise is surely eager to seize this commercially lucrative opportunity but for the legal impediments.

The body of existing space law comprising a couple of conventions and a few agreements has primarily envisaged of States and governmental agencies as players in the space arena. Further, the Outer Space Treaty treats space as common heritage of mankind. Other supporting and allied treaties reiterate the same stance and no private property rights are legally tenable on the celestial bodies. This is an admirable doctrine of public international law but bodes ill for many profitable yet peaceful uses. Space tourism is one of them.

First, if space travel is to become popular public service, as market research has shown enormous positive response, an operational regime of commercial space travel and its concomitant incidents will have to be put in place. The components of this governance could concern liability in case of accidents, support from insurance industry, liability for damage caused on surface of the earth, standardization of travel documents, technical standards for safety, space worthiness of vehicles, traffic control in space and numerous other related aspects. For some of these aspects support and collaboration can be sought from space agencies and national laws under State responsibility defined in the Outer Space Treaty.

Secondly, if space hospitality is to develop in tandem with space travel then it has to sprout as a commercially viable industry. Obviously for such a commercial purpose, initiative must emanate from private enterprise. It is equally important to note that ventures in this field would involve colossal investments and corporations would be hesitant to commit huge outlays unless they get certain guarantees of realty rights or modified ownership or leasehold possession in property.

Existing "convention law" of space brooks no such concessions. Hence the need to bring about suitable change in our legal convictions to provide scope for growth rather than stifle space hospitality industry and dry up an eternal well-spring of a new business frontier. Suitable measures, whenever and wherever necessary, could be imaginatively devised and effectively enforced rather than smother a promising field of limitless opportunities for sheer angst.

The doctrine of 'common heritage of mankind' has proved its wisdom in the law of seas and global commons; and legal intelligentia has been zealously eager to extend its prudence to the space law to arrest the possibility of fiercest competition in "occupation" and establishment of sovereignty over space entities. Mankind has thus escaped a reckless race. But under the on-going information and knowledge explosion of almost limitless peaceful uses of space, let us not be paranoid or dogmatic about the doctrine of 'common heritage of mankind.' It is strongly advocated that emphasis must suitably shift to the concept of "common benefit of mankind" for improvement in the quality of human life and welfare of living beings on the planet earth.

It is humbly suggested that the UN may consider an initiative through COPUOS (Committee on the Peaceful Uses of Outer Space) to draft suitable protocol to the Outer Space Treaty and other conventions like Chicago Convention 1944, Montreal Convention 1999 as suggested earlier. If deemed fit COPUOS may form a specialized sub-committee for this task. Protocols will be easy to negotiate and formalize. Thus the new legal matrix would be able to accommodate and enunciate the second generation of space law that perforce will be perceptibly liberal, intrinsically interactive, responsive to unanticipated contingencies and conducive to latent opportunities that can collectively benefit and commonly enhance global peace and prosperity.

In the end, it may be pointed out that the existing Office of Space Affairs (OOSA) is unequal to the future responsibilities and additional tasks due to expanding commercial space activities and increasing participation of private enterprise. The situation seems pregnant with conflict and needs a vigilant, empowered and potent set up in the form World Space Organization which can be treated as Trustee and Inspector of outer space and celestial bodies. Its functions and roles may encompass broad-spectrum duties of space governance, competent inspection of compliances and judicious dispute redressal. There is a need to build up political lobby, diplomatic thrust and legal opinion; and at the same time plan its complexion and structure as well as commence preparation towards its establishment by absorbing OOSA.

Chapter 7

Regulating Space Exploration & Tourism —A Study of SpaceX and Blue Origin

SAVITHRAN RAMESH*
ADITYA PRASAD**

Introduction

The definition of what is deemed possible in the realm of outer space has expanded exponentially in the last few decades. Since the launch of Sputnik I, the world's first man made satellite, in 1957, the landscape of this sector has changed dramatically, with concepts that were otherwise considered to belong in science fiction novels now fast becoming a reality with the rapid growth in technology. The archaic notion of space exploration being reserved to governmental entities and "envoys of mankind" is also fast changing, with the private sector fast playing an important role in the development of this sector.[1] This change is most notable in the commercial space exploration industry, with private entities like Richard Branson's Virgin Galactic, Jeff Bezos' Blue Origin and Elon Musk's SpaceX making strides in the development of cost effective and efficient methods

* Student, the WB National University of Juridical Sciences, Kolkata.
** Student, the WB National University of Juridical Sciences, Kolkata.

1 Adrian Taghdiri, *Flags of Convenience and the Commercial Space Flight Industry: The Inadequacy of Current International Law to Address the Opportune Registration of Space Vehicles in Flag States*, Boston University Journal of Science and Technology Law, 2013, vol. 19, p. 405 at p. 406.

to further space exploration for the masses.[2] Hence, the prism through which space exploration has been viewed is evolving, making this activity no longer reserved for trained astronauts and governmental entities but now promising to cater to a far wider demographic.

The history of Space Law

The development of the body of law that regulates the exploration and use of outer space can be traced back to the period after the launch of the Sputnik I satellite by the erstwhile Soviet Union and presently, there exists five main treaties that regulate the same. These are:

(i) *Treaty on Principles Governing the Activities of States in the Exploration and Use of Outer Space, including the Moon and other Celestial Bodies 1967* (hereinafter: "Outer Space Treaty"), that spelt out various fundamental principles relating to the use of outer space;

(ii) *Convention on Registration of Objects Launched into Outer Space 1976* (hereinafter: "Registration Convention"), that addressed the registration of any space objects launched by a particular space party. This Treaty specifically requires the *launching State* to register its space objects and defines this term. Moreover, the launching State exercises its jurisdiction over the object as well as any individuals on board.[3]

(iii) *Convention on International Liability for Damage Caused by Space Objects 1972* (hereinafter: "Liability Convention"), attributes differing standards of liability to the launching State for damage caused by their space objects either on the surface of the earth or in outer space to other space objects. Compensation must be given to affected parties by the launching State in accordance with this Convention.

2 Adrian Taghdiri, *Flags of Convenience and the Commercial Space Flight Industry: The Inadequacy of Current International Law to Address the Opportune Registration of Space Vehicles in Flag States,* Boston University Journal of Science and Technology Law, 2013, vol. 19, p. 405 at p. 407.

3 Article VIII of the Outer Space Treaty 1967.

(iv) *Agreement on the Rescue of Astronauts, the Return of Astronauts and the Return of Objects Launched into Outer Space* 1968 (hereinafter: "Rescue Agreement") deals with the return of astronauts and space objects landing in a foreign jurisdiction or beyond.

(v) *Agreement Governing the Activities of States on the Moon and other Celestial Bodies* (hereinafter: "Moon Treaty"), reaffirms and elaborates upon the provisions of the outer space treaties dealing with the use of the moon and other celestial bodies.

These treaties thus reflected a series of different laws that governed numerous different facets of a single "phylum": space law.[4] The climate, in which these treaties were negotiated, however, differed vastly from that which exists today. The above-mentioned space treaties were negotiated in the midst of a "space race" between the United States of America and the Soviet Union, with their primary goal largely driven towards ensuring that outer space was not used for military purposes, rather to promote the peaceful use of space.[5] Moreover, the possibility of private entities dealing with space exploration was considered largely improbable, given the cost and resources required for space exploration.[6] This can be seen by virtue of the fact that the responsibility of private entities has seldom been mentioned within the treaties, with the Rescue Agreement failing to accept the possibility of a private entity being the launching authority and the Outer Space Treaty failing to envisage the possibility of private entities participating in the use and exploration of outer space.[7] This notion has, as

4 Francis Lyall & Paul B. Larsen, *Space Law: A Treastise*, 2009, p. 479 (Routledge).

5 Paul G. Demling & Daniel M. Aarons, *The Evolution of the Outer Space Treaty*, Journal of Air Law & Commerce, 1967, vol. 33, pp. 419-456 at p. 427.

6 Myres S. Mcdougal, *et al.* (eds), *Law And Public Order In Space*, 5th Ed. 1963 (Yale University Press).

7 Brian Beck, *The Next, Small, Step for Mankind: Fixing the Inadequacies of the International Space Law Treaty Regime to Accommodate the Modern Space Flight Industry*, Albany Law Journal of Science & Technology, 2009, vol. 19(1), pp. 1 to 37 at p. 13.

mentioned above, changed dramatically in the recent past, with the "commercialisation" of outer space fast becoming a reality. Recent projects like SpaceX and Blue Origin have quickly begun to reduce the traditionally high price of space exploration by employing numerous novel methods like the use of reusable launch vehicles, potentially reducing the cost of each launch from $10,000 a pound to $1000 a pound.[8] These companies have proven to embody the term "disruptive industries," which will make outer space far more accessible to a far greater number of people by virtue of economies of scale. The growth in this sector has been acknowledged by many, with the Federal Aviation Authority of the United States of America predicting that the space tourism industry in isolation could be worth over $1 billion by 2022.[9] Parallels to the space industry are often drawn with the growth of the commercial aviation industry in the 1920's, wherein rapid innovation in technology led to an unprecedented rise in the popularity of this sector, with it quickly changing from an activity pursued by pioneering aviators to a common mode of transport for millions. This growth in the aviation sector, however, could not have been possible without the legal framework governing and fostering its growth, with the forward looking Warsaw Convention (Convention for the Unification of Certain Rules Renting to International Carriage by Air, 1929), that deals with the liability of air carriers and the Chicago Convention (Convention on International Civil Aviation 1944), that deals with the legal categorisation of air space, proving to be vital in encouraging the expansion of a fledging aviation industry.[10] In the same breath, there is a need to ensure that there exists clear, coherent and supportive legislations to

8 Roscoe M. Moore, *Risk Analysis and the Regulation of Reusable Launch Vehicles,* Journal of Air Law & Commerce, 1998, vol. 64, p. 245 at p. 251.

9 David Their, *FAA Predicts Space Tourism Will Be Worth $1 Billion In 10 Years,* available at <http://www.Forbes.Com/Sites/Davidthier/2012/03/22/Faahead-Predicts-Space-Tourism-Will-Be-Worth-1-Billion-In-10-Years/> last visited 6 May 2016.

10 Dr. Zhao Yun, *A Legal Regime for Space Tourism: Creating Legal Certainty in Outer Space,* Journal of Air Law & Commerce, 2009, vol. 74, p. 959 at p. 962.

foster the growth of this industry and currently, the archaic legislation that exists seems inadequate to encourage its growth. The chapter looks into the growth of the private space industry. Part I of the chapter deals with the goals and successes of two companies: SpaceX and Blue Origin, which have both made significant strides in increasing the accessibility of outer space. Subsequently, Part II compares some of the present and proposed activities of these companies with the existing legal structure in order to highlight the lacunae and the impediments that exist in *status quo* and Part III analyses a few possible solutions to these problems.

Part I: The Growth of Privatisation in Space Industry—A Look into SpaceX and Blue Origin

The last decade, as explained above, has seen immense growth in the commercial space industry and private space companies have made a valid case on how they can be the best suited candidates to pioneer the space frontier and catalyse the Space Age.[11] The benefits of these are many, be it the commercial incentive, scientific advantages or social justifications.[12] Private entities have now made it possible to fulfil the goals of national space agencies at a fraction of the cost, innovating new advanced methods as well as employing effective business techniques. This commercialization of outer space can largely be seen to have developed in the 1960s, with telecommunications satellites being sent into outer space by private players.[13] This trend has expanded significantly today due to advancements in technology and availability of large investments. Private players have penetrated the market on a far larger scale, with it being forecasted to further grow in the years to come. This growth is also predicted to expand across numerous sectors, be it the

11 Zach Meyer, *Private Commercialization of Space in an International Regime: A Proposal for a Space District*, available at <http://scholarlycommons.law.northwestern.edu/cgi/viewcontent.cgi?article=1705&context=njilb> last visited 6 May 2016.

12 *Ibid*, p. 244.

13 A Velocci, *Commercialization in Space: Changing Boundaries and Future Promises*, Harvard International Review, 2012, vol. 33, No. 4, pp. 49-53.

mining of asteroids for resources, transportation or orbital and sub-orbital space tourism. This has meant that the global space economy grew to a whopping $314.17 billion in governmental allocations and commercial revenues in 2013, a 4% growth from 2012 and growth that in no small way is attributable to the private industry.[14] This increase in participation can, in no small degree, be attributed to the driving down of costs of space travel by these entities, by using innovative mechanisms like reusable launch vehicles.[15] The two companies to achieve this critical breakthrough are SpaceX and Blue Origin. This part of the chapter aims to analyse the activities, goals and successes of these two companies that have grabbed the headlines in the recent past and have made significant strides in this field.

SpaceX

One such organization is the Space Exploration Technologies Corporation (hereinafter: "SpaceX"), that was established in 2002 and hopes to revolutionize the space industry by producing cost-effective mechanisms of reaching outer space.[16] SpaceX was established by the visionary entrepreneur Elon Musk, whose previous companies *PayPal* and *Zip2Corp* gave him the resources to proceed with this industry, and is currently his most high profile and exciting initiative. The inception of this project was largely driven by Musk's personal interest in increasing the accessibility of space exploration and his inability to procure rockets, leading him to begin the organisation to produce them

14 Space Foundation, 'Space Foundation's 2014 Report Reveals Continued Growth in the Global Space Economy in 2013', available at <http://www.spacefoundation.org/media/press-releases/space-foundations-2014-report-reveals-continued-growth-global-space-economy> last visited 7 May 2016.

15 Eric Berger, *Forget Blue Origin* v *SpaceX, the Real Battle is between Old and New Ideas,* available at <http://arstechnica.com/science/2016/01/forget-blue-origin-vs-spacex-the-real-battle-is-between-old-and-new-ideas/> last visited 6 May 2016.

16 Siemens, *SpaceX Delivers Outer Space at Bargain Rates,* available at <https://www.plm.automation.siemens.com/CaseStudyWeb/dispatch/viewResource.html?resourceId=5999> last visited 6 May 2016.

at what he believes will be a fraction of the cost.[17] Subsequently, the organization developed various stages of their Falcon rocket, and in 2010, the company successfully became the first private entity to launch a payload into orbit and successfully return the same to the surface of the earth: a feat which in the past only governmental agencies like NASA and Roscosmos could boast of.[18] Their latest version, the Falcon 9 rocket, was launched as recently as 2015, with the rocket successfully entering the geostationary orbit and successfully landing the first stage of the rocket upright on the surface of a drone ship in the ocean.[19] This innovation allows for such rocket components to be reused, thereby reducing their costs significantly. What has also gained traction is the cost of launching the Falcon 9, which was advertised to have cost around $57 million, a fraction of the traditional cost of such launches.[20] Furthermore, in 2008, SpaceX signed a $1.6 billion deal with NASA to transport cargointo orbit for NASA.[21] It was also around the time NASA decided to end the space shuttle program, making them dependent on Russia to transport their astronauts to complete their obligations in the space station.[22] This deal further grew to $2.8 billion in 2014, to transport astronauts by 2017 and ending NASAs reliance on the Russian Souyuz program. Moreover, SpaceX also aims to provide rocket launch services at the relatively low cost of $5 million to $7 million by using

17 Ashlee Vance, *Elon Musk: How the Billionaire CEO of SpaceX and Tesla is Shaping our Future*, 2015, pp. 227–228 (Virgin Books).

18 Jeffery Kluger, *10 Things to know about SpaceX*, available at <http://time.com/space-x-ten-things-to-know/>.

19 Irene Klotz, *SpaceX Falcon 9 Rocket Flies on Fifth Launch Attempt*, available at: <http://www.seeker.com/spacex-falcon-9-rocket-flies-on-fifth-launch-attempt-1770978020.html> last visited 6 May 2016.

20 Andrew Chaikin, *Is SpaceX Changing the Rocket Equation?*, available at <http://www.airspacemag.com/space/is-spacex-changing-the-rocket-equation-132285884/?no-ist> last visited 6 May 2016.

21 Lior Ronen, *SpaceX IPO: Successfully Disrupting the Aerospace Market*, available at <http://amigobulls.com/articles/spacex-ipo-successfully-disrupting-the-aerospace-market> last visited 6 May 2016.

22 *Ibid.*

reusable launch vehicles.[23] Furthermore, the development of its Dragon spacecraft to transport cargo, with the additional goal of being able to be certified to transport human beings in the near future, has proven to be a testament to the growth of commercial space tourism over the last decade.[24] Despite these successes and these targets, however, SpaceX's overall ambition is to colonize mars, with Elon Musk declaring that such an "outpost" in the red planet could be vital as an insurance policy, making humanity's extinction less probable and also for various scientific and technological benefits.[25] Furthermore, it has also been announced that a robotic Dragon spacecraft will land on its surface in 2018, followed by which human beings will be present in mars by 2026.[26] The proposed manned missions are visualized not to cater to trained astronauts, but towards ordinary civilians, leading to several grey areas within the legal framework that exists in *status quo*. Moreover, there are also various proposals by Musk that have proven contentious in the implementation of this plan, like his suggestion to essentially "nuke" the air above mars to increase the surface temperature and make the climate more hospitable.[27] While the technological, scientific and moral dilemmas of such issues are worth pondering upon, such fast emerging solutions also lead

23 Andrew Chaikin, *Is SpaceX Changing the Rocket Equation?,* available at <http://www.airspacemag.com/space/is-spacex-changing-the-rocket-equation-132285884/?no-ist> last visited 6 May 2016.

24 Marcia S. Smith, *SpaceX Aims to Land Robotic Dragon Spacecraft on Mars in 2018,* available on <http://www.spacepolicyonline.com/news/spacex-aims-to-land-robotic-dragon-spacecraft-on-mars-in-2018> last visited 6 May 2016.

25 Mike Wall, *Now is the Time to Colonize Mars Elon Musk says,* available at < http://www.space.com/31388-elon-musk-colonize-mars-now.html> last visited 6 May 2016.

26 Marcia S. Smith, *SpaceX Aims to Land Robotic Dragon Spacecraft on Mars in 2018,* available on <http://www.spacepolicyonline.com/news/spacex-aims-to-land-robotic-dragon-spacecraft-on-mars-in-2018> last visited 6 May 2016.

27 Loren Grush, *Elon Musk Elaborates on his Proposal to Nuke Mars,* available at <http://www.theverge.com/2015/10/2/9441029/elon-musk-mars-nuclear-bomb-colbert-interview-explained> last visited 6 May 2016.

to various questions regarding the existing space law regime and its ability to cope with such developments.

Blue Origin

Another private entity making demonstrable advancements in outer space exploration is Blue Origin, an organization aimed towards popularizing sub-orbital space travel. Established by Jeff Bezos, this company also hopes to reduce costs of space travel by reusing spacecraft and launch vehicles.[28] In its most recent attempt, the private space company launched and successfully recovered its *New Shepard* spacecraft for the third time, with the propulsion system making a vertical landing demonstrating the viability of such a method and reducing costs significantly.[29] While the latest flight was aimed towards space tourism at sub-orbital altitudes, the organization also hopes to propel travellers to orbit, with there being plans to develop larger spacecrafts to implement that goal.[30] Similar to SpaceX, Blue Origin hopes to send thousands of private citizens to outer space at a far lower rate, adding a great impetus to space tourism.[31] As mentioned above, while such initiatives have generated significant excitement, there is a need to assess whether or not the rapidly changing technology is regulated by a strong legal system. Through the course of the following section, the researchers hope to assess a few lacunae that exist within the aging legal structure governing outer space law.

Part II: Inadequacy of Current Space Treaty Regime

The previous part of the chapter dealt with activities that are currently undertaken and are proposed to be attempted in future

28 Calla Cofield, *Launch, Land, Repeat, Blue Origin's Amazing Rocket Liftoff & Landing in Pictures,* available at <http://www.space.com/32457-blue-origin-third-rocket-landing-pictures.html#sthash.Kk8t3hlR.dpuf> last visited 6 May 2016.

29 *Ibid.*

30 Elizabeth Howell, *Blue Origin: Quit Plans for Spaceships* available at <http://www.space.com/19584-blue-origin-quiet-plans-for-spaceships .html> last visited 5 May 2016.

31 Yoni Heilser, *Jeff Bezos' Plans for Space Travel includes 'Millions of People Living and Working in Space',* available at <http://bgr.com/2016/05/06/jeff-bezos-blue-origin/> last visited 7 May 2016.

by private space companies. While these companies may not necessarily pay much heed to the space legislations that govern them in contemplating these missions, they would be obligated to conform to the legal requirements that regulate and sometimes even prevent these activities. These would include at one level, the national legislation in the country they operate in, and to a greater level, the international treaties, specifically the outer space treaties mentioned earlier in the chapter. This part of the chapter will look into specific instances where the current space treaty regime would impede the activities proposed to be carried out.

Applicability of Treaty Regime to Private Enterprises

The space treaties were entered into at a time when there were only governmental organizations partaking in outer space activities. The text reflects the reality that existed back when they were signed. Most of the current innovations in space flight industry are coming from private corporations.[32] The Outer Space Treaty merely makes a mention of non-governmental organizations but does not go further in detailing their duties and responsibilities. Rather, it has put the onus on the States to monitor and supervise these private space activities. This could lead to problems for both the private corporations as well as the States. For instance, in relation to the Liability Convention that will be discussed in detail later, the State has to bear the burden for damages caused by the private corporations. The State may not always be able to retrieve this amount from the private corporations, especially considering the quantum of losses which a failed launch or mission entails. The private corporations may also be subject to more than necessary restrictions from the State due to latter's averseness to bear the burden of damages. A similar issue also arises from the Rescue Agreement where the private corporations are dependent on their State to retrieve the space object in the event of unintended landing in some other jurisdiction or no

32 Glenn H. Reynolds & Robert P. Merges, *Outer Space: Problems of Law and Policy*, 2nd Ed. 1997, p. 245 at pp. 275 & 279 (Westview Press Inc).

jurisdiction. It is necessary to adjust the treaty regime to specifically address such unique issues.

Rescue Agreement

The Rescue Agreement is important as it deals with instances when unintended events take place such that the space object and its passengers are forced to land or crash in some other State or non-state territories such as the high seas or Antarctica. This risk is a very likely scenario and it was seen to be important that an agreement was signed between States to indicate duties that are required to be performed by them in such a contingency. The Outer Space Treaty itself contains what can be considered a broad framework of this duty to provide all possible assistance to astronauts.[33] This requires States to regard astronauts as 'envoys of mankind' and provide assistance in the 'event of accident, distress or emergency landing on the territory of another State Party or on the high seas'.[34] The astronauts so rescued have to be safely and promptly returned to the State of registry of the space vehicle.[35] Similarly, with respect to space objects, the ownership and control of such objects continue to vest with the State Party on whose registry the object was launched.[36] If they are found beyond the limits of the State of registry, it has to be returned.[37]

The Rescue Agreement was signed "desiring to develop and give further concrete expression to these duties" expressed in the Outer Space Treaty with respect to providing assistance to astronauts and returning objects launched into outer space.[38] First, this expands on the earlier treaty by ensuring that assistance is provided in the event of accident, distress or unintended landing not just in the State's jurisdiction and the high seas, but also in 'any other place not under the jurisdiction

33 The Rescue Agreement, Preamble.
34 *Ibid.*
35 *Ibid.*
36 *Ibid,* Article VIII.
37 *Ibid.*
38 The Rescue Agreement, Preamble.

of any State'.[39] However, it is required for the personnel of the spacecraft to have alighted for this duty to be invoked, and it has been argued that this rules out any duty to rescue personnel stranded in orbit or deep space.[40] Secondly, instead of using the word 'astronauts', the Rescue Agreement uses the word 'personnel'. The word 'astronaut', especially when considered as connoting 'envoys of mankind', has a very narrow interpretation.[41] This view has been supported by various commentators who have argued that it only includes "the pilot, crew and any professional performing a service on board".[42] Perhaps to correct this narrow reading, the word 'personnel' was used in the Rescue Agreement to give a much broader interpretation. Thirdly, instead of returning the space objects and astronauts to State of registry which refers to one particular State, they are to be returned to the launching authority, which could include multiple States.

While the Rescue Agreement intended to broaden the scope of who is a space traveler and when and where a State is to rescue, it is still uncertain whether space tourists would fall within the ambit of personnel. Primary rule of treaty interpretations requires interpreting the treaty text using their 'ordinary meaning'.[43] Ordinary meaning of 'personnel' is 'people employed in an organization or engaged in an organized

39 The Rescue Agreement, Article III.

40 Paul G. Dembling & Daniel M. Arons, *The Treaty on Rescue and Return of Astronauts and Space Objects*, William & Mary L Review, 1968, vol. 9(3), p. 630 at p. 649; see also Carl Q. Christol, *The Modern International Law of Outer Space*, 1982, pp. 171-172 (Pergamon Press).

41 I.H. Ph. Diederiks-Verschoor, *Search and Rescue in Space Law*, in Proceedings of the Nineteenth Colloquium on the Law of Outer Space, 1977, pp. 152-159 at p. 156.

42 Stephen Gorove, *Interpreting Salient Provisions of the Agreement on the Rescue of Astronauts, the Return of Astronauts, and the Return of Objects Launched into Outer Space*, 1968, in Proceedings of the Eleventh Colloquium on the Law of Outer Space, 1969, p. 93; Elina Kamenetskaya, *"Cosmonaut" ("Astronaut"): An Attempt of International Legal Definition"*, in Proceedings of the Thirty-First Colloquium on the Law of Outer Space, 1989, pp. 177-178.

43 Vienna Convention on the Law of Treaties, Article 31(1).

undertaking',[44] and space tourists would not fall within the ambit of this definition as they are not engaged in any service or employment.[45] Yet, it is to be noted that some commentators argue that personnel is interpreted broadly enough to include even space tourists,[46] but the challenge is to bring this broad interpretation in line with the customary law of treaty interpretation.[47] Fortunately, this lacuna has not affected the seven private space tourists who have undertaken the journey into space. Nevertheless, considering the number of sub-orbital and orbital flights proposed to be carrying space tourists, it is likely that a spacecraft makes an unintended landing in another State or outside the jurisdiction of any State. In such instances, it would be necessary to receive the assistance of other States which might be in a better position to provide assistance than the launching State.

As regarding space objects, each Contracting State is required to take practicable steps to recover space objects and their components found within their territorial jurisdiction upon the request made by launching authority.[48] Similarly, upon request by launching authority, they are required to return the space objects found even beyond their territorial jurisdiction back to the launching authority or its representative.[49] The key difference between rescuing astronauts/personnel and recovering space objects is that in the latter situation, expenses borne by the State for recovery and return of space objects has

44 *Concise Oxford English Dictionary*, 12th Ed.

45 Stephen Gorove, *supra* note 42, p. 93. Bin Cheng, *Space Objects, "Astronauts" and Related Expressions*, in Proceedings of the Thirty-Fourth Colloquium on the Law of Outer Space, 1992, vol. 17, p. 165.

46 Gabriella Catalano Sgrosso, *Legal Status of the Crew in the International Space Station*, in Proceedings of the Forty-Second Colloquium on the Law of Outer Space, 2000, pp. 35, 36, 40; Steven Freeland, *Up, Up and . . . Back: The Emergence of Space Tourism and its Impact on the International Law of Outer Space*, Chicago Journal of International Law, 2005, vol. 6(1), p. 10.

47 Mark Sundahl, *The Duty to Rescue Space Tourists and Return Private Spacecraft*, Journal of Space Law, 2009, vol. 35, p. 163.

48 The Rescue Agreement, Article V(2).

49 *Ibid*, Article V(3).

to be borne by the launching authority.[50] The problem that arises for private companies from this provision is that the return of their space objects is subject to a request being made by the State responsible for launching, who may not be very forthcoming in making the request due to the costs. The private companies cannot unilaterally request the return of space objects, even if they are willing to bear the cost of the recovery.

Liability Convention

With the increase in number of daily launches once these space tourism companies start operating at maximum efficiency, even if the percentage of risk reduces, the number of actual instances of damage caused due to the spacecraft can increase. These accidents can happen in orbit when it collides with another space object, or within the earth, either in the territory of the launching State or in the territory of another State or outside the territory of States. Damage could be caused to both life and property in all these instances and the need to affix liability becomes an issue. Further, even the space tourists travelling in these spacecrafts will have to be provided to some recourse to claim compensation for any accidents.

At the time of entering into the Outer Space Treaty, it was expected that space exploration would be dominated by national space agencies.[51] While Article VI of the Treaty clearly indicates that even non-governmental entities were contemplated, it is also explicitly mentioned that the States Parties have to bear international responsibility for national activities in outer space.[52] The basis for this can be inferred from the Article itself which requires that States authorize and continuously supervise activities carried out by non-governmental entities.[53] Thereby, it can be argued that since the activities are controlled by the State, they can be held liable for the same.

50 The Rescue Agreement, Article V(5).

51 Dr. Zhao Yun, *A Legal Regime for Space Tourism: Creating Legal Certainty in Outer Space*, Journal of Air Law & Commerce, 2009, vol. 74, p. 960.

52 The Outer Space Treaty, Article VI.

53 *Ibid.*

The Liability Convention expands on this obligation by 'elaborating effective international rules and procedures concerning liability for damage caused by space objects'.[54] It establishes two regimes of liability. First, for damage caused by space objects on the surface of the earth or to aircraft, it is an absolute liability regime.[55] Second, for damage caused elsewhere, it is a strict liability regime.[56] The Liability Convention follows the same approach as in Outer Space Treaty and holds the launching States to be jointly and severally liable. It is for this reason that most States have national legislations to pass on the liability to private organizations.[57] It is also important to note that claims can only be brought by the State which suffers damage, or whose natural or juridical persons suffer damage.[58] This implies that space tourists would have to claim through their respective States and cannot bring a private claim under the Liability Convention.

The applicability of Liability Convention itself is an uncertain issue in situations where the space tourists are nationals of the launching authority. Article VII of the Liability Convention states that it shall not apply to situations where the damage is caused to its own nationals or foreign nationals during the time they are participating in the operation of that space object.[59] For instance, if a US Citizen takes a trip on board a Blue Origin Space Craft and during the journey damage is caused to this person, he will not be able to claim under the Convention. It has also been argued that space passengers would always be participating in operation of the space object and as a result, they would never be eligible to claim.[60] But it is a bit of a

54 The Liability Convention, Preamble.

55 *Ibid,* Article 2.

56 *Ibid,* Article 3.

57 Steven Freeland, *Up, Up and . . . Back: The Emergence of Space Tourism and its Impact on the International Law of Outer Space,* Chicago Journal of International Law, 2005, vol. 6(1), p. 10.

58 The Liability Convention, Article VIII(1).

59 *Ibid,* Article VII.

60 Stephan Hobe, *Legal Aspects of Space Tourism,* Neb L Rev, 2007-2008, vol. 86, p. 439 at p. 449.

stretch to say that space tourists are participating in the operation of the space object, so they should be allowed to claim through their States. There could also be a contradiction between the Rescue Agreement and the Liability Convention in this regard. As already discussed, one of the interpretation of 'personnel' under the Rescue Agreement is 'body of persons engaged in service of spacecraft'. Space tourists would have to fall within the ambit of this definition for them to be rescued. But if they do fall within the ambit, then Liability Convention would cease to apply to them by virtue of Article VII. It would imply that in the event of an accident, the space tourist can either be rescued or reimbursed, but not both.

Moon Agreement

The Moon Agreement in its current form brings about various questions and challenges with regards to the expansion of programs like SpaceX and Blue Origin. As has been pointed out, both programs hope to increase the access given to private citizens in outer space and this raises various lacunae, most specifically with the question of sovereignty.[61] Elon Musk's SpaceX has been resolute in laying down its ultimate objective of colonizing mars. However, the Moon Agreement clearly mandates that the moon and other celestial bodies will not be subject to sovereignty of any one State and will be the province of all mankind.[62] This carries forward the mandate laid down in the Outer Space Treaty and hence makes it impossible for such an initiative to prosper.[63] Moreover, with programs like Blue Origin gaining popularity, the number of private citizens in space would also lead to the establishment of services on celestial bodies and inevitably of property rights being vested on certain individuals.[64] With parties being unable to extend

61 Zach Meyer, *Private Commercialization of Space in an International Regime: A Proposal for a Space District*, Northwestern Journal of International Law & Business, 2010, vol. 30, Issue 1, pp. 241–261.

62 Moon Agreement, Article 4(1).

63 Outer Space Treaty, Article II.

64 Steven Freeland, *Up, Up and . . . Back: The Emergence of Space Tourism and its Impact on the International Law of Outer Space*, Chicago Journal of International Law, 2005, vol. 6(1), p. 13.

sovereignty and control over celestial bodies, the goals of such programs would be rendered futile and hence, no owner of land on such bodies will be in a position to exercise legal rights over the same.

Another issue that stems from the Moon Agreement is the imposition of the laws relating to placing nuclear devices or weapons of mass destruction on the moon and other celestial bodies or in their orbits.[65] As has been mentioned previously, the plans involving the colonization of mars involves subjecting the atmosphere above the poles of the planet to a nuclear pulse for a period of time to raise its temperature and to make it habitable for human beings.[66] Aside from the feasibility of such an action, the legality, given the current status of the law undoubtedly prohibits such an action and in that context, it becomes important to assess whether there is a need for a change, should such a situation arise.

Part III: Possible Changes to Treaty Regime

The previous part looked into the various treaties governing activities in outer space and identified specific provisions of the treaties which would impede the activities relating to space tourism and exploration. The primary stakeholders or the parties affected by the interplay between the proposed activities and the treaty regime are the States, private individuals in the States, private corporations engaging in the activities and private individuals participating in the activity. To give an illustration, an individual space tourist *A* from England uses the Blue Origin spacecraft from USA to make a sub-orbital flight and in return, the spacecraft makes an unintended landing in India, causing damage to property and also leaving the space tourist stranded and injured. Here, the States involved are USA, England and India. The individual *A* is also affected by the activity. Further, Blue Origin is also an important affected party in the illustration.

65 The Moon Agreement, Article 3(3).

66 Loren Grush, *Elon Musk Elaborates on his Proposal to Nuke Mars,* available at <http://www.theverge.com/2015/10/2/9441029/elon-musk-mars-nuclear-bomb-colbert-interview-explained> last visited 6 May 2016.

Finally, even people of India are affected by the damage caused to property as a result of unintended damage.

In the above illustration, if the treaty regime were to apply as it stands right now, Blue Origin requires USA to make a request if it requires the spacecraft to be recovered and returned. USA would have to bear the burden for this and pay India. The individuals of India whose property was damaged is dependent on India making a claim on their behalf against the USA. Also, India has to ensure that the space tourist is rescued and returned but would not be compensated for this. From this very illustration, it can be intuitively argued that the current regime would not effectively work as the stakeholder causing the effect and the one who bears the burden are almost always different.

The major reason for the conundrum presented above is the lack of recognition of private corporation and individuals in the treaties. The first proposal in this regard is the recognition of private enterprises and accordingly to substitute the duties of States with that of the private players when the activity is conducted by them. This could present problems as individuals of one State may not be able to institute a claim before another State's courts. This could be considered as infringement of sovereignty. Thus, an international body to adjudicate disputes would be useful for fair adjudication of claims and it would also absolve the States from bearing the cost of its private space flight industry. The recognition of private industry would also aid in implementing the Liability Convention and Rescue Agreement.

The Liability Convention imposes the liability on the States for any damage caused. Similarly, the claims would also have to be made through the State. With the grant of jurisdiction to private individuals or corporations to institute claims against private individuals or corporation before international body discussed above, it would make the process more accessible and independent of the political consideration of the States. It would also mean that States don't have to bear the burden of commercial failures. It has been suggested that Liability Convention be remodeled along the lines of Warsaw Convention as a model.[67] This, as suggested above, would include an international tribunal to hear disputes arising out of outer space incidents.[68] This would also mean a shift from absolute liability to negligence based liability with respect to injury to space tourists as they have voluntarily signed up for the activity.[69] With respect to damage caused to stakeholders not participating in the space activity such as the property owners in India in the illustration provided earlier, there is still a strong case for sticking to absolute liability regime.

To address the problem from the Rescue Agreement, it would be necessary to include space tourists within the ambit of 'personnel'. On the contrary, it would appear that these space tourists would have no recourse to be rescued and returned to their respective States. However, it would be necessary for the State to be reimbursed for the expenses resulting from the rescue and return.[70] It would be an inequitable expectation for States to bear the burden of rescuing space tourists engaging in commercial activities. The cost could be imposed on the space tourist itself, or the private space company or the insurer if any. This could either be regulated or left to private contract between the parties.

Finally, with regard to the Moon Agreement, instead of outright rejection of nuclear technology based on unfounded fear that existed back in the cold war days, the risk of any such

67 Van C. Ernest, *Third Party Liability of the Private Space Industry: To Pay What No One Has Paid Before,* Case Western Reserve Law Review, 1991, vol. 41(2), p. 503.

68 Brian Beck, *The Next, Small, Step for Mankind: Fixing the Inadequacies of the International Space Law Treaty Regime to Accommodate the Modern Space Flight Industry,* Albany Law Journal of Science & Technology, 2009, vol. 19(1), pp. 1 to 37 at p. 13.

69 Gabriella Catalano Sgrosso, *Legal Status of the Crew in the International Space Station,* in Proceedings of the Forty-Second Colloquium on the Law of Outer Space, 2000, 35, 36, 40; Steven Freeland, *Up, Up and . . . Back: The Emergence of Space Tourism and its Impact on the International Law of Outer Space,* Chicago Journal of International Law, 2005, vol. 6(1), p. 10.

70 Mark Sundahl, *The Duty to Rescue Space Tourists and Return Private Spacecraft,* Journal of Space Law, 2009, vol. 35, p. 163.

proposal need to assessed in a scientific way with respect to the threat of such a project. As Elon Musk argues, in the event of an existential threat to humans on earth, a safe haven in mars could be the only available alternative and unknown and unfounded fears of technology should not be a barrier. It should not become a situation where the barrier to exploration is not lack of technology but an out of context law.

Conclusion

In conclusion, it is apparent that there has been and will continue to be a surge in the participation of private entities in the exploration and use of outer space and the current legal regime that exists to govern these operations seem far from adequate. The space treaties in question were framed in an extremely different political climate and there is thus, a need to relook at their efficacy today. As argued, there is an undoubted need to update such laws and address the lacunae that exists with private space players in order to benefit all stake holders involved. Moreover, given that private citizens may soon play a major role in space exploration, there is a need to safeguard their rights and ensure that there exists an effective legal framework. Further, these dated legislations need to address the recent changes in technology as well as cater to any possible changes that could very much occur in the recent future, given the proposals of companies like Blue Origin and SpaceX. Lastly, while there is also a need, in this age of rapid advancements, to regulate the over exploitation of outer space, the avenues that are provided for space exploration by virtue of private entities entering the market is immense, as seen above, and there is a need to foster this growth by updating the laws that regulate them.

Chapter 8

Regulating Space Tourism and Space Habitation– Significance of Sustainable Development Concept

DEVA PRASAD M.*

Introduction

Outer space travel and tourism are interesting and exciting propositions for the mankind. Outer space travel has already being initiated by professional astronauts. Attempts are also in the pipeline by many private entities to make outer space travel a viable tourism venture.[1] Some non-professional astronauts have already travelled to outer space as part of adventure tourism. They have travelled to International Space Station and stayed there for short duration by paying large amount of money.[2] These people who have travelled to outer space for the

* Assistant Professor of Law, Indian Institute of Management, Kozhikode.

1 Private ventures such as Virgin Galactic are investing in space tourism ventures. Please see 'Virgin Galactic website', available at <http://www.virgingalactic.com> last visited 1 July 2016. Olly Barrot, *In Evaluation of the Potential Demand for Space Tourism within the United Kingdom*, available at <http://www.spacefuture.com/archive/an_evaluation_of_the_potential_demand_for_space_tourism_within_the_united_kingdom.shtml> last visited 1 July 2016.

2 Stephan Hobe, *Legal Aspects of Space Tourism*, Nebraska Law Review, 2007, vol. 86, No. 2, pp 439-458. Dennis Tito is the first person to go as a space tourist and till now around 5 others have also gone as space tourist.

purpose of adventure and leisure and for non-professional purpose could be brought under the ambit of "space tourists". But space tourism in an established manner is yet to take off. The concept of outer space tourism in that sense is still futuristic.[3]

The outer space habitation is another futuristic development expected due to the rapid advances in science and technology. Project such as 'Mars One' is planning to establish permanent habitat in outer space.[4] With the population explosion, natural resource exploitation and increase in human needs, the proposition of outer space habitation would become a necessity and reality in future. From the perspective of this chapter, it is to be highlighted that space tourism and space habitation are pertinent developments that would grapple the international space law and policy in the near future. Interesting legal issues also arise due to the proposal of outer space tourism and outer space habitation.

The present international space law does not have any specific legal mechanism relating to space travel and space habitation. This could be attributed to the lack of commercial exploration as an objective while drafting Outer Space Treaty 1967 and Liability Convention 1972. Regulating the space tourism and space habitation activities are necessary for the purpose of long term interest of mankind regarding outer space.

In this context, relevance and significance of the legal concept of sustainable development in enabling the international space law to regulate the legal concerns posed by space tourism and space habitation is analyzed. The concept of sustainable development has gained relevance in public international law

3 Ram Jakhu, *Space Tourism in India,* Report of the Interdisciplinary Research Study, 2010, (University of Petroleum and Energy Studies Publication). Also see Ranbir Singh, Srikrishna Deva Rao, *et al.* (eds), *Current Developments in Air and Space Law,* 2012 (Delhi: National Law University Press).

4 See Mars One Website, available at <http://www.mars-one.com> last visited 1 July 2016.

as an enabling norm[5] and as a tool to strike balance between conflicting interests of commercial-economic development and environmental protection.

Overview of Legal Issues Relating to Space Tourism

Space tourism being an emerging concept, there is no specific definition. Space tourism as mentioned earlier, has been more of an *ad hoc* practice and not an established one till now. Further, the existing international space treaties are drafted before the trend of space tourism had started. These factors would have contributed for the present situation, where there is no specific definition either for space tourism or space tourist.

According to eminent space law scholar Stephan Hobe, space tourism could be considered to include any activity, especially a commercial activity that attempts to provide the participants with "direct or indirect experience with space travel."[6] It is relevant to indicate that in this definition, Stephan Hobe has emphasized on the commercial nature of the activity. This would be a significant distinguishing feature for the space tourism from the space travel, which is generally undertaken for scientific purposes and for larger public interest.

In the case of space tourism, the commercial factor and adventure and leisure factors come into picture. This also calls for looking at the outer space from the perspective of travel and tourism. The international space law till now has perceived outer space exploration from the perspective of only scientific

5 The International Court of Justice decision in the cases of *Gabcikovo-Nagymaros Project (Hungary* v *Slovakia)* [1997] ICJ Reports 7 and *Pulp Mills on the River Uruguay (Argentina* v *Uruguay)* [2010] ICJ. Reports 14 have discussed in detail about the significant balancing character of sustainable development. Moreover, the inclusion of sustainable development concept and its underlying principles in the various conventions such as the Convention of Biological Diversity 1992, United Nations Framework Convention on Climate Change 1992 also provides evidence of the enabling norm function.

6 Stephan Hobe, *Legal Aspects of Space Tourism*, Nebraska Law Review, 2007, vol. 86, No. 2, pp. 439-458. Dennis Tito is the first person to go as a space tourist and till now around 5 others have also gone as space tourist.

exploration of outer space. It is important to note that the space tourism is a commercial activity devoid of any specific public interest, which lacks any larger benefit accruing to the mankind. This crucial fact would be relevant for international space law in deciding the law and regulatory mechanism governing the space tourism. The commercial and passenger travel angle attached with the space tourism would be posing new challenges for outer space law. Safety of passengers, activities of the passengers and pollution of outer space environment are certain issues, which need to be tackled by the international space law.

Space tourism could be sub-orbital space tourism or orbital space tourism. Sub-orbital space tourism basically intends to provide an opportunity for the tourist to experience the feeling of lack of gravity or micro gravity by taking the tourist to the altitude above the earth.[7] It is important for the international space law to clearly demarcate the air travel from the sub-orbital space. This calls for a clear solution to the demarcation of outer space for effective regulation of outer space tourism.

At the same time, in case of orbital space tourism, the outer space tourists are given an opportunity to be taken to the orbit and stay there for a brief period during which the persons get an experience to stay at 'space based habitat'[8] facilities such as the International Space Station. Based on the above discussion, it is clear that space tourism as a concept is posing significant challenges to the international space law. Certain important challenges are discussed below.

Legal Regulation for the Safety of Outer Space Passengers

The legal regulation regarding safety of passengers would be an important issue perplexing the international space law. Presently, the outer space flights are considered involving considerable risk attached with the process. The failure and accidents of

7 Ram Jakhu, *Space Tourism in India,* Report of the Interdisciplinary Research Study, 2010, p. 3 (University of Petroleum and Energy Studies Publication).

8 *Ibid,* p. 4.

space flight shuttles such as Challenger and Columbia of United States are primary reasons for the perception regarding risk attached with the outer space flights.[9] The accident of Virgin Galactic spaceship in December 2014[10] while attempting a test flight helps to remind mankind on the risk and concern regarding safety.

The international air law, which governs the airspace use by aircrafts also emphasizes heavily on the significance of safety.[11] Chicago Convention on International Civil Aviation 1944 and institutional mechanism of International Civil Aviation Organization (ICAO) form the basis for the safety mechanism in case of international air law. The International Civil Aviation Organization stipulates important safety standards such as airworthiness. The Standards and Recommended Practices (SARPs) help in streamlining and providing a uniform safety standard.

In this regard, emphasis could be made regarding the need for safety regulations and legal mechanism in case of space tourism. It is important for the international space law to evolve legal mechanism for effective control over the various commercial and private ventures involved in the space tourism. A high threshold of safety standards needs to be stipulated considering the high risk involved in space tourism.

Article VI of Outer Space Treaty 1967 would be relevant in the context of the safety standards that need to be adhered. Article VI of the Outer Space Treaty provides that non-governmental entities "require authorization and continuing supervision by the appropriate State Party to the Treaty". As required under the Article VI of Outer Space Treaty, States should constantly monitor all the space tourism activities.

9 Ram Jakhu, *Space Tourism in India,* Report of the Interdisciplinary Research Study, 2010, p. 27 (University of Petroleum and Energy Studies Publication).

10 *Spacecraft for Tourists Explodes on Test Flight,* The Hindu, available at <http://www.thehindu.com/news/international/spacecraft-for-tourists-explodes-on-test-flight/article6554849.ece> last visited 1 July 2016.

11 Jiefang Huang, *Aviation Safety, ICAO and Obligations Erga Omnes,* Chinese Journal of International Law, 2009, vol. 8, No. 1, pp. 63-79.

The international space law needs to lay down the threshold of safety standards. The precautionary principle, which is an underlying principle of sustainable development concept, could be applied in this context as a benchmark of the safety standard. The States should ensure that only those space tourism ventures maintaining the safety standard above the particular threshold mandated by the international space law are authorized.

For enabling the States to maintain a uniform standard of safety with regard to space tourism, it is pertinent for international space law to quickly evolve standards. The role which precautionary principle could play in this context requires to be highlighted.

Legal Regulation Needed for the Purpose of Outer Space and Earth Environment Protection

It is also important to ensure that due to space tourism, there is no adverse impact being caused to the earth and outer space environment. There are studies pointing to the fact that emissions from the increasing rocket launches are leading to climate change. The study highlights that "as few as 1,000 rocket launches per year would cause world wide climate change".[12] In case of the advent of space tourism, the impact on climate change due to the spacecraft and rocket launches would be adverse. This is because outer space tourism would constitute a large part of the rocket and spacecraft traffic in the times to come. Usually the rocket or spacecrafts are used for the purpose of launching satellites. But once the outer space tourism becomes feasible in a commercial manner, large number of spacecrafts would be launched for space tourism purpose. It is reported that emissions from large number of spacecraft launch would be contributing in an adverse manner towards the climate

12 Martin Ross, Michael Mills *et al*, *Potential Climate Impact of Black Carbon Emitted by Rockets*, Geophysical Research Letters, 2010, vol. 37(24), also see Jon Krois, *Onwards and Upwards: Space Tourism's Climate Costs and Solutions*, available at <http://www.columbiaenvironmentallaw.org/articles/onwards-and-upwards-space-tourism-s-climate-costs-and-solutions> last visited 1 July 2016.

change. This issue brings up the prime reason for regulating the space tourism rocket launches as that of ensuring outer space and earth environment are not adversely impacted and also ensuring that the long term sustainable use of outer space is protected.

It is important to strictly regulate the space activities conducted by the private entities and corporates for commercial purpose if there is no impending public and national interest being served.[13] The public interest space launches need to be clearly distinguished from those space launches which only serve the private interest. The space tourism activities are primarily private interest commercial activities for the purpose of entertainment and there is no imminent public interest being served.

The volume of solid and liquid waste in outer space could increase many folds due to the space tourism.[14] The outer space pollution is a critical issue that needs to be taken into consideration by international space law. Article IX of Outer Space Treaty 1967 highlights the requirement of absence of harmful contamination of outer space. Apart from these issues, the possibility of "outer space vandalism by an insensitive and self-centered space tourist"[15] also needs to be contemplated and tackled by the international space law. Outer space vandalism contemplates insensitive activities of polluting and destroying outer space resources. Outer space vandalism by deliberately polluting the outer space environment could lead to harmful contamination and might lead to accidents for future space tourist activities and adversely impact safety of future space tourist and might develop chances of forward contamination.

13 Jon Krois, *Onwards and Upwards: Space Tourism's Climate Costs and Solutions,* available at <http://www.columbiaenvironmentallaw.org/articles/onwards-and-upwards-space-tourism-s-climate-costs-and-solutions> last visited 1 July 2016.

14 Dirk C. Gibson, *Commercial Space Tourism: Impediments to Industrial Development and Strategic Communication Solutions,* 2012, p. 22 (Bentham Books).

15 *Ibid,* p. 23.

Hence it is important for the international space law to evolve standards that could normatively develop Article IX of Outer Space Treaty 1967's requirement of absence of harmful contamination of outer space.[16] In this regard, the private entities conducting the outer space tourist activities have to be regulated to function without adversely impacting the outer space environment.

Overview of Legal Issues relating to Outer Space Habitation and Space Settlement

The outer space habitation and space settlement is another important challenge being faced by the international space law. The establishment of a permanent habitation and space settlement might become a reality soon. In this regard it is important to factor in the various legal issues that might crop up. The pertinent legal implications posed by the proposal of space settlement are as follows:

The Legal Issue of Right to Private Property in Outer Space

The available literature[17] on space settlement and outer space habitation proposes right to private property as the way forward for effectively enabling the outer space habitation and space settlement. It becomes important to clarify the terminologies of space habitation and space settlement, as there is no legal definition of these terminologies that has evolved till now. The terminology 'space habitation' is used for either short-term temporary habitation (as in the case of space station) or long-term permanent habitation (as envisaged in the case of Mars One). However, 'space settlement', is usually referred for the

16 As pointed out by Lawrence D Roberts, lack of consensus towards an inferred understanding of harmful contamination makes it much more difficult to evolve standards. See Lawrence D Roberts, *Addressing the Problem of Orbital Space Debris: Combining International Regulatory and Liability Regimes,* Boston College International & Comparative Law Review, 1992, vol. 15, No. 1, pp. 50-60.

17 Alan Wasser and Douglas Jobes, *Space Settlement, Property Rights and International Law: Could a Lunar Settlement Claim Lunar Real Estate If needs to Survive,* Journal of Air Law and Commerce, 2008, vol. 73, pp. 38-78. See Thomas Gangale, *The Development of Outer Space: Sovereignty and Property Rights in International Space Law,* 2009 (Praeger).

long-term permanent settlement. For the purpose of this chapter, space habitation and space settlement are considered from a long-term permanent habitation perspective.

The legal issue of right to private property in the outer space arises in case of long-term permanent settlement/habitation. Allowing land claims in the outer space and recognizing the private property in the outer space is being put forward as an incentive measure.[18] The argument advanced by the private property proponents is that recognition of the private property would act as an incentive for the government as well as various private players to invest capital for the purpose of developing viable technology for outer space habitation and settlement. But this proposal is against the basic principle of non-appropriation,[19] which is a significant pillar on which the entire space law is being built.

The evolved State practice till now also indicates that non-appropriation principle is a cardinal principle for international space law. Except for the lone incident of Bogota Declaration 1976[20] by the equatorial States, there has been no attempt as of now challenging the non-appropriation principle. However, the recent trend of commercial focus on the outer space, especially for the purpose of outer space settlement, tries to de-bunk the relevance of non-appropriation principle. The future relevance of non-appropriation principle in the context of commercial and technological developments such as space settlement remains a contested arena.[21] The non-appropriation principle has helped in ensuring that conflict over outer space between the countries could be regulated and controlled to large extent until now.[22] The non-appropriation principle is

18 Alan Wasser and Douglas Jobes, *Space Settlement, Property Rights and International Law: Could a Lunar Settlement Claim Lunar Real Estate If needs to Survive,* Journal of Air Law and Commerce, 2008, vol. 73, p. 39.

19 The Outer Space Treaty 1967, Article II.

20 Declaration of the First Meeting of Equatorial Countries 1976.

21 Fabio Tronchetti, *The Non□Appropriation Principle under Attack: Using Article II of the Outer Space Treaty in its Defence,* available at <http://www.iislweb.org/docs/Diederiks2007.pdf> last visited 17 June 2015.

22 *Ibid.*

considered as part of the customary international law. The State practice and *opino juris,* clearly support the fact that the non-appropriation principle is a customary international law. There is widespread acceptance for non-appropriation principle by the States. There is no major persistent objection to the non-appropriation principle in international space law. The fact that no major space-faring country has claimed sovereignty in outer space elucidates the widespread acceptance for non-appropriation principle. As mentioned, except for the lone-standing incident of Bogota Declaration 1976, there is no other property right claim by States in the outer space.

In case the non-appropriation principle is compromised, there could be many contesting claims for outer space real estate amongst nations and other private entities participating in the outer space activities. This could lead to a situation of unregulated commercial exploitation of outer space. Once the right to property in outer space is accepted, space settlement would also lead to the situation of space colonization. With the space settlement participants occupying sites in celestial bodies, there would be claims of treating such sites as individual property. Further, countries having space-faring capacity would also be in a race for colonization of the outer space territory. Once the non-appropriation principle is compromised and property rights are allowed in outer space, the States would follow the old colonization method of 'doctrine of discovery'[23] for claiming the property.

The element of public interest[24] in the international space law might be compromised in such situation. The free-riding instinct[25] could lead to economic and profit making interest to overtake the long-term interest of mankind in the outer space. This would also lead to international space law putting forth

23 Robert Miller, *The International Law of Colonialism: A Comparative Analysis,* Lewis and Clark Law Review, 2011, vol. 15, pp. 847-921 at p. 851.

24 Ram Jakhu, *Legal Issues Relating to the Global Public Interest in Outer Space,* Journal of Space Law, 2006, vol. 32, pp. 31-110.

25 Garrett Hardin, *The Tragedy of the Commons, Science,* vol. 162, pp. 1243-1248.

the interest of only space-faring countries. Moreover, it would be breach of the customary international law. The need of the hour is to strengthen the non-appropriation principle with the aim of protecting the long-term sustainable interest of mankind in the outer space.

The Legal Issue Relating to the Impact on the Outer Space Environment Due to the Space Settlement and Outer Space Habitation

Since the outer space habitation and space settlement contemplate permanent habitation in outer space, issues of outer space environmental pollution and waste management due to anthropogenic activities might crop up. The day-to-day waste generation due to human life in the space settlement would have a major impact upon the outer space environment. The major concern would be ensuring that there is no forward or backward contamination.

The human health in space settlement would also be impacted due to the waste generation, if not managed properly. Building a human life sustaining system in the outer space environment for long-term settlement is a major challenge. Further, there is "lack of atmospheric and ecological system" in the celestial bodies such as moon.[26] The absence of well functioning ecosystem as on earth would lead to the absence of regeneration capacity exhibited by the earth's eco-system.[27] Hence any pollution caused by the space settlement would be difficult to tackle.

Contemplating and framing the rules and regulations for outer space environment pollution and waste by space settlement endeavours is an important agenda before the international space law. The issues mentioned regarding space tourism would be relevant in the case of outer space habitation also.

26 David Timothy and Michael Hall, *Sustainable Space Tourism: New Destination and New Challenges* in C. Michael Hall, Stefan Gossling, Daniel Scott (eds), *The Routledge Handbook of Tourism and Sustainability,* 2015, pp. 450-460 at p. 453 (Routledge).

27 *Ibid.*

Further, it is also important to look at the issues of outer space mining, as a source of resource for space settlement needs. There is need for regulating the outer space mining as part of the space settlement ventures. Space settlement ventures have to function within the ambit of international space law. The natural resources in the outer space cannot be over-exploited since they may adversely impact the outer space environment. Outer space settlement ventures would have to be regulated strictly based on the above consideration to the outer space environment.

The Legal Issue Relating to Safety of the Human Life in the Outer Space

The legal issue relating to safety of the human life in the outer space is much more relevant as the entire concept of space habitation prepares for permanent settlement of human beings in the outer space. It is important to understand that the outer space does not possess the conducive factors for sustaining human life. This requires enormous effort for ensuring that the human life is safe in the outer space habitation and settlements. The issues such as exposure to radiation, lack of gravity leading to health issues, lack of breathing air are important impediments that need to be overcome for the purpose of ensuring safety of human life in the outer space.[28] Apart from these impediments, the issues of the spacecraft and space habitation module being exposed to accidents also loom large on the human safety.[29] The risk involved in the space settlement venture would adversely affect the human life participating in the space settlement. Further, the space settlement ventures such as Mars One plans to have permanent human settlement in mars. Here, the significant question arises about safety of the participants in case of any accidents or mishaps during the mission. At present, there are no particular safety standards that the international space law provides for space settlement ventures.

28 Ram Jakhu, *Space Tourism in India, Report of the Interdisciplinary Research Study*, 2010, p. 3 (University of Petroleum and Energy Studies Publication).

29 *Ibid.*

Due to lack of safety in the case of space settlement ventures, the possibility of permitting the space settlement itself is in question.

From the discussion above, it is pertinent that the international space law needs to develop law and regulations for the purpose of ensuring safety of human life in the outer space habitation and settlement.

Legal Regulation Needed for the Purpose of Ensuring Long-term Sustainable use of Outer Space

The discussion provides for a clear understanding that the long-term sustainable use of outer space would be undermined if unregulated space tourism and space habitation is allowed, which may lead to free riding and tragedy of commons issue. In this regard, it is pertinent for the international space law to evolve a long-term sustainable solution for regulating outer space tourism and space habitation. The issues of safety of space tourism passengers and human life in space habitation are major concerns that have arisen. Apart from safety, another major issue is that of environmental concern regarding outer space and earth environment. The space tourism and space habitation and settlement could give rise to many concerns for the outer space environment and to a certain extent in case of earth environment also. These are the issues, which could affect the long-term sustainable use of outer space.

Safety concerns as well as the impact on the outer space environment and earth environment require evolution of a legal regulatory mechanism. Significant revamping of the existing free riding mechanism due to the gap in law is required. Balancing of the commercial interest with the long-term public interest in sustainable use of outer space is also required. This is the scenario in which the legal concept of sustainable development attains relevance as a balancing mechanism.

Legal Concern Regarding Impact of Space Settlement on Outer Space Natural Resource Exploitation

An important concern for international space law posed by the outer space settlement is the impact it would have on the outer space natural resources. An outer space settlement or habitat would require natural resources for their consumption and survival. A permanent outer space settlement would have to invariably bank upon the natural resource available on various celestial bodies for the purpose of survival. The absence of effective mechanism for the purpose of regulating and governing the natural resources exploitation remains a major concern for international space law.[30]

In this context, the claim that outer space settlement could impose on the natural resources over the outer space would be an additional legal issue. There could be issue of accessibility and over exploitation of resource. The space settlement participants may claim ownership over the natural resources. It is important for international space law to evolve legal standards to tackle the claim on outer space natural resources. This re-emphasizes the need for evolving a balancing concept for the purpose of regulating the outer space natural resources from being depleted and also having a legal mechanism for controlling the outer space settlement and habitation.

Significance of Applying Sustainable Development Concept to Space Tourism and Space Settlement

The sustainable development concept coupled with this normative value and practical applicability is found relevant in the sphere of public international law. The analysis of International Court of Justice's decisions in *Gabcikovo□Nagymoros*[31] and in the case of *Pulp Mills on River Uruguay*[32] helps in arriving at the conclusion that though the sustainable development concept is not accepted as part of the customary international law, there is clear understanding that the

30 Lack of consensus amongst the developed and developing states regarding treating the natural resources on moon and other celestial bodies as common heritage of mankind has led the failure of Moon Agreement 1979.

31 *Gabcikovo□Nagymaros Project (Hungary* v *Slovakia)* [1997] ICJ Reports 7.

32 *Pulp Mills on the River Uruguay (Argentina* v *Uruguay)* [2010] ICJ Reports 14.

sustainable development concept is identified as an integral and significant part of the international law.

Analysis of the Judge Weeramantry's separate opinion[33] in *Gabcikovo–Nagymoros* case also facilitated in identifying that the sustainable development concept has a normative character. This is expected to help sustainable development in acting as an enabling and modifying norm along with the already existing norms, which could be considered as an interstitial norm. The existing conflicting norms of economic development and the environmental protection could be balanced with the help of sustainable development.

According to the International Law Association's 'New Delhi Declaration of Principles of International Law Relating to Sustainable Development, 2002',[34] the sustainable development concept has the underlying principles, *viz.*, principle of sustainable use, principle of integration, principle of intra-generational equity, principle of inter-generational equity, principle of common but differentiated responsibilities, precautionary principle, principle of good governance and public participation.[35] 'Polluter Pays principle and 'environmental impact assessment' process are also identified as underlying elements of the legal concept of sustainable development.[36] The related and underlying principles mentioned above acts as instrumentalities for applying sustainable development concept to the international space law for tackling issues posed by outer space tourism and habitation.

33 Separate Opinion of Vice President Judge Weeramantry, available at <http://www.icj-cij.org/docket/files/92/7383.pdf>.

34 International Law Association's 'New Delhi Declaration of Principles of International Law Relating to Sustainable Development, 2002', available at <www.ila-hq.org/download.cfm/docid/65DD8DEF-E74D-4ED5-925EBC6D73F19C97>.

35 *Ibid.*

36 Principle 13 and Principle 17 of Rio Declaration on Environment and Development1992 helps in reiterating the significance of polluter pay principle and environment impact assessment process. Also see Niel Craik, *The International Law of Environment Impact Assessment: Process, Substance And Integration,* 2008, p. 11 (Cambridge University Press).

Principle of Sustainable Use and Principle of Integration

Principle of sustainable use and integration[37] has significance from the perspective of space tourism and space habitation. This principle could be used for the purpose of bringing responsibility upon the space tourism and space habitation endeavors to ensure that the outer space environment and resources are used in a sustainable manner. The over emphasis on commercial aspect of outer space tourism as well as the private property claims in space settlement could be balanced with the 'sustainable use' principle. Application of 'sustainable use' principle would help in emphasizing the public interest element of long-term interest in outer space.

Principle of sustainable use would demand the outer space tourist and also those enabling the outer space tourism to keep the outer space environment clean from pollution. The issue of unwanted vandalism of space tourist could also be regulated using the 'sustainable use' principle. The organizing entity of space tourism could also be brought under the ambit of sustainable use.

The 'sustainable use' principle would also require regulating the space tourism rocket launches for the purpose of ensuring that outer space and earth environment are not adversely impacted.[38] The number of space tourism rocket launches would have to be clearly restricted once the 'sustainable use' principle is strictly enforced. Moreover, the 'sustainable use' principle could also be applied to space habitation endeavors.[39] The space habitation endeavors could also lead to issue having adverse

37 Principle 3 and Principle 4 of Rio Declaration on Environment and Development 1992 helps in reiterating the significance of sustainable use and integration principle.

38 Principle 1, New Delhi Declaration, 2002. Wasteful use of natural resources would have to be ruled out. Further, States and the various stakeholders are under the obligation "to avoid wasteful use of natural resources and promote waste minimization policies", thus promoting sustainability in the use of resources.

39 Principle 1.3, New Delhi Declaration, 2002 extends the duty of States to ensure sustainable use of natural resources even to the outer space.

impact upon the outer space environment. In this connection, the waste management and pollution issues due to the space habitation could be controlled using the 'sustainable use' principle.

Further, the 'sustainable use' principle could be used for the purpose of ensuring that the space habitation and settlement endeavors would use the outer space natural resources in a sustainable manner. The principle of integration also brings responsibility on the international space law to ensure that the space tourism and space habitation legal mechanism has to consider the outer space environment also. The principle of integration also ensures that the economic and commercial ventures such as space tourism and space habitation could be regulated and environmental factor could be brought in for consideration.

Principle of Inter-generational Equity and Principle of Intra-generational Equity

Principle of inter-generational equity and Principle of intra-generational equity[40] have relevance for space tourism and habitation as they strengthen non-appropriation principle and provide for a theoretical base to analyze the claim for property rights in outer space. Inter-generational equity principle emphasizes upon the need for using resources in a manner keeping in mind the requirement of future generations.[41] The non-appropriation principle, which is the edifice of the international space law, could be further strengthened normatively by the inter-generational equity principle. Inter-

40 Principle 3 and Principle 6 of Rio Declaration on Environment and Development 1992 helps in reiterating the significance of principle of inter-generational equity and principle of intra-generational equity.

41 The Principle 2.1 of the New Delhi Declaration states "the principle of equity is central to the attainment of sustainable development. It refers to both inter-generational equity (the right of future generations to enjoy a fair level of the common patrimony) and intra-generational equity (the right of all peoples within the current generation of fair access to the current generation's entitlement to the Earth's natural resources)".

generational equity principle would be an appropriate mechanism for ensuring that there is no over-exploitation of resources, so as to ensure that future generations are not affected. Non-appropriation principle, which also intends to ensure that no State tries to establish ownership over outer space resources and establish monopoly, could be strengthened by the inter-generational equity principle.

Principle of inter-generational equity is an important instrument by which the space habitation proposal of right to property in the outer space could be evaluated. The right to property in the outer space without any proper regulation would lead to free riding and only certain space-faring nations to establish monopoly status. But this is against the idea of inter-generational equity as the need of future generations are also to be contemplated. Thus the space habitation proposal of right to property could be viewed as in conflict with the non-appropriation principle and also that of the inter-generational equity principle.

Principle of intra-generational equity would also be important in reiterating the need for non-appropriation principle and normatively strengthening the same. The intra-generational equity principle emphasizes upon the need for equity amongst the nations in accessing the outer space.[42] The non-appropriation principle also intends to ensure that powerful space-faring countries do not claim monopoly over ownership in outer space resources, including property rights. The application of inter-generational equity and intra-generational equity principle helps in countering the challenge of space colonization. Claiming outer space territory by States would be denial of equity among the States in accessing the outer space. Further, space colonization would also have adverse impact on the interest of the future generation in outer space. Application of the non-appropriation principle thus helps in providing a firm grounding for the non-appropriation principle in the context of claim for property rights in the outer space. Application of

42 *Ibid*, footnote No. 41.

the inter-generational equity and intra-generational equity principles help in highlighting the relevance of non-appropriation principle. The need for adding normative strength to the non-appropriation principle, in context of the right to property claim by space settlement ventures are succeeded with the application of the inter-generational equity and intra-generational equity principle.

Thus application of principle of inter-generational equity and intra-generational equity also impose responsibility upon the space tourism and space habitation activities to ensure that the outer space environment is protected to ensure long-term use of outer space for future generation as well as for other States.

Precautionary Principle

Precautionary principle[43] has a major role to play in the case of space tourism and space habitation. Precautionary principle is applicable to space tourism and space habitation as these two activities have an enormous amount of risk and uncertainty involved. Primary concerns regarding risk and uncertainty attached with human safety and outer space environment due to the space habitation and space tourism have to be properly addressed.

The precautionary principle stipulates that in case of lack of scientific certainty regarding activities involving high risk, such activities should be restricted for the protection of human health and environment.[44] The precautionary principle creates a burden of proof on the proposer that proposed activity does not constitute environmental harm or adversely affect human

43 Principle 15 of Rio Declaration on Environment and Development, 1992 helps in reiterating the significance of precautionary principle.

44 Principle 4 of New Delhi Declaration clearly states that "precautionary approach is central to sustainable development in that it commits States, international organizations and the civil society, particularly the scientific and business communities, to avoid human activity which may cause significant harm to human health, natural resources or ecosystems, including in the light of scientific uncertainty".

health.[45] In this regard, the precautionary principle would demand the technology to advance to a more evolved stage, where the safety of human life and the impact on the outer space environment would have scientific certainty. The space tourism and space habitation activities will have to be clearly indicated as activities having no irreversible damage upon the human health.

Hence application of the precautionary principle may require conditional licensing of the space habitation and space tourism activities in view of the safety of human life and concerns regarding impact upon outer space environment. Application of the precautionary principle would be enabling the States to monitor and authorize the activities by private entities as required under the Article VI of Outer Space Treaty 1967. Moreover, the application of precautionary principle would help in ensuring that the international space law could devise a mechanism for regulating the high risk and uncertainty related to space tourism and space habitation.

Principle of Common but Differentiated Responsibilities

The principle of common but differentiated responsibilities[46] would help in casting a responsibility on the space-faring States to balance the long-term public interest in the outer space for mankind with the commercial private interest in the outer space. The space tourism and space settlement ventures are basically driven by the commercial private interest.

Major space-faring nations should ensure that the outer space technological capability and financial resources should be used in the long-term public interest. Space tourism and space settlement ventures could lead to adverse impact on earth environment or outer space environment and such activities need to be regulated. Major space-faring nations have an

45 Lotta Viikari, *The Environmental Element in Space Law: Assessing the Present and Charting the Future*, 2008, p. 169 (Martinus Nijhoff).

46 Principle 7 of Rio Declaration on Environment and Development, 1992 helps in reiterating the significance of principle of common but differentiated responsibilities.

additional level of responsibility under the common but differentiated responsibilities principle as the space-faring countries have benefitted mostly from the outer space technology.[47] Since the space-faring countries have gained the maximum benefit from outer space technology, there is an additional responsibility to take pro-active leadership in ensuring that the outer space is protected from over commercialization and over exploitation by the private interest.

Further, to ensure that the outer space is kept intact for long term perspective, space shuttle launch for space tourism has to be regulated to the extent needed to ensure that the climate change impact due to such spacecraft launches are kept to the minimum. As pointed out earlier, only those outer space launches that necessitate national and larger public interest should be permitted at the first instance. Only those space tourism launches, which do not adversely cause carbon emission, should be permitted.

Application of the common but differentiated responsibilities principle would be helpful in regulating the orbital space tourism, which lead to creation of space debris. As the major space-faring countries have contributed to the creation of maximum amount of space debris, they have to take pro-active role in controlling the orbital space tourism and other space tourism/settlement activities, which lead to space debris creation.

Procedure of Environmental Impact Assessment

The procedure of environmental impact assessment[48] has major significance for the purpose of space tourism and space

47 The Principle 3 of the New Delhi Declaration states that: "Differentiation of responsibilities, whilst principally based on the contribution that a State has made to the emergence of environmental problems, must also take into account the economic and developmental situation of the State."

48 Principle 17 of Rio Declaration on Environment and Development 1992 helps in reiterating the significance of environmental impact assessment process.

habitation. The space tourism and space habitation are high-risk activities involving large-scale uncertainties. Hence the long-term impact upon the outer space environment as well as upon the earth environment due to space tourism and space habitation is yet to be understood.

Applying the procedure of environmental impact assessment to the space tourism and space habitation ensures that there is an obligation upon the States to conduct environmental impact assessment studies before allowing activities such as space tourism and space habitation. Since *ex ante* environment impact assessment need to be conducted, the proposed space tourism and space settlement activities are accorded permission as a result of which the States could control those activities, which do not follow the safety standards. Moreover, the environment impact assessment procedure would help the States to fulfill the responsibility under Article VI of Outer Space Treaty 1967 to monitor and grant authorization for the private space activities. The precautionary principle along with the procedure for environmental impact assessment would strengthen the international space law in keeping a strong guard upon the protection of outer space environment as well as the earth environment.

Polluter Pays Principle

The polluter Pays' principle[49] has major significance as a legal mechanism for controlling the space tourism and space habitation. Space tourism and space habitation could lead to major anthropogenic pollution and waste in the outer space as discussed earlier. Application of polluter pays principle to space tourism and space habitation could help in providing a legal mechanism for the purpose of regulating the pollution in outer space. Penalty measures could be imposed on the States and entities engaging in space tourism and space habitation leading to outer space environment pollution. Polluter pays principle

49 Principle 13 of Rio Declaration on Environment and Development 1992 helps in reiterating the significance of polluter pays principle.

could also be used to strengthen the Liability Convention 1972 to deal with the outer space pollution due to space tourism and space habitation. The present fault based liability for accidents in the outer space could be elaborated using the polluter pays principle. This is due to the fact that in case of application of polluter pays principle, the polluter would have to pay for the pollution and damage caused as well as for restoration to the previous condition to the extent possible.[50]

Hence for all the activities, which could lead to space debris creation, such as the orbital space tourism and space settlement activities, there could be clear regulations. Moreover, lack of ecosystem in the celestial bodies makes it difficult for waste management. Hence a strict principle such as polluter pays principle would be required to tackle the complex situations that may arise due to space settlement.

The polluter pays principle would require all the space tourism and space habitation ventures to have constant vigil regarding their activities in the outer space. The commercial interest of private parties would have to be balanced with the long-term public interest of mankind in outer space by application of polluter pays principle.

Principle of Good Governance and Participation

Principle of good governance and participation could be relevant for the purpose of ensuring that the law and policy making regarding space tourism and space habitation would be done with the participation of all the stakeholders such as entities involved in these ventures, States and space organizations. The good governance refers to presence of well-defined institutional mechanism to ensure the space tourism and space habitation are well regulated. Well-defined institutional mechanism would necessarily require the UNCOPUS to take major steps in this direction. Hence application of principle of good governance and participation would also help in strengthening the

50 Phillipe Sands, *Principles of International Environmental Law*, 2003, p. 253 (Cambridge University Press).

international space law to govern the space tourism and space habitation. It is important to take into confidence the private parties regarding the need for regulation of outer space tourism and settlement. The long-term interest of mankind in the outer space could be sustained only with the cooperation[51] of the all the States as well as the private ventures involved in space tourism and space settlement activities. Application of good governance and participation would require the development of institutional mechanism to consider the safety standards and environmental protection measure for the space tourism and space settlement.

Conclusion

This chapter portrays the absence of effective mechanism in international space law regarding space travel and space habitation. The chapter also displays how the applications of sustainable development concept to the space travel and space habitation try to bridge the gap in the international space law framework. It could be understood that the application of the underlying principles of sustainable development concept such as the sustainable use principle, precautionary principle, inter-generational equity and intra-generational equity would help in normatively strengthening the international space law to deal with the legal issues relating to space tourism and space habitation.

The above discussion could help to understand that the present international space law is not equipped to deal with the legal issues concerning space tourism and space habitation. It also helps to understand that the legal concept of sustainable development and its underlying principles could help in normatively strengthening the international space law to regulate and space tourism and space habitation.

Application of principles such as precautionary principle, polluters pays principle and procedure for environment impact

51 S. Bhatt, *Studies in Aerospace Law: From Competition to Co⃞operation,*1974 (Sterling Publishers).

assessment could help in addressing major concerns regarding the protection of outer space and earth environment due to space tourism and space habitation. The concerns relating to human safety in case of space tourism and space habitation could also be regulated to a large extent with the application of sustainable development concept and the underlying principles.

The application of sustainable development concept and the underlying principles also help in reiterating the non-appropriation principle and debunk proposal for right to property in the outer space.

Chapter 9

Obligation Towards Debris Remediation vis-a-vis Space Contamination and Fault Liability

PRANJAL SRIVASTAVA*

Introduction

Space debris in the outer space is posing threat to myriad functional space objects. Presently, under the space law regime, there is nothing that explicitly prohibits the creation of debris in the outer space. Debris, as small as the size of a peanut, has the potential to cause serious damage to a fully-functional satellite.[1] The problem is worse in the lower earth orbit (hereinafter "LEO") which is already inundated with the huge amount of debris. The orbit stands the risk of cascading effect of mutual collisions and chain reaction, which would result in causation of irreparable loss to the nations' space objects.[2] The influx of the debris in the lower earth orbit is to the extent

* 4th Year, BA, LLB (Hons), The West Bengal National University of Juridical Sciences, Salt Lake, Kolkata.

1 European Space Agency, <http://www.esa.int/Our_Activities/Space_Engineering/Clean_Space/FAQ_s> last visited on 19 March 2016.

2 J.C. Liou, A. Rossi & H. Krag, *et al.*, *Stability of the Future LEO Environment*, Inter-Agency Space Debris Coordination Committee, 2013, IADC-12-08 Rev 1.

that, NASA pursuant to its debris regulation estimate studies has concluded that it might take as long as two hundred years to stabilize the LEO.[3] This however, is subject to the active removal of five large intact objects per year from the orbit and strict adherence to debris mitigation guidelines by the space-faring nations starting from the present day.[4] There seems to be no relenting to the problem, given the fact that there is no accepted or unanimous definition of the space debris. Although, 'space debris' is now included within the scope of 'space objects', yet, there is no unanimity amongst the States as to its definition.

Various interpretations have been given to the virtue of Articles I, II and IX of the Outer Space Treaty to conclude that the presence and creation of debris in the outer space is the violation of principles of international law. However, there is no such interpretation that has been adopted by UN through any of the resolutions or endorsed by UNCOPUOS except the debris mitigation guidelines. For the same reason, the debris mitigation and debris remediation measures assume importance in the context of fault liability under Article III of the Liability Convention. If the principles are to be considered as the hard bound binding principles of international law, then their violation could be relevant for the purpose of determining fault liability under the space law regime. Any breach of the said violation shall be a determining factor in examining the due diligence as a fault liability standard under Article III of the Liability Convention.

Obligation to Not Create Debris under Outer Space Treaty

There is an obligation upon the States as per the space treaties which prohibit any contamination of the outer space environment, in the form of debris or otherwise. The Preamble

3 N.L. Johnson, N.M. Hill & J.-C. Liou, *Controlling the Growth of Future LEO Debris Populations with Active Debris Removal,* Acta Astronautica, 2010, vol. 66, No. 5, pp. 648-653.

4 *Ibid.*

and Article I of the Outer Space Treaty categorically mention that the exploration and the use of outer space ought to be for the benefit of all persons and in the interests of all countries. The debris creation of any form can in no manner be considered as beneficial to any country as it poses serious hazard to the satellites and the space objects in the orbit. Further, some scholars have also argued the presence of the debris in the outer space to be a violation of Article II of the Outer Space Treaty. The rationale for concluding the same is that, Article II is the extension of the States' right to explore outer space and when the object changes in to a debris (due to its non-functionality or otherwise), the exploration of outer space ends.[5] Therefore, the debris starts appropriating the outer space as it also poses serious danger to the presence of other functional satellites in the orbit.

Obligation of States to Actively Remove Debris under Fault Liability Regime

The extremely dangerous nature of the debris makes it imperative for States to undertake actions other than debris mitigation. The developed space-faring nations have been pondering over the nature of the operations involving the debris remediation.[6] However, the issue involves legal complexity with respect to the liability if any damage is caused in the precinct of the outer space. The damage caused to any person or property of a State is covered under Article III of the Liability Convention. Therefore, the issue of debris remediation and ADR, involves taking into account the fault liability which governs the damages caused in the outer space. However, the scope of Article III is not yet extended to impose any liability upon the State, to remove its non-functional object (debris) if the same is posing a threat to the other satellites present in the orbit. Therefore,

5 Christopher D. Wiliam, *Space: The Cluttered Frontier,* 1994-1995, vol. 60, J Air L & Com, p. 1152.

6 Debra Werner, *NASA's Interest in Removal of Orbital Debris Limited to Tech Demos,* 22 June 2015 last visited on 19 April 2016.

there is no incentive for a State to remove the satellite which may foster State's nonchalance towards actively removing its non-functional space object or debris as against the rights of the other States. Additionally, given the absolute nature of a States' jurisdiction over its space object under Article VIII of the Outer Space Treaty, any attempt of removal of the State's satellite without its prior permission shall constitute piracy even if the removal attempt was advanced in good faith to protect one's own satellite. This chapter focuses and analyses the above issues with an attempt to reconcile and balance the rights of a State in the event of threat caused to its satellite due to space debris. The author with a holistic approach would also attempt to determine the legal issues surrounding debris remediation measures under Outer Space Treaty and Liability Convention so as to prevent the contamination of outer space.

Debris Mitigation and Debris Remediation

Inter-Agency Space Debris Coordination Committee (IADC) and the subsequent UNCOPUOS Guidelines endorsed by UNGA Resolution 62/217 suggest the number of measures that the countries ought to take for mitigating the space debris. The debris remediation is, on the other hand, the steps that a State takes in furtherance of actively removing the defunct satellite or the space debris out of the outer space. While the former are the precautionary and preventive measures channelled towards not letting the debris form in the first place while the latter is more of a cure to the already formed debris in the space environment.[7] Could it however be concluded that the debris remediation by whatever feasible technology by a State is a step towards debris mitigation in effect? The answer to the same requires the comprehensive standing mitigation guidelines.

7 Natalie Pusey, *The Case for Preserving Nothing, The Need for a Global Response to the Space Debris Problem,* 2010, vol. 21, Colo J Int'l Envtl L & Pol'y, p. 432.

Debris mitigation guidelines provide for the comprehensive steps for the States to undertake in their space mission so as to shun any debris creation in the outer space environment and especially in the LEO. To gain a very basic understanding of the guidelines, it requires the States to take steps involving passivation, de-orbiting, re-orbiting and avoiding any measure or step that would result in the break up or the creation of debris in the outer space environment. The listed measures include within it the prohibition of intentional action of destructing the other satellite which might involve self-destruction or intentional collision of the satellites. The break-up of the satellite in order to reduce the debris ought to be undertaken so as to reduce all the associated dangers with the creation of debris in the outer space environment.[8] The active removal of the space debris from the outer space might inevitably involve the breaking up of the satellite if it qualifies to be space debris. Despite the breaking up of the satellite would be the measure of the actively removing debris but there is a slight and in some cases even a significant probability that this action might result into creation of further debris fragments. If that is the case, then rather than the removal or reduction of the space debris from the outer space, the State might end up in creating the further debris fragments. Therefore, there is a significant overlap and contradiction between the two and there might be instances where the both could run counter to each other as the steps towards debris remediation might result into consequences that run directly against the debris mitigation guidelines. Therefore, despite the debris mitigation and debris remediation seem to accomplish the reduction of space debris from the outer space *prima facie*, they need not necessarily do so.

The further distinction between the two might be drawn with regards to the liability that would be imputed upon the States for undertaking or not undertaking the debris mitigation

8 IADC Guidelines.

and debris remediation measures. The space debris mitigation guidelines are recommendatory in nature and therefore do not qualify as hard-law principles of international law.[9] Therefore the debris mitigation guidelines are the principles of soft-law, if not adhered by the States would not impose any liability upon them, under the normal circumstances.

Further, it is a known and well-concluded fact by the scholars that the space activity is the ultra-hazardous activity and thus naturally requires higher degree of care and due diligence to be undertaken before any space flight could be advanced. However, any ultra-hazardous activity would be one which involves within its functionality an exceptional risk of the severe damages.[10] Like all hazardous activities, any space mission or activity is considered to include danger that is rarely expected to materialise but if so, then would cause disproportional and irreparable harm. The harm could also be a series of harm if the result of the space activity is the creation of debris as the debris so created may cause further debris fragments. The prospects of danger and risk in any space-flight is not solely related and limited to the creation of debris. Any space flight or space

9 Inter Agency Space Debris Coordination Committee (IADC), Space Debris Mitigation Guidelines, 2002; revised 2007; Space Debris Mitigation Guidelines of the United Nations Committee on the Peaceful Uses of Outer Space, UNGA Res. 62/217, 22 December 2007; European Code of Conduct for Space Debris Mitigation, Issue 1.0., 28 June 2004. The guidelines were endorsed by UN General Assembly Resolution and the EU guidelines for the mitigation of debris are all sets of recommended measures that a space-faring nation should incorporate in any of the space mission so as not to further contaminate the outer space environment by creating more debris in it. The problem is worse with respect to the debris that is present in LEO. It is an established fact that LEO contains the most number of satellites and consequently the space debris in it and therefore any further creation of space debris might result into the series of collision creating unimaginable number of debris in the LEO making it unviable any further usage.

10 Nandasiri Jasentulyana, *The Legal Dimension of the Sustainability of Outer Space Activities: The Draft Code of Conduct on Outer Space Activities,* Proceedings of the Fifty-fifth Colloquium on the Law of Outer Space, in Sergio Marchisio, Ed. 2012, p. 11.

mission involves tremendous prospects of risk and danger with it. First and foremost reason for the same is the amount of energy required and stored in the space objects to undertake any space flight is enormous. Needless to mention is the consequences if any accident is caused due to any mishappening on the earth. The space activity involves a similar or even bigger risk in the outer space as the outer space contains ample satellites with tremendous amount of energy stored within them. Therefore, any mishappening would result into serious consequences graver than the formation of space debris. Due to the same very reasons, space activities are concluded to be inherently dangerous and therefore, proper assessment and due diligence should be prerequisite of every space flight.[11]

Fault Liability under Article III of the Liability Convention

Article III of the Liability Convention enlists the liability upon the State in the event of damage caused to the person and property of another State in the space. Article III of the Liability Convention is based on the fault liability and hence a State is only liable to the extent that the fault is attributable to the State. Therefore, the State stops becoming liable to the damages caused when the wrongful act done by the State is not the reason for the damages caused to another State's person or property. This could be linked to the concept of causal link which in essence lays down that there needs to be an immediate and necessary link of the wrongful act committed by the State and the damages caused. Only once the wrongful act could be attributable to the State and it is established that the damages caused to the person or the property was attributable to those wrongful acts of the States, could the State be made liable under Article III of the fault liability. Not all the wrongful acts are relevant for the purpose of determining the liability of the State under Article III of the Liability Convention. Therefore, it can

11 Dr. Michael Mineiro, *Space Debris Remediation: The Public International Legal Status of Jurisdiction and Control of Space Objects*, Presented to the International Interdisciplinary Congress on Space Debris Remediation in Montreal, Q.C., 11 November 2011.

be concluded that only the breach of established principle of hard law would be relevant in determining the liability of the State.[12]

Articles on State Responsibility shall determine whether a wrongful act could be attributed to a State. A State shall not be liable for the damages caused if it is not responsible for the wrongful act which is the reason of the damages caused. The responsibility in this regard as per Prof. Bing Cheng at a very fundamental level would mean the authorship over an act.[13] Thus, if the State cannot be held responsible for an act which means if the act is not attributable to the State then State would not be liable under Article III of the Liability Convention. However, even if the State's authorship over an act is to be established the fault liability would not be applicable unless the authored act by the State is wrongful. The wrongful nature of the act shall be decided by the established principles of international law which would include the space law treaties signed between the countries.[14] However, there exists no consensus amongst the authors that whether the breach of all provisions and clauses of the treaties be relevant for the purpose of determining fault liability under Article III of the Liability Convention.

Determining Liability under Article III of the Liability Convention

The reason for no unanimous position of law regarding the determination of the fault liability under Article III of the Liability Convention is no definite definition of 'fault'. The definition of fault is not provided for in the treaty and therefore, different views and opinions have emerged amongst authors regarding the acts that would make a State liable under

12 Hamid Kazemi, Hadi Mahmoudi & Dr. Ali Akbar Golroo, *Towards a new International Space Liability Regime Alongside the Liability Convention 1971*, Proceedings of the Fifty-fifth Colloquium on the Law of Outer Space, in M. Schwartz, 2012, p. 606.

13 Bin Cheng, *Studies in International Space Law*, 2004, p. 603 (Oxford University Press).

14 Hamilton DeSaussure, *The New Era in Outer Space*, 1979-1980, vol. 13, Akron L Rev, p. 594.

Article III of the Liability Convention. Article III is *lex specialis* with regard to the damages that occur in the outer space to any State's person or the property. One of the interpretations is with respect to the fault liability under Article III of the Liability Convention is that there exist two prongs to the fault liability under the Article. To determine the breach of fault under Article III of the Liability Convention there needs to be either a violation of international law or breach of duty of care.[15] The duty of care owed is that of higher due diligence as per Article 3 of the Draft Articles on the Responsibility of States for Internationally Wrongful Acts 2001 (hereinafter "Articles on State Responsibility"). Further the same has also been confirmed and concluded by various jurists that the due diligence standard relevant for determining fault under Article III of the Liability Convention shall be extremely high due to the ultra-hazardous nature of any space activity. Therefore, the hypothesis in itself precludes any frivolous exclusion from Article III of the Liability Convention by virtue of *force de majeure*. Taking in regard the ultra-hazardous nature of any space activity, the duty of due diligence would include within it the duty to comprehensively examine the size of operation, the special weather condition prevalent in the outer space etc. Any State failing to undertake comprehensive examination of even the extraordinary circumstances prevailing in the outer space and earth would be liable under Article III for any damage caused in the outer space. Because of the ultra-hazardous nature of the space activities a State is presumed having knowledge of the special conditions prevailing in the outer space. As the result of the knowledge, the State is obliged to act diligently to resist the extraordinary circumstances that might be prevailing in the outer space.[16]

15 Martha Mejia-Kaiser, *ESA's Choice of Futures: Envisat Removal or First Liability Case*, Proceedings of the Fifty-fifth Colloquium on the Law of Outer Space, in M. Schwartz, 2012, p. 606.

16 Leslie I Tennen, *Outer Space, A Preserve for All Humankind*, 1979-1980, vol. 2, Hous J Int'l L, p. 155.

Causal Link between the Wrongfulness of the Act and the Damages Caused

Therefore the main questions that are needed to be answered are that, what violation of international law would be considered to be relevant for the determination of fault under Article III of the Liability Convention? Further, would any violation of international law make a State liable under Article III of the Liability Convention? If any international law violation were to be considered for the purpose of determining fault under Article III of the Liability Convention then even a single delay or non-registration of the space object would make a person liable under the Registration Convention 1975 and consequently under Article III of the Liability Convention. Would the violation of the aforementioned provision then mean that a State is liable under Article III of the Liability Convention as well? The authors were in disagreement to the same and proposed that although the violation under Registration Convention might make a State liable under international law, the violation would not be relevant for the purpose of determining fault under Article III. There seems to be a great obfuscation in this regard as to what violation would result into breach of Article III of the Liability Convention. The other school of thought suggest that the international law violation shall not be relevant for the purpose of determining fault under Article III of the Liability Convention. The sole parameter for determining the existence of fault under Article III of the Liability Convention ought to be the breach of due diligence violation by the State. However, if a State violates any principle of international law then it could be liable for the breach of international law but not under Article III of the Liability Convention. The reason as follows is, if the interpretation that the violation of international law would result into violation of Article III is to be followed then any violation of Public International Law would result into a violation of Article III which was not envisaged by the drafters of the treaty.[17]

17 Ronald E Alexander, *Measuring Damages under the Convention on International Liability for Damages Caused by Space Objects*, 1978, vol. 6, J Space L, pp. 153-157.

To resolve the dilemma it was suggested that both the due diligence violation and international law violation must be considered relevant for the purpose of determining fault under Article III of the Liability Convention as long as the causal link between the international law violation in question and the damages suffered could be established. The requirement of establishing the causal link was also said to be an important factor for considering the violation of due diligence.[18] Therefore, it was proposed that the causal link needs to be established by the State taking resort of Article III of the Liability Convention. Therefore, not every violation of international law and due diligence shall make a State liable under Article III of the Liability Convention. The fault liability standard required to be established under Article III is higher and not every auxiliary violation could establish fault liability under Article III. Therefore, there needs to be a violation of hard law principles of international law which would be considered to be relevant for fault liability standards under Article III of the Liability Convention.

There should not be such high standard of fault liability under Article III of the Liability Convention. The previous provision that covered the liability for the damages in the outer space was Article VII of the Outer Space Treaty. Under the regime of liability under Article VII of the Outer Space Treaty, a State would be strictly liable for any damage caused to the person or property in the space.

Presumption of Causal Link in Space Related Activities

The important question that emerges out is could the creation of debris in the outer space be considered to be the violation of Article III of the Liability Convention, especially given the high fault liability standard under Article III? The change of liability standard was from strict liability to fault liability where

18 Sergio Marchisio, *The Legal Dimension of the Sustainability of Outer Space Activities: The Draft International Code of Conduct on Outer Space Activities*, Proceedings of the Fifty-fifth Colloquium on the Law of Outer Space, in M. Schwartz, 2012, p. 606.

the term 'fault' was not defined. Therefore, Article III needs to be interpreted in view of the background of the liability standard for the damages caused in the outer space under the regime of Article VII of the Outer Space Treaty. Albeit the standard of liability has been changed to the strict liability, it has to be interpreted in the favour of the State which has suffered damages in the outer space. In light of the above, the causal link in the event of the space activity needs to be assumed which means that there is a presumption of causal link in the event of damages in the outer space.[19] The nature of the presumption is rebuttable but it is for the respondent State to prove that there was a break in chain of causation or the causal link, if there is any alleged damage done by the State in the outer space.[20] It can be reasoned that when liability concerning the ultra-hazardous activity is in question then the burden to establish the causal link is to be with the accused respondent State. If the respondent State could prove that there is no causal link between its activities and the damage so caused, then it could preclude its liability under Article III of the Liability Convention. However, the other way to preclude the liability under Article III is by establishing that there is a substantial intervening act committed by the applicant, which is the reason of the damage caused to the State. If it can be established that if not for the intervening act of the State that has suffered the damages, the damages would not have been caused to it, then the accused State would not be liable under Article III of the Liability Convention.[21]

At this point it becomes imperative to note that the liability under Article III cannot be precluded by establishing contributory negligence. The standard of proof for the purpose of rebutting the causal link is higher and it has to be proved

19 Summary Records of the 18th meeting, UNGAOR, 58th sess., U.N. Doc. A/C.6/58SR.18, p. 41.

20 Summary Records of the 19th meeting, UNGAOR, 58th sess., U.N. Doc. A/C.6/58SR.19, p. 43.

21 Howard A. Baker, *Space Debris: Legal and Policy implications*, 1989, p. 25 (Netherlands: Springer).

that the State is not liable because of the intervening act of another State. However, if the State fails to prove so and is only able to prove the intervening act as a measure of contributory negligence then the accused State shall be liable under Article III of the Liability Convention.[22]

To answer the question that was raised regarding the interpretation of Article III of the Liability Convention to prohibit the creation of debris within the outer space, the mechanism of Article III was to be understood. The interpretation is a step before the damage caused to the outer space. Therefore, the liability that is sought to be placed upon the respondent State is of precluding damages to the outer space by non creation of debris. However, the plain reading of Article III suggests that liability under Article III can only be realised after the damages have been caused in the outer space.[23] The interpretation would be in light of the Article 31 of the Vienna Convention on the Law Treaties 1969 according to which the provision of the treaty is to be read as per its literal plain meaning unless there is an absurdity or obfuscation in the provision of the treaty in question. Therefore, wider interpretation to Article III of the Liability Convention under Article 32 of the Vienna Convention on the Law Treaties 1969, seems difficult due to the unequivocal meaning of Article III of the Liability Convention, which would only give rise to the liability if the damage in the outer space is realised or eventuated.[24]

Obligation to Mitigate Space Debris

However, the other school of thought seems to suggest that it is imperative to include the non creation of debris in the outer space within the scope of Article III of the Liability Convention due to the innumerable space objects and space debris in the

22 Micheal J. Listner, *The Ownership and Exploitation of Outer Space: A Look at Foundational Law and Future Legal Challenges to Current Claim*, 2003, vol. 1, Regent J Int'l L, p. 83.

23 Nathan C. Goldman, *American Space Law: International and Domestic*, 1988, pp. 66-67 (Iowa State University Press).

24 Marboe, *et al.*, *Article III*, Cologne II, 2009, (Stephan Hobe, *et al.* eds.).

outer space and especially in the lower earth orbit (LEO). In furtherance of the conclusion it is stated that, if the same is not done then the State which has created the space debris or has launched any space object in the outer space, would wait for the liability to eventuate without taking any steps to preclude the damage posed to the outer space. There would not be any incentive for the State whose space object is posing threat to the other State's object in the outer space to remove the object from the outer space. Further, the problem does not stop here, the States might misuse their right provided to them by virtue of Article VIII of the Outer Space Treaty. Article VIII of the Outer Space Treaty vests a State with an absolute jurisdiction over the space object in the outer space ad otherwise. Therefore, if the scope of Article III of the Liability Convention is not extended then the States would continue creating debris as there is nothing in the space law regime to prohibit States from creating debris.[25] IADC Guidelines subsequently sponsored by UNCOPUOS and further by UNGA Resolution are only the instances of soft law that could which would not be relevant for the purpose of determining the liability under Article III of the Liability Convention. The mentioned guidelines and EU Guidelines are not binding in nature and are only suggested principles of debris mitigation. This makes the guidelines discretionary in nature for the States to follow or not. However, presently more than twenty States including the large space-faring nations such as USA, UK and Russia are abiding by the UNCOPUOS guidelines. Additionally, more than 150 satellites are fitted with the space faculties in accordance with the space debris mitigation guidelines. Therefore, it could be argued that the guidelines have become customary international law and therefore, the non-realisation of the guidelines ought to be considered as the international law violation. Moreover, scholars such as Martha Mejia Kaiser[26] have argued that the guidelines

25 N. Jasentuliyana, *Regulation of Space Salvage Operations: Possibilities for the Future,* 1994, vol. 22, J Space L, pp. 9-16.

26 Martha Mejia-Kaiser, *ESA's Choice of Futures: Envisat Removal or First Liability Case,* Proceedings of the Fifty-fifth Colloquium on the Law of Outer Space, in M. Schwartz, 2012, p. 606.

do not only include debris mitigation as a measure prior to the launch of the space object, but also include the space remediation and active debris removal steps that ought to be taken by the States to reduce the space debris in the outer space environment.[27]

The violation of measures enshrined under the guidelines could therefore be considered to be relevant for the determination of fault under the regime of Article III of the Liability Convention. This gives way to the interpretation that a State would be liable under Article III even if the fault is not realised into the outer space. Further, States by not adhering to the debris mitigation guidelines shall be in violation of Article III of the Liability Convention. Therefore, Article III of the Liability Convention need not necessarily need to work in the defence and could also be a measure of prevention of damages in the outer space. It might be a bit soon to suggest that the debris mitigation guidelines have been realised into customary international law as the aspect of *opinio juris* is missing in concluding the same.

Conclusion

The biggest dilemma under the space law regime seems to be the absence of any law regulating the creation or the active removal of space debris if created by the States while pursuing any space activities. The presence of the space debris in the LEO and the outer space in general continues to be a looming problem, which if not resolved would cause unfathomable damages to the outer space. The presence of space debris and the further risk of debris creation might make the usage of the outer space unfeasible for the future usage. This gives rise to the imperative need to regulate the creation and remediation of debris from the outer space. Even though there is nothing in

27 Article 6 of the UNCOPUOS, Space debris mitigation guidelines which provides for limiting the long term presence of the space object after the end of life mission include within it the removal in a controlled manner which could be interpreted to give way to a interpretation towards space debris remediation or active debris removal.

particular which prohibits the creation of space debris but different Articles of Outer Space Treaty and Liability Convention are suggestive of obligating the States to avoid creating space debris in the outer space. Article III of the Liability Convention could be construed to impose a liability on a State for the mere creation of debris and not necessarily causation of damages due to the debris so created. The interpretation might not be a very favoured one amongst the various scholars in light of the fact that the Article III of the Liability Convention requires actual realisation of fault, which is only in the case of damages being caused to the space object of the other State and not the mere creation of space debris. The construction of Article III whereby liability is imputed for mere creation of debris shall go a long way in obligating them to remove the debris so created and be more cautious of their space programs so as to preclude the formation of debris in the first place. This would also be a step towards obligation of debris remediation and active debris removal from the outer space.

Chapter 10

Liability Sharing Mechanism for Commercial Outer Space Activities in Different National Space Jurisdictions– A Comparative Study for Framework in India

BISWANATH GUPTA*
K.D. RAJU**

Introduction

The Space Foundation in 2016 reports that global space economy has grown up by nine per cent annual rate in 2015, which contributed $323 billion worldwide (Space Report 2016). Following the same trend, India's Antrix Corporation has shown a record growth in commercial activities, such as mission support, space object selling, remote sensing data and especially in commercial launching.[1] When commercial outer space activities are picking height, the sharing of liability is very important.[2] Almost all the space advance nations are allowing and encouraging private parties to engage more into outer space commerce. The issue of liability sharing covers major question

* Research Scholar, Rajiv Gandhi School of Intellectual Property Law, IIT, Kharagpur.

** Associate Professor, Rajiv Gandhi School of Intellectual Property Law, IIT, Kharagpur.

1 Antrix, available at <http://www.Antrix.gov.in/> last visited 17 September 2015.

2 Edythe. E. Weeks, Ayodele. A. Faiyetole, *Science, Technology and Imaginable Social and Behavioral Impacts on Outer Space Develops*, Acta Astronautica, 2014, vol. 95, pp. 163-173.

in private commercial activities. Though, internationally a State is liable for commercial outer space activities, but practically the States are developing mechanism for sharing the liability with the private parties.[3] Coming to Indian scenario, the Government of India is seriously planning for enacting national space legislation with a focus on promotion of commercial activities. At this juncture, it is important to discuss the liability sharing mechanism for India for the development and control of commercial outer space activities in the national legal framework. While speaking at the inaugural session, Mr. Madhavan Nair, former ISRO chief, at Space Law Conference in Trivandrum on April 2015, emphasized the importance of liability associate with space activity. He shared an incident that ISRO usually face during satellite launching. He said that, ISRO launches its satellites from India without any insurance coverage. So, if any unfortunate situation arises, Government of India will be liable for damage.

Liability occurs, when there is no violation of international law *per se*, but damage had occurred due to the lawful activity. On the other hand, responsibility means, when there is a violation of international law *per se* and damage had occurred. Both the concepts are very well established principles in international law.[4]

Liability and responsibility both the words are used in the Outer Space Treaty 1967 and Liability Convention 1972.[5]

3 Huang Huikang, *Space Law and the Expanding Role of Private Enterprises, with Particular Attention to Launching Activities'*, Sing J Int'l & Comp L 2001, vol. 5, pp. 55-62 at p. 55.

4 Biswanath Gupta & Raju KD, *Product Liability in Outer Space: Need for Legal Regime,* Indian Journal of Air and Space Law, 2015, vol. 1, pp. 278-289.

5 Treaty on Principles Governing the Activities of States in the Exploration and Use of Outer Space, Including the Moon and Other Celestial Bodies, 27 January 1967, 18 UST 2410, 610 UNTS 205 [hereinafter OST 1967]. Convention on International Liability for Damage Caused by Space Objects, 29 March 1972, 24 UST 2389, 961 UNTS 187; G.A. Res. 2777 (XXVI) (29 November 1971) (adopted on 29 November 1971, opened for signature on 29 March 1972, entered into force on 1 September 1972).

Article VI of the Outer Space Treaty speaks about responsibility and Article VII of Outer Space Treaty speaks about liability. Article VI of the Outer Space Treaty discusses that the State has to take responsibility for any activities carried out by the State or any non-governmental entities under the jurisdiction of that country. The provision has incorporated one more principle, *i.e.* supervision clause. By this clause, a nation has the right to supervise the activities of private parties. It gives power to State to control the activities of private parties. Therefore, Outer Space Treaty gives power to the State for protection of outer space against any violation of international law *per se*. Article VII of the Outer Space Treaty is crucial from the point of view of liability. According to this Article, the launching country is liable for any damage results from outer space activities. Similar kinds of provisions are also available in Liability Convention. Articles II and III of the Liability Convention, directly punch for the enduring of liability for outer space activities. It clearly says, launching country is liable for any damage done during outer space activities. It incorporates fault-based liability on outer space and absolute liability on air and earth. Apart from this, the concepts of joint and separate liability are incorporated in the Liability Convention in case of joint launching.[6]

It is important to note that, none of above-mentioned principles has expressly dealt with the liability for the non-governmental entities in commercial space activity. Therefore, both the responsibility and liability lies with the launching country for any kind of space exploration. The author argues here that, Articles VI and VII of the Outer Space Treaty 1967 have made a clear demarcation between liability and responsibility. Most importantly, Articles II, III, and IV of the Liability Convention 1972 have followed the Outer Space Treaty 1967 principles. It clearly lay down that, the State is liable for

6 Stephan Hobe, *The Impact of New Developments on International Space Law (New Actors, Commercialization, Privatization, Increase in the Number of Space-faring Nations)*, 2010, Unif L Rev 869, vol. 15, pp. 869-881.

any space activity may it done by State or non-governmental entities.[7]

Absolute liability means, the party is completely liable for any damage without any exception. Separate liability means, though the damage occurs due to same cause of action but parties at fault are disjointedly liable. Their liability extends up to the limit of participation into the damage. Joint liability means, if two or more parties are there in any activity, both are together liable for such activity. Fault-based liability means; the party who is at slips is liable for the damage. Taking a hint from these liability principles, different nations have drafted national space legislation with a provision for sharing the liability in case of commercial activities.

Different Nations and Their Liability Regime

As we already discussed, launching country is liable for any damage done by space activities of government or non-government entities. But national space laws of Australia, US, UK, French, and Russia has made provision for shifting and sharing the liability in case of private space activities. The concept of sharing liabilities that has reflected in the domestic legislations is cross-waiver, limited liability, asset security and compulsory insurance or third party mechanism. The detailed discussions on these principles are made below.

Article 20 of the French Space Operation Act 2008, Article 5(*f*) of the UK Outer Space Act 1986 and Article 26 of the Law of the Russian Federation About Space Activity 1993 prescribe the system of sharing liability in case private party indulges into space commerce. Almost, all the space legislations have incorporated the provision of compulsory insurance coverage for private parties entering into the space business. Section 63, Part 4 of the Space Activities Act 1998 of Australia, section 50915 of the US Commercial Space Launch Act 1984, Article 25 of the Law of the Russian Indexation About Space

7 Stephan Hobe, *The Impact of New Developments on International Space Law (New Actors, Commercialization, Privatization, Increase in the Number of Space-faring Nations)*, 2010, Unif L Rev 869, vol. 15, pp. 869-881.

Activity 1993 and Article 6 of the French Space Operation Act 2008 make provisions for compulsory insurance coverage for space activities. The US and UK legislation have done mandatory provision for asset security in case of an application for the license for commercial activity. Section 69 of Space Activities Act 1998, Article 15 of the French Space Operation Act 2008, Article 50914 of the Commercial Space Launch Act 1984 have prescribed limited liability to the private parties. In case the damage exceeds the specified limit, the State will bear the liability. These provisions, in one way, promote and secure the private parties investment in outer space.

India and Space Law

Though there is no law in India relating to outer space activities, still Government of India passed Satellite Communication Policy 1997 (SATCOM) for facilitating space commerce in India. By the year 2000 the government has issued implementation mechanism of SatCom Policy 1997. SatCom Policy 2000 allows 74% of FDI in the space business.[8] It also allows the functioning and lease of a foreign satellite in India. But for the last fifteen years, except one initiative (though it failed) has not seen any light of the day. Other important policy related to space activities is Remote Sensing Data Policy 2011. Though, it was first published in the year 2006, but this policy is revised and freshly written in 2011.[9] Except the size of the remote sensing data, nothing has been changed in the policy.

By establishing Antrix in the year 1992, India started an initiative for state-centric business venture for commercial activities. Till date, space commerce in India includes commercial launching, mission support, space object selling and remote sensing data (national remote sensing agency). All the above-mentioned activities operate through the Antrix Corporation of India. The statistical data of Antrix shows a clear uptrend of

8 Indian Space Research Organization, available at <http://www.isro.gov.in/isro-receives-gandhi-peace-prize-2014> last visited 23 September 2015.

9 *Ibid.*

commercial exploration of outer space in India. One of the prime reasons behind the rise is the cost effective space exploration by ISRO. Prof. Sridhara Murty, Prof. Mukund K Rao (both are well known writer in space law and policy) and Chief Policy Analyst of ISRO, Mr. Gopal Krishnan emphasized the need for an initiative for commercial exploration.[10] Prof. Sridhara Murty and Mr. Gopal Krishnan said clearly that ISRO is designed for research and development in space exploration. It is not a manufacturing hub for commercial exploration. Farther they said, ISRO doesn't have the intention to lead the market for commercial exploration or have any capacity to do so. It is a historical truth that, the growing of space technology in US and Europe is possible because of the participation of private parties. Both these countries from the very beginning allowed the private parties to run space business in their country. The national agencies of these countries initially helped private parties with technologies. It resulted with the huge success of space industry in those countries.

But, there is no doubt that, ISRO is moving fast and engaging industry house to take the commercial space activities in India successfully. It is coincident that, in 'Make in India' week (which held at Mumbai in 2016), ISRO chairmen have expressed DOS's intention for the privatization of Polar Satellite Launch Vehicles (PSLV, the most successful Indian launcher). Not only this occasion, in different occasion also, ISRO has shown its interest for the growing of space industry in India.

Different literature and interview reveals that, drafting national space legislation is very essential from the point of view of India. More significantly, legislation must contain provisions for promoting commercial aspect. India has signed and ratified all the important treaties relating to space law except Moon Treaty 1979. This ratification demands for a national application of those treaties by enacting national space legislation in India. So, it is important to discuss the liability sharing mechanism for India when DOS is planning to draft

10 They made this observation speaking to the authors privately.

national space legislation for India. Control of space industry and promotion of space industry are two vital points need to address in space legislation. Law has to make a balance between these promotion and control. International conventions have put extra importance to the liability as one of the important aspects of space activity. It is evident that not only international conventions but also, different national space laws are given extra importance to liability for the growing and controlling of the space industry.

Antrix and ISRO are rapidly engaging in commercial activities such as launching vehicle, satellite launching, mission support, satellite industry, and space object selling. Proposals are there for the private production PSLV for private commercial launching. No doubt, this decision has an enormous impact on Indian space industry. The success of 'Make in India', 'Digital India' initiative is not possible without the active support of space commerce.

Due to increasing trend of communication industry in India, there is a huge demand for transponder supply. But, the capacity production of transponder by ISRO is very limited. Therefore, unless the private parties are joining into it, it is impossible to fulfill the demand. Other than 'Make in India'[11] and 'Digital India'[12], 'Startup India' is an important policy for growing of space industry in India. Using this policy, ISRO will encourage industry house to start business in India.[13] For growing of space business in India, ISRO should help industry to get technology and other allied support. The success story of Arian Space, XOR, Boeing, SpaceX, Virgin Galactic, etc. is possible because of the initiative done by NASA and ESA.

11 Make in India is a program started by Government of India to make India a global manufacturing hub. Make in India, available at <http://www.makeinindia.com/sector/space> last visited 20 September 2015.

12 Digital India is a program started by Government of India for connecting India through digital link My Government, available at <https://mygov.in/group/digital-india/> last visited 20 September 2015.

13 Mr. Gopal Krishnan also viewed that ISRO will encourage 'space startups' for growing and engaging more and more industry with ISRO for space manufacturing and business.

While attending the round table conference at NLSIU Bangalore,[14] industry openly criticizes the role of ISRO that it plays for facilitating technology or other logistic support.[15] They accuses ISRO for their over protective nature in space technology transfer. On the contrary, ISRO countered their claim by saying; presently there is hardly any industry house in India which is having infrastructure facility for technology transfer. It is true that, presently there is no industry in India which is having any infrastructure for space activities. But proper technology transfer can impress the big industry houses for investing in space business in India. The prime reason behind the claim is, telecommunication industry in India has huge future. So, industry house will definitely look forward for investing in space commerce.

But the real hurdle between space business and Indian industry is the liability for space business. In India, as there is no law or policy is at place, industries are uncertain about the extent of their liability for commercial outer space activities. Still ISRO is conservative about the allowance of private party in space business in the name of security. This type of isolation will cause India losing the opportunity for growing space business in India.

There is no doubt that India is already late in enacting national space law. So never the late, it is the correct time to enact a space legislation for India. Mr. YMS Prasad, former director of SHAR (Sriharikota High Altitude Range) and the present chairmen for drafting space legislation for India, viewed that the most important reason behind the enactment of national space legislation is the international commitment that India made by ratifying the international treaties on space law. According to him, the second important argument behind

14 Round Table Conference on Commercialization and Privatization of Outer Space, Held on June 2015.

15 Mrs. Sushmita Mohanty, the CEO of Earth2orbit, an initiative for space business, accuses ISRO of not properly helping business initiative citing the reason for security.

enacting space legislation is commercial exploration.[16] Though India started its space program for socio-economic development, but presently it is approaching for commercial activities in outer space. Therefore, enactment of law is important for regulating and promoting space activities.

But the authors see the above sequence other way around. The second reason put forward by Mr. MYS Prasad should come first and the first argument put forward by should come second. The first and foremost point for enacting national space legislation is controlling and promoting space commerce in India. The argument follows like this, if any country is only engaging in sovereign space activities, there is no need for any space legislation. International law clearly says, launching State is liable for any activity. So, in case of accident the State has to bear full liability for their act. On the contrary, if State is involving the private parties in the space business, the sharing of liability comes into the picture. In no case the State will bear the full damage for the private parties. Therefore, there is a need for a domestic liability sharing mechanism between government and private parties. Space legislation is vital for controlling and regulating the non-governmental entities. For promotion of space industry also, domestic legislation is important. Until and unless the private bodies are clear about the extent of their liability and governmental support in the space business, they will not get encouraged to invest into space commerce. So, enactment of space legislation is only needed, if any State is engaging for space commerce. The second important point is the international commitment and its application in domestic level.

Historically, enactment and amendment of legislation is very difficult in India. So in case of any emergency amendment is required in space law, for flourishing and controlling the space commerce in India, it will be very difficult job for DOS. The space industry in India is at very nascent stage. It is better to

16 This view is taken from the personal interview of Mr. YMS Prasad. Mr. Prasad gave this interview to the author while talking about the drafting of national space law.

enact elaborate policy for promotion and control of space business in India. So in emergency and experimental time, government can take required step.

Interestingly, it is pertinent to mention that, countries those are leading in space commerce such as US, France, Russia, UK and Australia has enacted domestic space legislation with special reference to commercial space activity. All the countries have made explicit provision for sharing of liability in space commerce. These legislations largely follow the cross-waiver, compulsory insurance, limited liability, asset security or the combination of all. So, the later part will discuss the models or combination of models for better liability mechanism for India.

Limited Liability and National Space Legislation

The concept of limited liability mainly comes from partnership law. The term 'limited liability' means, liability restricted by law or contract. But in the case of outer space law, the concept of limited liability is entirely different. Limited liability in space law means, the liability of the private party is limited up to a certain extend.[17] On the other way, it can be understood as a ceiling of liability. State fixes the upper limit of private parties' liability for damage. Exceeding this liability, the State takes the responsibility for damage.

The Commercial Space Launch Act 1984 has also enumerated the monetary limits of liability by stating that the maximum limit of a third party liability is up to $500,000,000 (in the case of death, injury or destruction of private property). The limit is up to $100,000,000 in the event of damage done to the governmental property. However, if the amount of the damage exceeds the prescribed upper limits, the burden shall shift upon the US Government bear the excess amount after approval from US Congress.

Section 69 of the Space Activities Act 1998 of Australia also prescribes the limited liability provision. If the private party

17 Biswanath Gupta & Dr. K.D. Raju, *Studying Paradigms in National Space Legislation: Searching for a Basic Legal Framework in India,* Indian Journal of Air and Space Law, vol. 2, pp. 187-210.

paid the compulsory insurance and paid the statutory required compensation, rest will be beard by Australian Government.[18] But this liability of government does not exceed 3 billion. According to section 30 of the Act, the Russian Federation will bear full responsibility for any accident, if the activity is carried out with the full compliance of the Law of the Russian Federation About Space Activity 1993. The responsibility for damage will be conducted by the organization or the individual who did the space activity (Article 30.2).[19] Sub-clause 3 of the earlier Article 29 of Law of Russian Federation About Space Activities 1993 states that, if an accident has occurred due to an error in creation or an error in technology, then a part of the damage will be borne by the manufacturing agency.[20] According to Article 14 of the French Space Operation Act 2008, except in case of willful misconduct or gross negligence, operator's liability is limited to sixty million Euros.[21] If the damage exceeds sixty million Euro, the French Government will be liable to pay the rest of the compensation.[22]

The above inclusion of the Articles of different national space legislation shows that, almost all the major space power nation has inserted the provision for limited liability. The concept of limited liability has some inherent advantage. Limited liability assures the industry house against unlimited monetary liability in space commerce. It allows them to take risk and to go for significant achievement in space. The limited liability concept helps industry to grow faster and allows inventing and investing more in outer space.

Compulsory Insurance

Compulsory insurance is another mechanism for paying damage done by space activities. Almost all the space laws have made provisions for mandatory insurance coverage for space explorations. Compulsory insurance means, in case of accident,

18 The Space Activities Act 1998.
19 Law of the Russian Federation "About Space Activity" 1993.
20 *Ibid.*
21 The French Space Operation Act 2008.
22 Article 15, *Ibid.*

the third party will pay the damage on behalf of the party at fault. It is like general insurance scheme, the party has to pay the premium and in the case of accident occurs, insurance company will pay the damage.

The Space Activities Act 1998 states that the launch permits require insurance coverage or direct financial responsibility for granting the launching of space objects permits. The launching party is required to ensure the maximum amount of probable loss. The amount of probable loss was determined by section 7.02 of the Space Activities Regulations 2001. The Australian Government is not required to take insurance. It is the holder of the license or party holding launch permits that are required to make insurance for the third party for the coverage of liability. Articles 30.4 and 25 of Space Activities Act 1988 prescribe for mandatory insurance.[23] Article 25 directs the creation of a corpus Space Fund, that will collect the insurance premium money and in the unfortunate case of any incident, the Fund shall release the compensation amounts. Furthermore all insurance companies are required to have a license for the purpose of insuring such space activity.[24] Article 25 of the Space Activities Act 1988 further states that the organization which will carry limited insurance for risk coverage. If the compensation is in excess of the risk coverage, the compensation will have to be realized from the property of the organization/person.[25]

Under section 5(2)(*f*) of the Outer Space Act 1986 of UK, it is required to insure against liability incurred in respect of damage occurred due to outer space activities in UK or any place authorized by the Act. If an incident happens, the UK Government is liable to pay the compensation and the person who carries out the said operation shall indemnify the Government of UK for the said damage.[26]

In the US a key consideration in commercial space activities on insurance is, as per § 50914 of the Commercial Space Launch

23 The Space Activities Act 1998.

24 *Ibid.*

25 *Ibid.*

26 Section 10, the Outer Space Act 1986.

Act 1984, private parties are required to take insurance for any outer space activities. The holder of the license ought to take the maximum probable insurance for carrying out outer space activities. The Act has also incorporated the concept of limited liability and cross-waiver claims. Under limited liability, parties have to bear financial liability up to certain limit. Anything which is more than the said limit will be incurred by the State. The Commercial Space Launch Act 1984 has also enumerated the monetary limits of liability by stating that the maximum limit of a third party liability is up to $500,000,000 (in case of death, injury or destruction of private property). The limit is up to $100,000,000 in the event of damage done to the governmental property.[27]

The French Space Operation Act 2008 requires an operator to obtain an insurance of up to sixty million Euro in the case of loss. According to section 14 of the French Space Operation Act 2008, except in case of willful misconduct or gross negligence, operator's liability is limited to sixty million Euro.[28] This indemnification is applicable to contractors, sub-contractors, customers and insurers.[29] Further, if any other State sues the French Government under the Liability Convention 1972, the international law will be applicable.

Asset Security and Cross-waiver

Asset security is a process, where the private party gets the licenses for space commerce on the basic of asset that they are having in a country. In case of accident, the government will pay compensation and in later on they will realize from the asset that private party is having in the country. Countries like US and UK have made this kind of provision for granting license for outer space activities. Another liability mechanism is cross-waiver. In this system, both the parties waive their liability for space activities. While analyzing different bilateral agreements of ISRO with foreign countries puts this kind of provision. In

27 The Commercial Space Launch Act 1984.

28 Law of the Russian Federation "About Space Activity", 1993.

29 *Ibid.*

this sort of clause, no party is liable for paying the compensation. While talking to ISRO officials, they told to the authors that, generally the launching carried out by ISRO from India doesn't have any insurance. But, if India launches any satellite from French Guiana, ISRO has to take compulsory insurance coverage.

The Civil Liability for Nuclear Damage Act 2010

Outer space and nuclear exploration both are considered very high risk activities and have lot of similarity. The damage that occurs for an accident in both cases is enormous. Nuclear and space, both give the opportunity for human development. Some of the principles of liability mechanism of nuclear law and space law are similar. The contrast is, in case of nuclear accident, mainly it comes within national jurisdiction. But space jurisdiction is extraterritorial or terrestrial. So, jurisdiction for enforcement of law is a problem in case of space activities. But in nuclear law, this is not huge problem, until accident affects any neighbouring States.

It is important to mention that, section 2(*g*) of the Civil Liability for Nuclear Damage Act 2010 of India has defined the term nuclear damage. Any damage to property, life or economic loss will cover the damage. Section 4 of the Act clearly puts burden on the operator for liability for any accident.[30] The operator will be liable for any damage caused by nuclear accident. This is same as, in case of any space accident, the operator will be liable. But, it puts particular restriction where the operators are not liable for damage. Such as act of the God and war or terrorism. Both the provisos are necessary for space law. As in case of Act of the God or war or aggression, there is no doubt that, private party should not make liable. Sections 5, 6 and 7 of the Act are more important, where the Act inserts the provision of limited liability and compulsory insurance coverage.[31] The Act says, the private party or the operator's liabilities are limited. After a certain limit, the Central Government is liable for any compensation (section 6).

30 The Civil Liability for Nuclear Damage Act 2010.
31 *Ibid.*

Section 7 of the Act prescribes for compulsory insurance coverage of the activities.[32] Unless parties doesn't have insurance coverage, will not get license for operation in India. Parties enter into nuclear exploration must have insurance coverage for their plant. All these principles are also helpful for drafting space liability mechanism for India.

Conclusion

India is planning for enacting national space legislation with a focus on commercial activities promotion in outer space. While drafting national space law, it is important to insert the provision for liability sharing mechanism. According to Article VI of the Outer Space Treaty 1967 and Articles II and III of Liability Convention 1972, launching country is liable for any activities in outer space. Even, in the case of non-governmental activities, the launching State is liable. Therefore, in the event of any commercial activity from India, the State is liable for any accidents and consequential damages. But countries like Australia, US, Russia, UK and France have developed liability sharing mechanism with private parties for controlling and promoting commercial activities. India is rapidly venturing into commercial exploration in outer space without having any domestic mechanism for liability sharing with private parties. This poses the serious question of liability for any accidents and related damages to human beings or property. The lack of legal provisions to regulate space activities in India has made the issues more critical.

The comparative study of different national jurisdictions showed Australia, France, Russia, UK and US have developed liability sharing mechanism through the mandate of legislations at the domestic level. The mechanisms adopted are; cross-waiver, compulsory license or third parties liability, asset security and limited liability for the private parties.

This chapter explored the liability mechanism available in different space laws of different jurisdictions to formulate a

32 The Civil Liability for Nuclear Damage Act 2010.

better mechanism in India for sharing liability in commercial outer space activities. It is argued that India can adopt a liability sharing mechanism with mandatory provision for limited liability and compulsory insurance provision. Common liability fund similar to the Civil Liability for Nuclear Damage Act 2010, can be another option for sharing liability for damages.

Even the ISRO officials agree that, the SatCom and Remote Sensing Policies are not sufficient to deal space commerce in India. The growing size of communication and broadcasting in India, require a robust policy backing. Though efforts are taken long back in 2000 for drafting space law for India, but it didn't see the light of the day. There was always lack of consensus among the officials on the subject of drafting space legislation. Many of them are skeptical about drafting any legislation for India. They view that; drafting legislation will curve the efficacy of ISRO.

Mr. YMS Prasad, the Chairmen of the Drafting Committee has hinted that, very soon ISRO will go for mass public consultation for drafting national space legislation for India. He viewed that; the legislation will take care for the promotion of commercial activities in India.

Considering the promotion and control of commercial outer space activities, some suggestion for the development of liability mechanism in India are as follows:

1. There must be limited liability concept in the framework. Limited liability will give assurance to the industry to take risk in outer space exploration. It will help as a positive catalyst for growing space industry in India. This concept will help private companies from entering into contract with foreign companies interested in space business.
2. Another important idea is shared pool. The concerned party for space business will deposit minimum amount of money (as prescribed by government) to develop a common fund. This fund can be used for emergency purpose in case of accident.

3. Compulsory insurance is no doubt an important mechanism for liability sharing. The government has to force private parties to take compulsory insurance coverage up to certain limit. But getting insurance in India for space business is unpredictable. So, until the space business grows and insurance become comfortable, assets security can be a good option for India.

Chapter 11

Space Insurance

Shraddha Srivastava*
Sourav Kumar*

Introduction

The increased venturing in the space has brought forth many risks. These risks however includes major financial loss which may be due to physical damage to satellites, space vehicles and ground property, losses to parties and services related to commercial space endeavors and third-party liability. This chapter largely covers the satellite insurance and also has glimpses of the space vehicle insurance. The space market covers satellites and other space vehicles.

The satellites have been with the mankind since 1950 and now they are becoming more and more prominent. Previously the expenses were incurred by the government but slowly the private market has extended its hands over the space. The planet presently is orbited by many such satellites built by the private giants.

The cost of building and launching a satellite can be as great as many billion dollars. Also, even after incurring such heavy costs the risk factor remains huge as many satellites fail in their initial stages of operation. Even after the high cost and associated high risk, the larger good these satellites do for the

* 2nd Year students of BBA, LLB (Hons), Chanakya National Law University, Nyaya Nagar, Mithapur, Patna.

mankind cannot be overlooked. Thus, steps are needed for the insurance market to secure the satellites. Also the space law holds the State liable for any damage, so the State has now made it somewhat obligatory for space carriers to buy insurance.

The market has to be huge and should have many insurers because most insurers do not have individual capacity and interest to cater to the potential loss of failure. Thus, the satellite insurance market is broadly prospective.

Then comes the insurance of the space vehicle which also needs to be insured against the risks associated with the construction, testing and transportation of the vehicle. Thus, after recognizing the need of the insurance in the vast commercialized space, we need to look at how the market has evolved.

Evolution of Space Insurance Market

Space insurance market means the business of buying and selling the insurance related to space ventures and the companies which are doing this business. This insurance can be satellite insurance, space vehicle insurance or any other kind of insurance. Coverage tends to be split between launch risk and "in orbit" risk.[1]

With its first appearance in Anglo-Saxon countries, the space insurance market had mostly been developed in the USA through aviation insurance. It is evident that French, German and Italian insurance companies were eager quite earlier in evaluating space risk and insurance market in the context of the efforts of both European Launcher Development Organization (ELDO) and European Space Research Organization (ESRO). Thus they entered the market with the coverage of an ARIANE Launch.[2]

For the first time satellite operators resorted to insurance in the year 1965 when Lloyd's of London was to cover physical

1 Justyn Harding, *The Aviation and Space Insurance Market*, Working Party Membership, August 2000, p. 34, available at <file:///C:/Users/welcome/Downloads/aviation_wp.pdf> last visited 18 February 2017.

2 M.G. Bourley, *L'assurance des activities spatiales*, Annuaire de Droit Maritime et Aerien, 1983, vol. VII, pp. 360 & 361.

damages on pre-launch for the "Early Bird" satellite Intelsat I. The first policy covered only third party liability and damages to the satellite during the pre-launch phase.

The concept of third party liability was put forth by the Article VII of the Outer Space Treaty and later elaborated by the Liability Convention on international liabilities for damages caused by space objects. This made the insurer liable to pay damages to the third party and also towards the damage occurred to the satellite during the pre-launch phase on behalf of the insured. The probability of insuring a satellite or a space vehicle depends on two variables:

(1) risk associated with them, and

(2) the capacity available in the space insurance market.[3]

The risks are determined after evaluating the risk management carefully whereas the second one depends on both the history of satellite insurance, claims paid and impact of the external factors on the confidence of the industry.

In the initial phase, because the government carried out most satellite endeavors and insured their risks, the space insurance policies were limited from 1965 to early 1980s. But in the early 1980s the commercial satellite industry began to resort to insurance as the tool for major risk management. It was in 1982 when for the first time the total sum of payment surpassed the total sum of all premiums paid to the insurance companies.[4]

The loss and the failure of the Challenger, Titan, Delta and Ariane, all in mid 1980s eroded the confidence of insurance companies (even though only the Ariane launch was insured) and as a result the space insurance industry underwent heavy losses. The high number of incidents of claims resulted in the downfall of capacity and increase in premiums, to which clients

3 Julian Hermida, *Space Insurance*, in Sandeepa Bhat B. (ed.), *Space Law in the Era of Commercialisation*, 2010, p. 114 (Eastern Book Company).

4 M.G. Bourley, *L'assurance des activities spatiales*, Annuaire de Droit Maritime et Aerien, 1983, vol. VII, p. 361.

could not maintain the pace. In 1985 insurance capacity has been reduced from $180/200 down to $120 million. Premiums went up to around 16-18% of the insured value and even higher according to some experts.[5] Also, the premium for third-party liability increased even when no successful claim was made. Hence, space insurance market collapsed. As a consequence of these tragic and unexpected events, the United States amended its legislation in order to offer alternatives to the existing space insurance and those changes persist even today with minor modifications. Other States like Russia, Australia, and France followed the steps taken by US and they did similar legislative reforms to assist the space market. Fortunately, In the 1990s the space insurance market recaptured its confidence and its capacity increased from US $300 million to around $1.2 billion by the end of the decade. The increase in competition amongst the insurers led to decreased rates, however, it continued to react immediately to launch failure.[6]

The time and again failure or loss of satellites like the event of 9 September 1998 when launch of 12 GlobalStar satellites failed and all were lost or the incidents of 11 September 2001 compounded by six Boeing 702 satellites which suffered in-orbit losses due to solar array anomalies drastically influenced the space insurance market again. As a result, these circumstances acted as compelling force to make major changes in rate, terms, capacities and conditions of space insurance market. These are the reasons why space insurance market prolonged to be delicate and fragile.

Space Market Status

The global space insurance market consisting of satellite owners, manufacturers, launch-service providers, insurance broker,

5 Chappez J., *Les systemes de transport*, in Dutheil de la Rochere (ed.), 1998, p. 139 (Paris: Droit del'Espace).

6 Julian Hermida, *Space Insurance*, in B. Sandeepa Bhat (ed.), *Space Law in the Era of Commercialisat*ion, 2010, p. 113 (Eastern Book Company). See also "Committee on Commerce, Science and Transportation, US Senate, Insurance and the US Commercial Space Launch Industry", July 1998 at p. 6 (US Government Printing Office).

underwriters, financial institutions and government agents, has changed overtime and will continue to change rapidly. The market provides varied type of coverage including pre-launch insurance, launch insurance, in-orbit policies, third-party liability and government policies insurances. There is also an emerging dimension of re-launch guarantee where the launch company is an insurance-provider and in case of a launch failure the customer agrees to accept a re-launch in lieu of cash payment. The present form of market is a small specialty business under the umbrella of multinational insurance companies located in tax-haven environments. If these companies are located in tax-friendly environments they can invest their premium income and can return high profits on these investments. Often the underwriters also seek additional financial backing and this insures that the risk is spread in the larger insurance industry.

For insuring a satellite, the satellite owner or manufacturer chooses an insurance broker who acts as an agent and transmits information between the insurance-party and underwriters. The broker presents various financial and technical information to the underwriters and ascertains what kind of coverage they can offer. The broker takes bids from the underwriters along with their capacities, premiums, terms and conditions and offers their client with the best feasible solution.

The entire amount of coverage that insurance companies are willing to underwrite for a single satellite launch is known as the capacity. The capacity is decreasing; the stated capacity for the whole space insurance market has collapsed from $1.3 billion in 1999 to $840 million in 2002.

The premiums for both have been steadily rising. In good economic conditions, the space insurers are able to provide high- capacity and low-rates. Contrarily the capacity drops and premium rises.

There is also a great requirement for tighter underwriting and technical scrutiny. There has to be necessarily exclusions for losses resulting from terrorism and generic defects in a particular model of satellite.

The coverage periods also have been decreasing. In 1998 it was five years after the launch, but due to in-orbit losses from 1998 to 2001, the coverage period is just for one more year after the launch.

The space insurance market is cyclical in nature where the insurers charge lower premium at the start of the cycle but when the profits begin to fall the capacity falls, firms raise their prices to increase revenue. The cycle is affected by many factors. Interest-rate and time-lags in information used to set pricing both contribute to cyclical nature of industry.[7] More importantly, insurance markets are believed to be "capacity-constraint" [8] where changes in capacity occur due to changes in demand and supply of capital. An unexpected loss, which results in payment of claims, and reduces capital available to these companies, may lead to capacity-crunch. Due to this reason, the insurance companies generate revenues internally, increase the prices of their policies for which the insurance profit raises. Thereafter the insurer offers higher capacity and begins to lower their rates. The trend continues till another unexpected shock. Thus, the insurance cycle is highly volatile.

There has been a general declination in the launch activity and so in the available premium income. Thus, capacity-offer has fallen leading to premium rates to rise. The failure of one launch vehicle can drastically affect the entire market which can alter the capacity and premiums for all. In 2001, an Ariane 5G upper stage failure led to the loss of the Artemis and BSAT-2B satellites, resulting in $75 million in claims.[9] If the US State department does not give license to a client or broker to share the technical details of a satellite or launch vehicle, the

7 Neil A. Doherty and James R. Garven, *Insurance Cycles: Interest Rates and the Capacity Constraint Model*, Journal of Business, July 1995, vol. 68(3), pp. 383-404.

8 Anne Gron, *Capacity Constraints and Cycles in Property-Casualty Insurance Markets*, 1994, vol. 25(1), The RAND Journal of Economics, pp. 110-127 (Spring).

9 International Space Brokers, *An Update on the Space Insurance Market*, presentation to the Commercial Space Transportation Advisory Committee (COMSTAC), 23 May 2002.

international insurers generally ignore the risk or offer policies on less technical information which reduces the capacity for that insurance.

The present market needs to take into account the new technologies that are entering into the market. New technologies have to be scrutinized by the underwriters. Establishing reliability is a mounting battle that all launch vehicles must initially undergo, and usually 3 to 4 successful launches are required in order for a launch vehicle to be judged commercially insurable at reasonable terms and conditions.

There are different ways for the launch vehicle manufacturers to tackle the current market condition. It may be by way of relaunch guarantees or by way of self-insurance. One such example is EchoStar which has resorted to the method of self-insurance after disputes with underwriters. An executive from EchoStar estimated that the current cost of all insurance expenses for one satellite launch could just as easily pay for a second launch of an equivalent backup vehicle.[10]

Risk Factors for Satellites Operation

There are different factors which can obstruct the operation of satellite. The pre-launch failure, launch failure or post separation failures are the stages where any satellite can drop its existence. Among them, launch failure has shown high probability of satellite failure, *i.e.* around seven per cent of satellites have failed or lost during its launch phase. Satellite loss or failure is least probable in its pre-launch phase whereas the post-launch failure has also significant chances. Generally, it is about five per cent of satellites which suffer failure in its first six or twelve months but probability of failure increases after that. The different factors which can cause satellite failure in post-launch phase are:

Loss of Fuel

Satellites move with a certain amount of fuel with them. The fuel is necessary for its continuous operation. In certain

10 Peter B. de Selding, *Insurance Underwriters Using Rate Hikes to Recover Losses*, Space News, 13 May 2002, p. 19.

situation, the rate of consumption of fuel may be higher than the calculated. Therefore, the same can lead to subsequent failure in the operation of satellites.

Electrostatic Discharge

The most rampant post-separation/in-orbit threat to a satellite is electrostatic discharge, which can be tempted by solar movement or by the formation of plasma clouds due to development of charges on meteoroids colliding with a satellite.[11]

Solar Storms

Solar storms can obstruct the accurate functioning of a satellite's electrical components and can influence satellites over a large percentage of the sky.

Collisions with Space Debris

Satellites in low earth orbit may be lost due to collisions with space debris. There have been several incidents of space debris colliding with and damaging windows on the space shuttle.[12]

Electromagnetic Interference

The placing of satellites too close together can cause degradation in the expected operation of a satellite due to electromagnetic interference from the neighbour.

Satellite Insurance

Satellite insurance market has been widened because of the prominent increase in the space activity. Many insurers participate directly and even more participate through the insurance contracts. The satellite insurance takes within its ambit, payment for two kinds of claim:

(*a*) property loss taking place largely in three stages, that is, pre-launch, launch and initial post- separation and satellite life.

11 Sarah Goddard, *Satellite Owners Take Precautions for Meteor Storm*, Business Insurance, vol. 32(43), pp. 65 & 66.

12 Bill Coffin, *Lost in Space*, Best's Review/Proper Vr'-Casualty Insurance Edition, November 1997, vol. 98(7), pp. 68-72.

(*b*) third party liability (regulated by international and domestic outer space liability regulations).

(a) Property Loss

Talking about the insurance of the satellites, it is very important both for the insurer and the insured to first understand the kind of loss one may incur. Though the losses are majorly categorized in its three stages (pre-launch, launch and post-launch) there may be other general losses that might occur. The nature of the space market may be depicted by the following saying: "The biggest difference of space risk in comparison to conventional market segments might be the fact that you can actually watch your future loss live on television"- Thierry Colliot.[13]

The satellite can suffer the fury of ground as well as the orbit. The production sites and launch facilities are exposed to great risk and such risk factors contribute to the estimation of satellite insurance. The complicated functioning of the spacecrafts and objects can lead to certain obstructions in the whole operation. Many kinds of functions have to work simultaneously and even if one of them gets altered, it can change the entire design of the work. Such delays can prove to be very costly risks in the commercial space missions. The estimation of satellite insurance has to take into consideration that the malfunctioning of the tiniest part may lead to catastrophic losses. Further venturing deeper into the risks associated, we see it separately in its three life stages.

Pre-launch Insurance

Pre-launch insurance covers damage to a satellite during the creation, transportation, and processing phases prior to launch. The insurance provisions tend to cover all the losses that might occur from the manufacturing place or from the place of storing

13 Thierry Colliot, *Deputy General Manager at SpaceCo, an Allianz Global Corporate & Specialty Subsidiary and Leader in the Space Insurance Market*, see <https://www.agcs.allianz.com/assets/PDFs/GRD/GRD%20individual%20articles/GRD-2008-02-en-SpaceCover.pdf>, last visited 5 February 2017.

associated objects or the place from where it is launched. All the casualties during the process of integration, launching test, pre-ignition moment etc. are protected by the policies of the satellite. Talking conclusively, the policies cover the stages from manufacturing up to the point the satellites are placed on the launch vehicle. From an insurance perspective, the risk evaluation of the launch preparation, large amounts of highly explosive materials are used when the missile is gassed up for e.g. requires an extensive and highly specialized knowledge which is to be found in space travel insurance market.[14]

Launch Insurance

Launch failure has historically represented the greatest probability of loss and about seven percent satellites have failed on launch.[15] Many of the satellites fail in their launch phase and so it is the stage which requires the most risky-management, may be in terms of insurance coverage. The ending of the pre-launch section and the beginning of the launch session might coincide in many cases and such coincidence is often the ignition of the engine. Some agreements extend the launch-phase up to the time the satellites reach the intended orbit. Some policies also define launch phase as a definite period of time after the launch attempt.

Respective national telecommunications authority assigns the slot in which a satellite needs to be placed for a successful launch to be completed. The terms of the insurance contract also suggest the performance specification which the satellite needs to meet in order to have a successful launch. The losses excluded from coverage are those which result from or are due to war, anti-satellite weapons, confiscation, radio-active

14 Oliver Schöffski & André Georg Wegener, *Risk Management and Insurance Solutions for Space and Satellite Projects,* The Geneva Papers on Risk and Insurance. Issues and Practice, April 1999, vol. 24, No. 2, pp. 203-215 at p. 205.

15 Allen J. Gould & Orin M. Linden, *Estimating Satellite Insurance Liabilities,* available at <https://www.casact.org/pubs/forum/00fforum/00ff047.pdf> last visited 5 May 2016.

contamination, electro-magnetic or high frequency disturbances and intent.[16]

This section does not cover the entire satellite life but it certainly takes into cognizance any event or occurrence during the launch phase which may hamper the entire commercial life of the satellite.

Post-launch Insurance

This insurance includes in-orbit policies which insure satellites for in-orbit technical issues and damages once a satellite has been positioned by a launch vehicle in its intended orbit. The in-orbit insurance, also called as "life insurance", is a risk policy with pre-set total loss limits.[17] While launch comprises the greatest chance of failure as satellite failures can occur at any moment during orbital life, such failures may result in a total loss or partial loss of functionality, where the satellite continues to operate but at a lessened capacity.

Instantly following the successful operation of a satellite into a practical orbit there is hardly five percent probability that the satellite will undergo a total or partial failure in one year. This period is termed as the post-separation phase. As orbital losses commonly occur during the post-separation phase, it is highly probable that they can occur in the later years of its life as well. But nowadays the post-launch insurance covers the period of one year of satellite's life provided the satellite has experienced no damage during the pre-launch and launch phase. For new satellites the policy period is, most of the times limited to three years. For the renewal of policy, in general every year, the insurer demands a "health certificate", which involves an extensive reassessment of the satellite's condition (physical and technical) and all previous functional disturbances.

16 Oliver Schöffski & André Georg Wegener, *Risk Management and Insurance Solutions for Space and Satellite Projects*, The Geneva Papers on Risk and Insurance, Issues and Practice, April 1999, vol. 24, No. 2, pp. 203-215 at p. 205.

17 H. Zocher, *Neuere internationale Entwicklungen in der Raumfahrt und ihrer Versicherung (IV)*, Versicherungswirtschaft, 1988, vol. 43(4), pp. 284-290.

(b) Third Party Liability

The provisions of Liability Convention of 1972 and the domestic regulations which the respective State has adopted both govern the third-party liability policy. Different States have adopted different provisions in order to manage the risk its space sector is facing. For example, national laws determine who needs to be covered – the State, the launch services provider, contractors, employees etc., the type of damages that need to be covered, the maximum amounts of insurance, the exclusions, and time periods of insurance, among other issues.[18]

The policy's coverage starts either with the satellite's integration on the launcher and the launching pad or at the moment of the intentional ignition of the launch vehicle. It ends either with the complete destruction of the launch vehicle, or with the expiration of a certain delay after which a satellite is considered as destroyed.[19]

In cases where a launching State extends its launching services to another State, both the States are liable under the Liability Convention and the former, usually asks the latter to get a third-party liability insurance policy.

This was the case when NASA offered its launching services to other States like Canada, UK, France, Japan, or to international organizations like ESA, INTELSAT etc. NASA obliged its clients to take an insurance policy covering the U.S. liability obligations in case of damage. Initially, insurance coverage was of $100 million, and towards the end of the 1970s it rose to more than $300 million. Given the rare damages to third-parties and the important preventive measures taken by NASA, the premium required for a $100 million coverage was of $25.000 per launching.[20]

18 Julian Hermida, *Space Insurance*, in Sandeepa Bhat B. (ed.), *Space Law in the Era of Commercialisat*ion, 2010, p. 119 (Eastern Book Company).

19 M.G. Bourley, *L'assurance des activities spatiales*, Annuaire de Droit Maritime et Aerien, 1983, vol. VII, p. 367.

20 *Ibid*, p. 366.

Recent Insurance Claims

There have been few incidents recently which paved the way for claims. For instance, Amazonas 4A launched in March 2014 faced an anomaly due to power related issues resulted into claim of approximately $135million. Another is the claim of $215 million due to failure of six Russian ku-band beam transponders. The launch failure of Express-AM4R gave rise to claim of $217 million. In fact, total incidents in 2014 led to the claim of $650 million (including the claims of Orb 3 and Yamal 201). In the year 2013, 38 out of 81 satellites were insured in which the claim was made successfully for one satellite launch failure.

With the advent of insurance market there have been some incidents that gave rise to claims based on liability, but, of course they are enough to have their significant effect on the insurance market. One of the most important is the explosion of Long March. On 14 February 1996, Long March explosion after lift-off resulted into killing of four by-standers and destroying the Intelsat 708 satellite and thus led to demand for claim in order to recover the damages.

Another incident took place on 10 February 2009, a Russian satellite registered as COSMOS 2251 collided with Iridium-33, an iridium satellite in low earth orbit. This incident had become a conflicting issue even if neither satellite had been insured for in-orbit losses as its effect on insurance premiums was significant.

The insurance market is still in a developing stage, and hence, has difficulty in overcoming the claims on incidents and reducing its effect on insurance premiums.

Liability of States under International Space Law

States are responsible and liable internationally for any damage caused during their space activities as in accordance with Outer Space Treaty 1967. They are put under obligation to authorise, control and supervise any of the space activities conducted by its nationals.[21] Article VII empowers the State to exercise its

21 The Outer Space Treaty of 1967, Article VI.

jurisdiction in any space activity[22] whereas Article VIII[23] makes it obligatory for States to register their space objects.

The doctrine of international liability has been used in the Liability Convention of 1972 and it asserts that even if there is no wrong done by the State it is still liable for the damage caused by the acts over which the State exercises the control. Although the Liability Convention does not explicitly attribute international liability to the launching State for the damages caused by the non-governmental entities, from the interplay between the responsibility and liability provisions of the Outer Space Treaty and the Liability Convention, it follows that under the Liability Convention, the States are liable for damages caused by the space objects of their national private entities.[24]

From an insurance standpoint, the international space law has made it obligatory neither for States nor for launch service providers to insure launch vehicles but States can do the same by the way of their national regulations. Some States like USA, Russia, Australia etc. have implemented insurance obligations for their nationals including pre-launch, launch, post-launch and third party liability insurance.

Possible Coverage in Future

The insurance possibilities are not only limited to the insurance of a satellite or the insurance of a space vehicle but they follow a major scope. A financial loss or a business casualty can also be insured by the satellite companies. If we talk about financial loss, we tend to cover all the damages that are caused due to an external force. Any risk posed to the customers is covered by such insurance policy. The concept of third-party liability analyzed above caters to such insurance policies. This insurance is useful for small business enterprises that depend on the government for their business. The satellite system operator needs to depict their prospective lenders, their degree of care

22 The Outer Space Treaty of 1967, Article VII.
23 *Ibid,* Article VIII.
24 Julian Hermida, *Legal Basis for a National Space Legislation,* 2004, p. 23 (Dordrecht, Boston, London: Kluwer Academic).

and control and their risk management system after which they can be financed. This type of coverage protects from any adverse circumstances that might take place due to change in governmental circumstances or due to paucity of funds of the government or due to cancellation or delay in launch. These types of risks are generally referred to as financial risks and are difficult to anticipate and quantify and so a proper risk management system requires insuring such risks. There might be business interruptions or casualty that leads to shortage of funds/revenue and so such losses also need protection against potential risk. Business casualties may include satellite loss, damage or failure and such policies may cover all phases of the satellite.

Conclusion

The evolution of space insurance market depicts how the space has commercialized in its own specific way and how it led to greater opportunities for the new market. The first insurance agreement in 1965 had surely not explored the wide and vivid array of damages that might occur in a satellite. From the naïve times of realizing only the third-party liability, the insurance market has grown up to cover the complexities of the current times.

The volatility of space insurance can be estimated by the fact that one satellite launch can generate ten percent of annual premium whereas one loss or failure can smear out full annual premium. That's why the space insurance market is very soft and delicate.

Characterized by high volatility and fragility, the space insurance market has many times lost the confidence and people had to resort to alternative risk tools such as self-insurance. But soon the high costs and increased risks pulled the market back and recovered its capacity. They have given new shapes to the coverage availability, rates, exclusions, deductibles, and alternative risk management tools.

The insurance coverage has crept into the damages associated with property loss and also claims coming out of third-party liability. Various international and national regulations have initiated legislative provisions to determine the distribution of risk and liability between the launch service providers and the respective government. Therefore, it is important for space carrier to analyze the alternative risk management tools and the availability of claims in cases of loss or damage. The business or the financial risks associated with this sector offers prospects and opportunities to the new insurance market. What is needed in present time is that the space insurance market offers more vivid protection at lower rates so that the innovation at space venturing is encouraged more and more. Further, apart from risk management tool, space insurance also constitutes a precious element of financing. The expansion of space insurance market will be in the interest of science and largely in the interest of mankind.

Chapter 12

Settlement of Disputes Arising in Space Activities

BAYAR GOSWAMI*

Introduction

Dispute settlement is one of the primary objectives of law and the domain of international law is no different. Though it is often argued that international adjudicating bodies have no enforcement mechanism but past is the evidence to contrary where most of the decisions have been considered binding and have been enforced in letter and spirit. International law in many of its aspects remains nascent and one such field is international space law, recently where existing laws have started to become obsolete and they do not match the pace of development.[1] Dispute settlement in space related activities is multi-faceted. It not only raises questions pertaining purely to law but also involves concerns with regard to technology, commercial interest and in contemporary times, increasing involvement of private entities.[2] Various efforts have been taken

* Research Scholar, McGill University, Canada.

1 Karl-Heinz Böckstiegel, *Arbitration and Adjudication Regarding Activities in Outer Space*, Journal of Space Law, 1978, vol. 6, No. 3, pp. 5-7.

2 Gerardine Meishan Goh, *Dispute Settlement in International Space Law: A Multi-Door Courthouse For Outer Space*, 2007 p. 10 (Leiden, Brill Publications).

in last thirty years by various scholars and even international bodies like the International Law Association and International Court of Justice to address the lacunae of dispute settlement system in space activities. This chapter tries to encapsulate all the major proposals made for providing a dispute settlement system in international space law. Part I of the chapter attempts to define the term *space activity*, international actors involved in space activities, application of space treaties[3] to these actors by drawing nexus to States for all space related activities and the complexity arising due to interplay of such actors in a space activity. Part II elaborates on international space law regime pertaining to dispute settlement procedures flowing from the *corpus juris spatialis*. It also elaborates on adequacy of dispute settlement mechanisms established in the space treaties and whether they need to be revised to meet the need of present scenario. Part III focuses on specific dispute settlement mechanism that have been discussed and proposed. It elaborates specifically on three methods of settlement *viz.* Settlement under General International Law, ILA's Final Draft of the Revised Convention on the Settlement of Disputes related to Space Activities and PCA's Optional Rules for Settlement of Outer Space Disputes. Part IV of the chapter concludes the discussion and specific suggestions with regard to best suitable settlement mechanism have been provided.

3 Treaty on Principles Governing the Activities of States in the Exploration and Use of Outer Space, Including the Moon and Other Celestial Bodies, *entered into force* 10 October 1967, 18 UST 2410, 610 UNTS 205 [hereinafter Outer Space Treaty]; Convention on Registration of Objects Launched into Outer Space, *entered into force* 15 September 1976, 28 UST 695, 1023 UNTS 15 [hereinafter Registration Convention]; Convention on International Liability for Damage Caused by Space Objects, *entered into force* 9 October 1973, 24 UST 2389, 961 UNTS 187 [hereinafter Liability Convention]; Agreement on the Rescue of Astronauts, the Return of Astronauts, and the Return of Objects Launched Into Outer Space, *entered into force* 3 December 1968, 19 UST 7570, 672 UNTS 119 [hereinafter Return and Rescue Agreement]; Agreement Governing the Activities of States on the Moon and Other Celestial Bodies, *entered into force* 11 July 1984, 1363 UNTS 3 [hereinafter Moon Agreement].

Dispute–Subject matter & International Actors

Settlement of disputes of – "Outer Space Activities" or "Space Activities" or "Space Law"?

The definition of the term *space activity* is essential as it defines the scope of applicable law, the kind of dispute and the required dispute settlement procedure. A question often arises as to what is sought is a dispute settlement for outer space activities dealing only with disputes arising from activities occurring in the outer space or dispute settlement of space activities comprising of any activity in connection and furtherance of exploitation and exploration of outer space irrespective of its location or dispute settlement of activities only covered by international space law.

To answer the first two questions, the meaning of the term 'space activity' must be identified if not *per se* defined and this has been a task before scholars and the international community. Till date only a few texts have attempted to define the term 'space activity' and perhaps in my opinion the main reason to not define exactly what space activity comprises of is to leave it open to interpretation and be decided on circumstantial basis particularly in a dispute settlement process.

Spatialists have often used the term 'space activity' with different association to context. Some, while using the term 'space activity', mean activities which are wholly taking place in outer space and not in the airspace or the earth,[4] others are of the opinion that space activity includes everything connected with exploration and exploitation of outer space, including activities conducted on earth.[5] Thus, an ambiguity persists as

---

4 Henri A. Wassenbergh, *A Launch and a Space Transportation Law, Separate from Outer Space Law?*, Journal of Air and Space Law, 1996, vol. 21(1), pp. 28-32.

5 Article 2, Sofia Guidelines for a Model Law on National Space Legislation, International Law Association, 75th Conference, Res. No. 6/2012 (2012) [hereinafter ILA's Model Law], defines 'space activity' which includes the launch, operation, guidance, and re-entry of space objects into, in and from outer space and other activities essential for the launch, operation, guidance and re-entry of space

to whether the term 'space activity' is all inclusive term or only refers to activities in outer space.

National space legislations of various countries like Austria,[6] Russia,[7] South Africa,[8] Ukraine[9] and USA[10] have attempted to define space activity for the purpose of their national legislation and through understanding of which it can be said that most of them include activities conducted on the surface of the earth, in air and outer space. However, application of such definition remains limited to respective countries and there exists no internationally accepted definition of space activity.

---

objects into, in and from outer space. However the comment by secretary on the article dealing with definition of space activity itself states "Arguably, one could add that activities at an altitude of 100 km above sea level are considered space activities."

6 Austrian Outer Space Act 2011 (28 December 2011, Austria), s. 2(1) defines *space activity as*: the launch, operation or control of a space object, as well as the operation of a launch facility.

7 Law of the Russian Federation "About Space Activity", No. 5663-1, Article 2(1) states that ".....space activity shall be defined as any activity immediately connected with operations to explore and use outer space, including Moon and other celestial bodies. Space activity shall include- space researches; remote sensing of the Earth from outer space, including environmental monitoring and meteorology; use of navigation, topographical and geodesic satellite systems; piloted space missions; manufacturing of materials and other products in outer space; other kinds of activity performed with the aid of space technology."

8 Space Affairs Act (South Africa, 1993), section 1 defines *space activities* as –the activities directly contributing to the launching of spacecraft and the operation of such craft in outer space and *space-related activities* as –all activities supporting, or sharing mutual technologies with, space activities.

9 Ordinance of the Supreme Soviet of Ukraine, on Space Activity Law of Ukraine of 15 November 1996, No. 503/96-BP, Article 1 defines *space activity* as scientific space research, the design and application of space technology and the use of outer space.

10 The National Aeronautics and Space Administration Authorization Act 2010, Pub. L. No. 111–31 124 Stat. 3328, section 20103(1) defines *aeronautical and space activities* as - research into, and the solution of, problems of flight within and outside the earth's atmosphere; the development, construction, testing, and operation for research purposes of aeronautical and space vehicles; the operation of a space transportation system including the space shuttle, upper stages, space platforms, and related equipment; and such other activities as may be required for the exploration of space.

While it can be said looking at the State practice through national legislations and the drafting of International Law Association's Model National Space legislation[11] that the term 'space activity' ought to include activities conducted on earth, air and outer space, there exists scope for interpretation that one may avail to elude liability or claims based on understanding contrary to this definition. Thus, before delving into procedures of dispute settlement the definition of subject matter of dispute needs to be identified and set out clearly. An effective procedure can only be established once we are clear with what kind of activities are we trying to encompass by providing an international settlement mechanism for 'space activities,' or 'space-related activities' or even 'commercial space activities' or 'commercial space-related activities'.[12]

The third question is more literal than legal - whether it should be *settlement of space law dispute* as has been used by few scholars[13] and is also found in the title of the first draft of Draft Convention on the Settlement of Space Law Disputes,[14] though the Convention applies to all activities in outer space and all activities with effects in outer space,[15] the use of the term *settlement of space law dispute* rather appears to be casual and was later in the Final Draft changed to *Convention for the Settlement*

11 Sofia Guidelines for a Model Law on National Space Legislation, International Law Association, 75th Conference, Res. No. 6/2012 (2012) [hereinafter ILA's Model Law].

12 V.S. Mani, *Development of Effective Mechanism(s) for Settlement of Disputes Arising in Relation to Space Commercialization*, Singapore, Journal of International & Comparative Law, 2001, vol. 5, pp. 191-213 at p. 210.

13 Gérardine Meishan Goh, *The Multi-Door Courthouse: A Proposed Mechanism For Dispute Settlement In International Space Law*, Proceedings of the 50th Colloquium on the Law of Outer Space, 2007; Karl-Heinz Böckstiegel, *Proposed Draft Convention on the Settlement of Space Law Disputes*, Journal of Space Law, 1984, vol. 12, p. 136 [hereinafter Böckstiegel Proposed Draft].

14 International Law Association's Draft Convention on the Settlement of Space Law Disputes (ILA Paris Conference, 1984) (available in Böckstiegel Proposed Draft) [hereinafter ILA's First Draft].

15 *Ibid*, Article 1.

of Disputes Related to Space Activities.[16] In literal sense if it is taken to be settlement of space law dispute, this leads to definitional question as to what constitutes space law and what is its applicability.[17] Francis Lyall has defined space law as law which comprises all the law that may govern or apply to outer space and activities in and relating to outer space.[18] Which, in turn, again raises the same question as to what extent the phrase '*activities relating to outer space*' shall be interpreted, is it limited to outer space or should it cover activities like launching or transportation is unclear.

On the other hand if we consider only space treaties to mean space law, this would be an approach taken only to narrow the applicability against the rapidly growing space developments. Professor Böckstiegel has rightly pointed out that the application of space law has shifted from exploratory stage to practical use of space which in turn, reflects a shift from dispute in academic opinion to dispute in actual practical interests,[19] and poses actual challenges before space law.

Therefore, at the outset of having an international settlement system of any kind, we must identify what exactly comprises of space activity, which shall be governed by which exact framework of law. However, for the purpose of this chapter space activity, shall mean activity inclusive of all - earth, air and outer space activities carried out in furtherance of exploration and exploitation of outer space.

16 Final Draft of the Revised Convention on the Settlement of Disputes related to Space Activities, International Law Association, Report of the 68th Conference, Taipei, Taiwan, Republic of China, 1998, pp. 249-267 [hereinafter ILA's Final Draft].

17 Frans G. von der Dunk, *Space For Dispute Settlement Mechanisms - Dispute Resolution Mechanisms For Space? A Few Legal Considerations,* Proceedings of the 44th Colloquium on the Law of Outer Space, 2001, pp. 448-452.

18 Francis Lyall & Paul B. Larsen, *Space Law: A Treatise,* 2009, p. 10 (United States: Ashgate Publishing).

19 Karl-Heinz Böckstiegel, *Arbitration and Adjudication Regarding Activities in Outer Space,* Journal of Space Law, 1978, vol. 6, No. 3, p. 3.

International Actors Involved in Space Activities and Disputes thereof

Dispute settlement as much about law, is also about parties to disputes. There are three different types of actors involved in space activities. Sovereign States are the first known actors in space activities and it started with Soviet Union's launch of the world's first artificial satellite, Sputnik I which triggered the race between States to explore and use outer space to achieve their ends. Sputnik's launch on 4 October 1957, also in some form crystallized space law which had been only a subject of speculation for international lawyers.[20] International space law has developed for and primarily due to Sovereign States and they still continue to play a dominant role in setting the principles, as they are the prime makers of space law through the creation of and adherence to treaties and customary law as well as breakers thereof.[21] Till today, space treaties are State centric and primarily talk of rights and obligations of the States.

Second category of actors involved in space activities are international Intergovernmental Organizations (IGOs). international Intergovernmental Organizations have an international legal personality and States which are member to such organization for achieving goals, are realized better as group than individually. IGOs are governed by their own legal instrument which is ratified by States for grant of rights and obligations. Basic idea behind IGOs, particularly in space activities is pooling of resources and technological know-how and space activities are known to be a unique example in international field where States have come together (in form of IGOs) to share resources and knowledge to such a great extent.[22] Perhaps the most important feature of IGOs is that they are

20 M.S. Firestone, *Problems in the Resolution of Disputes Concerning Damage Caused in Outer Space*, Tulane Law Review, 1984, vol. 59, p. 747.

21 Frans G. von der Dunk, *Space for Dispute Settlement Mechanisms - Dispute Resolution Mechanisms for Space? A Few Legal Considerations*, Proceedings of the 44th Colloquium on the Law of Outer Space, 2001, pp. 448-452 at p. 445.

22 *Ibid.*

recognized as separate international legal personality which has two benefits – *first*, they can be a party to international instruments just like Sovereign States, if the instrument so allows and *second* – they can be a separate party to the dispute under international law. Space treaties have recognized international intergovernmental organizations and extended their applicability to IGOs as well.[23] In the case of Rescue Agreement, Liability Convention and Registration Convention, IGOs are given opportunity to become party to respective treaty by declaring acceptance of rights and obligations. Till date, only European Organization for the Exploitation of Meteorological Satellites (EUMETSAT) and European Space Agency (ESA) are known to have made declaration of acceptance of and under Rescue Agreement, Liability Convention and Registration Convention while European Telecommunication Satellite Organization (EUTELSAT) has declared its acceptance for Liability Convention and the Registration Convention.[24] Regarding IGOs being a separate party to dispute, it has been widely accepted since the advisory opinion in the *Reparation for Injuries Case*[25] that IGOs being a separate international legal personality are capable of being party to a dispute in international law.[26]

Third category of actors involved in space activities are private entities, though the involvement has increased only in recent past but they stand to be a notorious case in view of international space law.[27] Not many private entities existed at the time when

23 The Outer Space Treaty, Article XIII.

24 Status of international agreements relating to activities in outer space as on 15 March 2017, A/AC.105/C.2/2016/CRP.3 available at <http://www.unoosa.org/documents/pdf/spacelaw/treatystatus/AC105_C2_2016_CRP03E.pdf.> last visited 15 March 2017.

25 Reparation for Injuries Suffered in the Service of the United Nations, Advisory Opinion, [1949] ICJ Reports 174, 11 April 1949.

26 Frans G. von der Dunk, *Space for Dispute Settlement Mechanisms—Dispute Resolution Mechanisms for Space? A Few Legal Considerations*, Proceedings of the Forty-fourth Colloquium on the Law of Outer Space, 2001, pp. 448-452 at p. 446.

27 Gijsbertha C. M. Reijnen, *Outer Space Law and Private Enterprise in Outer Space: An International Perspective*, Houston Journal of International Law, 1979, vol. 2, p. 65; Yun Zhao, *The 1972 Liability Convention: Time for Revision*, Space Policy, 2004, vol. 20, p. 117.

international space treaties were being drafted, and not much involvement of private entities was imagined by the drafters. Today, where commercially viable, participation of private entities has become dominant, for example, in launching services, development of spacecrafts, operation of satellites etc. Of course, States in this scenario play an important role of *trait d'union*,[28] between these treaties and private entities through Article VI of the Outer Space Treaty[29] which mentions that every State shall be responsible (not liable)[30] for activities carried on by non-governmental entity. Also, Article VII of Outer Space Treaty[31] and Liability Convention, in general, specify international liability for space activity being categorized as ultra-hazardous activity. This nexus between space treaties and private entities is drawn through States on two primary approaches,

28 Frans G. von der Dunk, *Space for Dispute Settlement Mechanisms–Dispute Resolution Mechanisms for Space? A Few Legal Considerations,* Proceedings of the Forty-fourth Colloquium on the Law of Outer Space, 2001, pp. 448-452 at p. 445.

29 The Outer Space Treaty, Article VI: States Parties to the Treaty shall bear international responsibility for national activities in outer space, including the Moon and other celestial bodies, whether such activities are carried on by governmental agencies or by non-governmental entities, and for assuring that national activities are carried out in conformity with the provisions set forth in the present Treaty. The activities of non-governmental entities in outer space, including the Moon and other celestial bodies, shall require authorization and continuing supervision by the appropriate State Party to the Treaty. When activities are carried on in outer space, including the Moon and other celestial bodies, by an international organization, responsibility for compliance with this Treaty shall be borne both by the international organization and by the States Parties to the Treaty participating in such organization.

30 Frans G. von der Dunk, *Liability versus Responsibility in Space Law: Misconception or Misconstruction?*, Proceedings of the Thirty-fourth Colloquium on the Law of Outer Space, 1992, at p. 363.

31 The Outer Space Treaty, Article VII: Each State Party to the Treaty that launches or procures the launching of an object into outer space, including the Moon and other celestial bodies, and each State Party from whose territory or facility an object is launched, is internationally liable for damage to another State Party to the Treaty or to its natural or juridical persons by such object or its component parts on the Earth, in air space or in outer space, including the Moon and other celestial bodies.

first – jurisdictional approach, where if the private entity falls within the jurisdiction of the State (territorially or by nationality), the State becomes responsible for activities of such entities and *second* – registration based approach flowing from Article VIII of the Outer Space Treaty and Registration Convention as an extension of the same. In this approach, the State becomes *state of registry* for activities conducted by private entities and is internationally responsible for same.

Having identified the international actors, we must now understand the interaction between these actors and foresee disputes that may arise. In this regard, Professor Frans G. von der Dunk has commendably identified the dynamics of dispute between these three actors by drawing a matrix and specifying the possibility of kind of dispute and its settlement mechanism. According to which, there are six possible combination of actors among which dispute can arise and are put briefly as under:[32]

(i) *State versus State.* These disputes are generally subject matter of general international law and are resolved by dispute settlement procedures available *lex generalis* or *lex specialis* (space treaties for our context).

(ii) *State versus IGO.* These kinds of disputes can be further sub-categorized into two, Member State of IGO versus IGO and non-Member State of IGO versus IGO, while in the first category internal dispute settlement mechanism of such organization comes into play, however, for the second category options available through international law in general will have to be availed.

(iii) *State versus Private Entity.* These kinds of disputes can also be further sub-categorized into two based on jurisdiction, the first among this would be disputes between States and private entities falling within the

32 Frans G. von der Dunk, *Space For Dispute Settlement Mechanisms - Dispute Resolution Mechanisms For Space? A Few Legal Considerations,* Proceedings of the Forty-fourth Colloquium on the Law of Outer Space, 2001, pp. 448-452 at pp. 444-447.

States jurisdiction and the second category would be of State and private entities outside the jurisdiction of State. These disputes in both the cases are resolved through national jurisdictions.

(iv) *IGO versus IGO.* These kinds of disputes would be rare, but however would involve complex situation due to different and overlapping Member States of IGOs. These could be solved by internal mechanism or might also be based/or solved using national mechanisms.

(v) *IGO versus Private Entity.* These kinds of disputes would be perhaps complex and national law mechanism seems to be a viable option to resolve such dispute, however much would depend on whether the private entity falls within the jurisdiction of Member State to IGO or outside the jurisdiction of Member State.

(vi) *Private Entity versus Private Entity.* These disputes are inherently resolved at national level however, problem of numerous available methods of resolving the dispute, multiplicity of jurisdiction and lack of substantive space law pose challenge in achieving an effective dispute settlement method.

These are possible interaction between the international actors involved in space law, but considering the practical application and complexity of relations, various new dimensions may arise which are not contemplated and can be understood better in actualities.

Existing Law–Space for Binding & Mandatory Settlement Mechanism

Travaux Preparatories of the five international space treaties reflect a consensus based approach, meaning thereby, primary goal sought was conflict avoidance and not dispute settlement.[33] States while debating over drafts of space treaties had very

33 Geìrardine Meishan Goh, *Dispute Settlement In International Space Law: A Multi-Door Courthouse For Outer Space*, 2007, pp. 18-42 (Leiden, Brill Publications).

little knowledge of actual practical interests and thus, what was at the table was only an academic dispute which could be resolved through conflict avoidance mechanisms as opposed to compulsory procedures.[34] Conflict avoidance basically intends to reduce possibility of disagreement in the use of outer space whereas dispute settlement refers to a system which resolves disagreement after they have arisen. Therefore, it can be said that conflict avoidance approach is a stage prior to dispute and on failure of which dispute settlement mechanisms are required. Outer Space Treaty primarily focuses on cooperation and consultation procedures while Liability Convention as an exception to space treaties provides for establishment of Claims Commission for the purpose of settlement of claims of one State against another, however none of the treaties provide for a mandatory and binding dispute settlement system. A detailed analysis of existing space law for dispute settlement is required in order to understand how the space for binding and mandatory settlement system is to be filled.

Provisions under Outer Space Treaty 1967

The Outer Space Treaty was first amongst other space treaties drafted by United Nations Committee on Peaceful Uses of Space, and due to non-realization of actual practical interest and reluctance to submit dispute to third party, mandatory and binding dispute settlements were out of purview of Outer Space Treaty and treaties drafted thereafter.[35]Any farfetched resemblance to dispute resolution encompassed in Outer Space Treaty was use of words like *cooperation*[36] and *consultation.*[37] In a sense it can be said that an import of procedures from UN Charter[38] *via* Article III of Outer Space Treaty has been imbibed in the treaty.

34 Karl-Heinz Böckstiegel, *Arbitration and Adjudication Regarding Activities in Outer Space*, Journal of Space Law, 1978, vol. 6, No. 3, pp. 5-7.

35 Geìrardine Meishan Goh, *Dispute Settlement In International Space Law: A Multi-Door Courthouse For Outer Space*, 2007, pp. 24-31 (Leiden, Brill Publications).

36 The Outer Space Treaty, Article III.

37 The Outer Space Treaty, Articles IX and XII.

38 The Charter of United Nations, *entered into force* on 24 October 1945, 892 UNTS 119 [hereinafter UN Charter].

(i) Cooperation under Article III of the Outer Space Treaty 1967[39]

Article III provides for compliance with the general international law, including the UN Charter in the interest of maintaining international peace and security and promoting international cooperation and understanding. This can be understood to mean that all the procedures for maintaining international peace, provided in UN Charter and generally in international law can be applied to outer space activities by virtue of this Article. Therefore, primarily for settlement of disputes, Chapter VI[40] and Chapter VII[41] of the Charter come into play and perhaps the most important provision for the context is Article 33(1) of the Charter which provides that the parties to any dispute "... shall seek a solution by negotiation, enquiry, mediation, conciliation, arbitration, judicial settlement, resort to regional agencies or arrangements, or other peaceful means of their own choice." [42] This import of UN Charter is the most important feature for dispute settlement of space activities until a settlement mechanism is crystallized.

(ii) Consultation under Article IX and Article XII of the Outer Space Treaty 1967

Article IX of the Outer Space Treaty provides State Parties with an option of consultation. The State carrying out any potentially harmful activity or experiment in outer space shall consult international community beforehand if it has reason to believe that the activity or experiment might interfere with the use of outer space by other State Parties to the treaty, on the other hand the request for consultation can also be made by any State

39 The Outer Space Treaty, Article III: States Parties to the Treaty shall carry on activities in the exploration and use of outer space, including the Moon and other celestial bodies, in accordance with international law, including the Charter of the United Nations, in the interest of maintaining international peace and security and promoting international cooperation and understanding.

40 The Charter of United Nations, Chapter VI – Pacific Settlement of Disputes.

41 *Ibid*, Chapter VII – Action with Respect to Threats to the Peace, Breaches of the Peace, and Acts of Aggression.

42 The Charter of United Nations, Article 33.

Party if it has reason to believe that activity of another State in outer space would cause potential harmful interference.

Article XII of the Outer Space Treaty provides that any practical question arising in connection with activities carried on by IGOs in exploration and use of outer space shall be resolved by States Parties to the treaty with the appropriate international organization or with one or more Member States of that international organization, which are Parties to this Treaty.

All the three provisions of Outer Space Treaty, *viz.* Articles III, IX and XII do not provide a mandatory and binding dispute settlement procedure and only act as method of conflict avoidance, thus, there is a need for establishing binding and mandatory procedure.

Provisions under Liability Convention 1972

Liability Convention is the only existing space treaty which provides elaborate procedure for arriving at settlement of claims of parties who have suffered a damage as defined in the Liability Convention. The Convention lays down two methods for claiming compensation for damages; first method requires a State to present a claim for compensation for damage from launching State through diplomatic channels[43] and if within one year no settlement of claim is arrived through diplomatic negotiation, parties concerned shall establish a Claims Commission for arriving at a settlement.[44] Elaborate procedure is laid down for both the methods detailing limitation,[45] manner of payment,[46] composition of Claims Commission[47] and appointment of members of Claims Commission.[48]

Rather than delving into detailing of procedures laid down in Liability Convention, there are few aspects of the provisions

43 Article IX of the Liability Convention.
44 *Ibid,* Article XIV.
45 *Ibid,* Article X.
46 *Ibid,* Article XIII.
47 *Ibid,* Article XV.
48 The Liability Convention, Articles XV and XVI.

of Liability Convention that require academic attention, these are as under:

(i) Is Settlement of Claim the only Kind of Dispute in Outer Space Activity?

While under the purview of Liability Convention, reparation of liability through monetary claims is the only available option, but situations where claims are not the only dispute are practical and existing in international field. The Liability Convention determines and pins the liability to launching State, of any damages suffered on the surface of the earth or in air or outer space[49] and thus, in view of its rationale, Claims Commission addresses the questions limited to liability. However, while it is the only existing elaborate procedure to resolve dispute in outer space activities, it lacks jurisdiction to resolve dispute which are beyond the settlement of claims of one State to another. Disputes other than settlement of claims are not contemplated under Liability Convention and Claims Commission is not the solution to diverse dispute that may arise in outer space activity.

(ii) Representation of Claims

Only States being party to the Liability Convention may or may not represent claims of natural or juridical person who suffered damages as defined under Liability Convention. Therefore, discretion of the relevant State exists and such claim would rather be governed by the political climate than on the basis of substance of law. Private entities thus are still dependent on States to initiate action for claims under the Convention.[50]

Further, the procedure for presentation of claim by State is similar to that of diplomatic negotiations and where no diplomatic relation exists between the Claimant State and the launching State, a third State can act as the representative of

49 The Liability Convention, Articles II and III.

50 Geìrardine Meishan Goh, *Dispute Settlement In International Space Law: A Multi-Door Courthouse For Outer Space*, 2007, p. 38 (Leiden, Brill Publications).

one of the parties.[51] However, the Liability Convention is not clear on whether the third State has to be a party to the Convention or not, merely acting in accordance with the provisions of the Convention would mean binding applicability of provisions on third State[52] is bit difficult to understand. One of such other concern is that a claim can be made against international organization and the power to present such claim vests with the Secretary General of the United Nations, but one may argue legality of this provision as international organizations are not members of the United Nations.

(iii) Non-binding Decisions of Claims Commission

During the negotiations while drafting of the Liability Convention few of the proposals like those from the Belgian and the US delegations did propose compulsory arbitration[53] and the Hungarian drafts backed by Soviet Union and European Unions also had provisions for establishment of an arbitral tribunal.[54] However, after much consideration and reluctance to accept compulsory settlement procedures, compromise was arrived at a draft which became Liability Convention[55] providing settlement of claims through diplomatic negotiation and failing

51 The Liability Convention, Article XIX.

52 Bin Cheng, *International Liability for Damage Caused by Space Objects*, in Nandasari Jasentuliyana and Roy Lee (eds), *Manual on Space Law*, 1979, vol. I, (New York: Oceana Publications).

53 Belgium: Proposal for a Convention on the Unification of Certain Rules Governing Liability for Damage Caused by Space Devices to Third Parties on the Surface of the Earth and to Aircraft in Flight, Committee on the Peaceful Uses of Outer Space, Article 4, p. 3, UN Doc. A/AC.105/C.2/L.7/Rev. 3 (1967); USA: Proposal Convention Concerning Liability for Damage Caused by the Launching of Objects into Outer Space, Committee on the Peaceful Uses of Outer Space, Article X, at pp. 5-6, UN Doc. A/AC.105/C.2/L.19 (1967).

54 Hungary: Proposed draft agreement concerning liability for damage caused by the launching of objects into outer space, Committee on the Peaceful Uses of Outer Space, Article XII, at p. 4, UN Doc. A/AC.105/C.2/L.10/Rev.1 and paragraph 17 of UN Doc. A/AC.105/37; UN Doc. A/AC.105/C.2/SR.101, p. 128.

55 See elaboration on political climate while drafting of Liability Convention in M.S. Firestone, *Problems in the Resolution of Disputes Concerning Damage Caused in Outer Space*, Tulane Law Review, 1984, vol. 59.

which establishment of Claims Commission with non-binding decision unless agreed by the parties. Article XIX provides that the decision of the of the Commission shall be final and binding only if the parties have so agreed, otherwise the Commission's decision shall be of recommendatory nature which the parties shall consider in good faith[56] and this is known to be a major deficiency of the Liability Convention.

Provisions under Moon Agreement 1979

Moon Agreement is yet another conflict avoidance procedure and lays down a non-binding dispute settlement option with no obligation on State Parties to accept the settlement proposals. Article 15 of the Moon Agreement provides that State Parties should act in manner compatible with the provisions of this agreement and the framework of the United Nations in the exploration and use of the moon.[57] In event of any conflict or non-adherence of the provisions of the Moon Agreement, State Parties shall enter in consultations and arrive at a mutual resolution to be submitted to the Secretary General of the United Nations.[58] Further, if such consultations fail to arrive at mutually acceptable resolution, States shall take all measures to settle the dispute by peaceful means of their choice appropriate to the nature of the dispute.[59]

Moon Agreement is heavy on the role of Secretary General of the United Nations in resolving such disputes and fundamentally it is negotiation and mediation by the Secretary General which is not mandatory and binding. Therefore, Moon Agreement can be understood to be a step further than the Outer Space Treaty where some procedures have been laid down for negotiation and mediation but the applicability of these procedures is limited to activities carried on the moon or other celestial bodies leaving activities elsewhere in outer space beyond its scope of application.[60]

56 The Liability Convention, Article XIX.
57 The Moon Agreement, Article 15(1).
58 *Ibid*, Article 15(2).
59 The Moon Agreement, Article 15(3).
60 *Ibid*, Article 1(1).

Dispute Settlement Procedures–Options in Space Disputes

The need for mandatory and binding dispute settlement mechanism in space activities has been a topic of relevance since long time now. In late 1970s scholars began to understand the lacunae of international space law particularly regarding dispute settlement procedure. Professor Böckstiegel has contributed enormously to this topic and has suggested methods which can be utilized for resolving space disputes.[61] One of the earliest initiatives of international character is the International Law Association's Draft Convention on the Settlement of Space Law Disputes 1978[62] which was later adopted in 1998 as Final Draft of the Revised Convention for the Settlement of Disputes Related to Space Activities.[63] International Court of Justice while celebrating its 50th anniversary by an international colloquium also included a session on space law disputes to make the procedure in sync with space disputes.[64] Over the time many proposals and solutions to address the lacunae of dispute settlement procedures have been suggested by scholars and it

61 Karl-Heinz Böckstiegel, *Arbitration and Adjudication Regarding Activities in Outer Space*, Journal of Space Law, 1978, vol. 6, No. 3, pp. 5-7.; Karl-Heinz Böckstiegel, *Proposed Draft Convention On The Settlement of Space Law Disputes*, Journal of Space Law, 1984, vol. 12, p. 136. [hereinafter Böckstiegel Proposed Draft]; Karl-Heinz Böckstiegel, *Settlement of Disputes on International Regimes Applicable to Space Activities*, Proceedings of the 33rd Colloquium on the Law of Outer Space, 1980, p. 123.; Karl-Heinz Böckstiegel, *Developing a system of Dispute Settlement Regarding Space Activities*, Proceedings of the 35th Colloquium on the Law of Outer Space, 1992; Karl-Heinz Böckstiegel, *Settlement of Disputes Regarding Space Activities*, Journal of Space Law, 1993, vol. 23, p. 1; Karl-Heinz Böckstiegel, *Arbitration of Disputes Regarding Space Activities*, Proceedings of the Thirty-sixth Colloquium on the Law of Outer Space, 1993, vol. 136.

62 International Law Association's Draft Convention on the Settlement of Space Law Disputes (ILA Paris Conference, 1984), ILA's First Draft.

63 Final Draft of the Revised Convention on the Settlement of Disputes related to Space Activities, International Law Association, *Report of the 68th Conference, Taipei, Taiwan, Republic of China*, 1998, pp. 249-267 [hereinafter ILA's Final Draft].

64 Roy S. Lee & Connie Peck, *Increasing the Effectiveness of the International Court of Justice: Proceedings of the ICJ UNITAR Colloquium to Celebrate the 50th Anniversary of the Court*, 1997 (Netherlands: Springer).

is important to analyze all of such options which can be availed once a space dispute has arisen.

For purpose of this chapter, focus would be on the following methods –

A. Dispute Settlement under General International Law,

B. International Law Association's 1998 Taipei Final Draft of the Revised Convention on the Settlement of Disputes Related to Space Activities, and

C. Permanent Court of Arbitration - Optional Rules for the Arbitration of Disputes Relating to Outer Space Activities.

Dispute Settlement under General International Law[65]

Dispute settlement in general international law is primarily governed by the principles laid down in the UN Charter, more particularly in Article 33 of the Charter. The Outer Space Treaty makes an import of these general principles extending the applicability of these principles to outer space activity[66] but as discussed, none of the mandatory and binding mechanisms have been adopted by the space treaties *per se*. Under general international law there are two approaches *viz.* resolution of disputes through diplomatic procedures and adjudication. While diplomatic procedure is non-binding and is a procedure amongst parties to dispute themselves, adjudication means submission of dispute to disinterested third party for settlement by arbitration or judicial body.[67]

As discussed, space treaties follow a consensus based approach and make use of diplomatic procedures for resolution of disputes. Traditionally there are five major methods of resolving dispute through diplomatic procedures – negotiation, consultation, inquiry and fact finding, mediation and good offices

65 Elaborately discussed in Handbook on the *Peaceful Settlement of Disputes Between States*, United Nations Publication, OLA/COD/2394 (1992).
66 The Outer Space Treaty, Article III.
67 Malcolm N. Shaw, *International Law*, 2003, pp. 914-915 (Cambridge: Cambridge University Press).

and conciliation, all of which are not mandatory and non-binding settlement (conflict avoidance) system.

(i) Negotiation

Negotiation can be said to be the heart of diplomatic procedure for dispute settlement. International Court of Justice has recognized negotiation as fundamental method of settlement in the *North Sea Continental Shelf Cases;*[68] further court also noted that parties are under an obligation so as to conduct themselves that the negotiations are meaningful.[69] Negotiation is a method where parties remain in contact, exchange views at different stages and even afterward to implement the final settlement.[70] It is a process limited to parties themselves and no third party intervention is required, however rules to conduct such negotiations do exist as practice in international law and parties are obliged to act in good faith, especially when such negotiations are flowing from a treaty obligation.[71] Negotiations are low-risk mechanisms, make parties responsible to settle dispute themselves and most likely result into acceptable and stable outcome[72] and hence negotiation is an effective mechanism to resolve disputes.

(ii) Consultation

Consultations are pre-emptive resolution mechanism for avoidance of conflict rather than settlement of disputes. As discussed earlier, obligation for having consultation with international community or a particular State has been instilled in space treaties,[73] where a State has reason to believe that its

68 North Sea Continental Shelf Cases (*F.R.G* v *Den., F.R.G.* v *Neth.*) 1969 ICJ 3 (February 20), p. 48.
69 *Ibid,* at p. 47.
70 Geìrardine Meishan Goh, *Dispute Settlement In International Space Law A Multi-Door Courthouse For Outer Space,* 2007, pp. 94-98 (Netherlands: Brill Publications).
71 United Nations Convention on the Law of the Sea, *entered into force* 16 November 1994, 1833 UNTS 3, Article 283 [hereinafter UNCLOS].
72 Geìrardine Meishan Goh, *Dispute Settlement In International Space Law A Multi-Door Courthouse For Outer Space,* 2007, pp. 94-98 (Netherlands: Brill Publications).
73 The Outer Space Treaty, Articles IX and XII.

activity may create potential harmful interference with use of outer space by another State. Consultations are fundamentally conducted before a policy decision or an action that might adversely affect another party or international community in general. Particularly in international environmental laws, consultations hold an important position, in cases as early as *Lac Lanoux*[74] arbitration, the tribunal concluded that France had the duty to notify and consult with Spain with regard to works planned on Lake Lanoux. International Court of Justice has also endorsed the duty to consult as implied in Fisheries Jurisdiction case.[75] Various international instruments including space treaties have obligated State Parties to consult with other States or international community before proceeding with any activity which may interfere with rights of other States. Space activities being recognized as ultra-hazardous activity,[76] consultations are of primary importance to avoid conflict.

(iii) Inquiry and Fact Finding

Inquiry and fact finding is a method to resolve dispute not of law but of facts and questions of technical nature. This can serve as effective means and aid to resolution of dispute particularly in space law where technological issues are often in question, for example harmful interference through satellite signals can be resolved on fact finding basis. Such technological dispute require high expertise and because of which fact finding and interpretation of such findings would play vital role in dispute settlement, especially when the alleged State denies to initiate a fact-finding mission at its end. UN Security Council

74 Lake Lanoux Arbitration (*France* v *Spain*) [1957]12 RIAA 281; 24 ILR 101.

75 Fisheries Jurisdiction [*United Kingdom of Great Britain and Northern Ireland* v *Iceland*] 1974 ICJ 3 (July 25).

76 Jenks, C., *Liability for Ultra-Hazardous Activities in International Law,* Recueil des Cours de l, Academie de droit International, 1966, vol. 117, p. 107 - Ultra-hazardous refers to - the consequences (of an) ... exceptional and improbable event ... may be so far reaching that special rules concerning the liability for such consequences are necessary if serious injustice and hardship are to be avoided.

has extensively utilized this method and the General Assembly has endorsed this method at various points.[77]

(iv) Mediation and Good Offices

Mediation and good offices involves confiding in a third party to resolve settlement, however it is different from arbitration and adjudication as it is not of binding nature. This method "involves the use of third party, whether an individual or individuals, a State or group of States or an international organization, to encourage contending parties to come to a settlement."[78] The basic objective behind mediation can be understood as reconciling the opposing claims and appeasing the feelings of resentment which may have arisen between the States at variance.[79] There is a slight difference between mediation and good offices, in the former the third party plays an active role while in the latter third party just plays a supervisory role and acts as an initiator of the procedure. Good offices are usually approached by a State to use its influence on the other party to dispute to enter into a dispute resolution mechanism.[80] Mediation on other hand not always initiated by both the parties, but almost always is successful only if parties at dispute accept the mediation proceedings.

(v) Conciliation

Conciliation is a method which has features of both inquiry and mediation. It allows the conciliator to find facts relevant to dispute based on inquiry and then mediate the dispute as in

77 UN Security Council sent a fact finding mission in 1984 to Iran-Iraq Gulf War UN SC Res. 598 (1987); UN Security Council sent a fact-finding mission to the Seychelles in 1981 to investigate the involvement of mercenaries in an invasion UN SC Res. 496 (1981); UN General Assembly passed a resolution on fact-finding in the maintenance of international peace and security - UN GA Res. 1967 (XVIII).

78 Malcolm N. Shaw, *International Law*, 2003, pp. 921-923 (Cambridge: Cambridge University Press).

79 International Convention for the Pacific Settlement of International Disputes, The Hague, 18 October 1907, 36 Stat. 2199, Article 4.

80 Malcolm N. Shaw, *International Law*, 2003, pp. 921-923 (Cambridge: Cambridge University Press).

mediation. Conciliation was first devised in the 1913 Bryan Treaties which granted competence to make non-binding decisions.[81] Arbitration and conciliation are often coupled in international instruments, and recently have been ubiquitous in majority of international instruments having dispute settlement mechanism.[82] This procedure like other non-binding disputes settlement system is availed on agreement between the parties.

The above discussed methods are all non-binding and non-mandatory dispute settlement mechanisms, flowing from Article 33, other two mandatory and binding settlement mechanisms are arbitration and adjudication. Various scholars have proposed arbitration and adjudication by formulating different opinions and approaches. While on one hand establishment of specific space dispute settlement organization like International Court of Air and Space Law[83] has been proposed, on the other hand many scholars have suggested effective use of existing settlement system opposing establishment of new organizations to address the lacunae of dispute settlement procedures in space law.[84]

ILA's 1998 Taipei Final Draft of the Revised Convention on the Settlement of Disputes Related to Space Activities

International Law Association in its conference held in Manila in 1978 recognized and recommended the problem of settlement of space law disputes to be addressed by the Space Law

81 Gerardine Meishan Goh, *Dispute Settlement in International Space Law A Multi-Door Courthouse for Outer Space*, 2007, pp. 94-98 (Netherlands: Brill Publications).

82 United Nations Convention on the Law of the Sea, *entered into force* 16 November 1994, 1833 UNTS 3, Article 283; Vienna Convention on the Law of Treaties, entered into force 23 May 1969, 1155 UNTS 331; Vienna Convention on the Protection of the Ozone Layer, *entered into force* 22 September 1988, 1513 UNTS 293.

83 Doo Hwan Kim, *Proposal for Establishing an International Court of Air and Space Law*, German Journal of Air and Space Law, 2010, vol. 59, p. 362.

84 V.S. Mani, *Development of Effective Mechanism(s) for Settlement of Disputes Arising in Relation to Space Commercialization*, Singapore Journal of International & Comparative Law, 2001, vol. 5, p. 191 at p. 211.

Committee. The committee was asked to present a report in the next ILA conference following which, discussions and research was ongoing until the conference of Montreal in 1982, where a resolution was passed recommending Space Law Committee to start the drafting of Convention on the Settlement of Space Law Disputes.[85]

In the 60th Conference held in Montreal in 1982, basic principles to be incorporated in the Draft Convention were adopted as resolution and are as under—

"1. The Convention should permit States to choose for its application between:

  (*a*) all space law disputes with other States Parties;

  (*b*) application to specific areas of space law as may be dealt with in specific bilateral or multilateral treaties;

  (*c*) certain categories of disputes or certain sections of the Convention, subject to such exceptions that the State may wish to claim.

2. The Convention should in one section provide for non-binding settlement methods, including advisory awards, but should in another section provide for binding methods of settlement upon application by one of the parties, if the other party does not agree with the consequences of such non-binding methods;

3. The Convention should provide States with a choice from among different settlement methods which, in the case of a binding settlement, should include adjudication by the International Court of Justice as well as administrated and *ad hoc* arbitration;

4. The Convention should provide that States Parties must select one method for binding settlement within the choices given;

85 Karl-Heinz Böckstiegel, *Proposed Draft Convention on the Settlement of Space Law Disputes*, Journal of Space Law, 1984, vol. 12, p. 136 [hereinafter Böckstiegel Proposed Draft].

5. The Convention should stress that States Parties have an obligation to satisfy the decisions of the tribunal chosen;
6. In the Convention or as an annex thereto a 'disputes settlement clause' should be drafted which could serve as a model to be included in future bilateral or multilateral treaties on space law."[86]

Professor Böckstiegel played a key role in drafting of the convention and presented the first draft to the Space Law Committee which was elaborately discussed in the 1984 Paris Conference of the ILA and admittedly much of it was inspired from the experiences of the United Nations Convention on the Law of the Sea, 1982.[87] Finally after further considerations in ILA Conferences of 1990, 1994 and 1996, ILA in 1998 Taipei Conference adopted the "Final Draft of the Revised Convention for the Settlement of Disputes Related to Space Activities."[88]

(i) Applicability of the Convention

The Convention is applicable to all activities in outer space and all activities with effects in outer space which are carried out by States and international organizations which are Party to the Convention.[89] It seems to provide a wider and all inclusive meaning to the term 'space activity', with the use of phrase *activities with effects in outer space*, this should ideally cover all the activities conducted on the surface of the earth, in air and outer space.

86 *Resolution on Space Law Adopted by the 60th Conference of International Law Association*, Journal of Space Law, 1982, pp. 256-257.
87 Karl-Heinz Böckstiegel, *Proposed Draft Convention on the Settlement of Space Law Disputes*, Journal of Space Law, 1984, vol. 12, p. 136 [hereinafter Böckstiegel Proposed Draft].
88 Final Draft of the Revised Convention on the Settlement of Disputes related to Space Activities, International Law Association, Report of the 68th Conference, Taipei, Taiwan, Republic of China, 1998, pp. 249-267 [hereinafter ILA's Final Draft].
89 *Ibid*, Article 1(1).

Applicability of the Convention is limited to States and International Organizations which may while ratifying, by means of a declaration further exclude a specific kind of activity from the scope of this Convention or choose specific activities to be governed by specific bilateral and multilateral treaties described in the declaration. Also, reservations to provisions of the Conventions are allowed.[90]

(ii) Non-binding Dispute Settlement Procedures

The Convention in "Section II–Non-Binding Settlement Procedures" specifies two traditional non-binding dispute settlement methods – negotiation and conciliation. Under the Convention, once a dispute has arisen, the parties are under an obligation to exchange views regarding its settlement by negotiation or other peaceful means.[91] While mention of negotiation is explicit, at the same time settlement by any other peaceful means is kept open to the choice of parties, what is made obligatory is expeditious exchange of views before and after the procedure for the settlement of dispute has been terminated with or without settlement.[92] Second method provided in the Convention is conciliation where parties in dispute may invite the other party(ies) to submit dispute to conciliation in accordance with "Section IV–Conciliation Procedure"[93] of the Convention or another conciliation procedure.[94] A list of conciliators has to be drawn up and maintained by the Secretary General of the United Nations and every contracting party is entitled to nominate four conciliators.[95]

Section IV of the Convention further provides constitution of the conciliation commission which shall consist of five

90 ILA's Final Draft, Article 1(2).
91 *Ibid,* Article 3(1).
92 ILA's Final Draft, Article 3(2).
93 Section IV deals with conciliation procedure.
94 ILA's Final Draft, Article 4.
95 *Ibid,* Article 15.

members and shall determine its own procedures unless otherwise agreed by the parties to reach an amicable settlement.[96] The Convention also elaborates on functions of the commission, report of the proceedings, termination of the commission, fees and expense and right of parties to modify procedure.[97]

(iii) Binding Dispute Settlement Procedures

Once procedures laid down in section II have failed to arrive at a settlement, any party to the dispute can submit the dispute to the court or tribunal having jurisdiction as specified in "Section III–Binding Settlement Dispute Procedures" of the Convention.[98] Article 6 offers choice of procedure to the Parties, which they shall choose by means of written declaration while signing, ratifying or acceding to the Convention or anytime thereafter and such declaration remains in force until three months after the notice of revocation has been deposited to Secretary-General of the United Nations.[99]

The Convention offers three choice of procedure for submission of dispute *viz.*

(*i*) International Tribunal for Space Law,

(*ii*) The International Court of Justice and

(*iii*) An Arbitral Tribunal.

It is further provided that if a party to the Convention has not declared its choice of procedure and is party to a dispute, it shall be deemed to have accepted arbitration in accordance with the provision of the Convention. The Convention also provides arbitration as a default choice in case where parties have not chosen any settlement method or have chosen

96 ILA's Final Draft, Articles 16, 17 and 18.
97 *Ibid,* Articles 19, 20, 21, 22 and 23.
98 *Ibid,* Article 5.
99 *Ibid,* Article 6.

different procedures, unless otherwise agreed by the parties.[100] Section III elaborately provides procedure regarding jurisdiction of the court or tribunal, provision for consultation with expert by the court or tribunal and provisional measures which a court or tribunal can prescribe.

(iv) Establishment of International Space Tribunal under the Convention

Provisions of the Convention are drafted as closely as possible to the dispute settlement procedure of the, UN Convention on the Law of the Sea 1982 because of the similarities of sea law with space law and also because sea law represented what was acceptable as State practice during that time and it had not been subject to any controversy in the later stages of the Law of the Sea Conferences.[101] However, unlike the compulsory establishment of International Tribunal for the Law of the Sea[102] establishment of International Tribunal for Space Law is contingent on two conditions – *first*, it may be established only once 30th ratification or accession to the ILA's Convention has been deposited and *second*, at least 21 of the contracting parties agree to establish the tribunal.[103] Detailed procedure regarding organization and administration of the tribunal have been given in Article 6(1) of the Convention which are fundamentally similar to the International Tribunal for the Law of the Sea, however for relevance of the context, Article 6(2) and 6(3) are of importance, which deal with competence and procedure of the tribunal.

The competence of the tribunal is to deal with all the cases submitted to it according to the provisions of the

100 ILA's Final Draft, Article 6.

101 Karl-Heinz Böckstiegel, *Proposed Draft Convention on the Settlement of Space Law Disputes*, Journal of Space Law, 1984, vol. 12, p. 136. [hereinafter Böckstiegel Proposed Draft].

102 Article 188 and Annex VI, United Nations Convention on the Law of the Sea, *entered into force* 16 November 1994, 1833 UNTS 3 [hereinafter UNCLOS].

103 ILA's Final Draft, Article 37.

Convention and any other agreement specifically providing jurisdiction to the tribunal for settlement of disputes.[104] It is also provided that if all the parties to a treaty (treaty concerning subject matter of the convention) already in force agree to submit a dispute to the tribunal, it shall have jurisdiction to settle such disputes.[105] The tribunal shall decide all disputes and applications by applying provisions of this Convention and other rules of international law not incompatible with the Convention as well as any other rules of law that the parties to a dispute have agreed.[106]

Procedure for settlement by tribunal is similar to traditional court procedure where initiation of the proceedings is by special agreement or a written application addressed to the Registrar.[107] The tribunal is empowered to grant provisional measures conduct the case by deciding form and time, making arrangements connected with taking evidence and hear the case *ex parte*, and all the proceedings shall be public in nature unless otherwise agreed by the parties.[108] An important feature is embedded in Article 65,[109] which provides that a contracting party having interest of a legal nature may be allowed to intervene the ongoing procedure between parties in dispute, however such intervention is only allowed at the discretion of the tribunal. The decision of the tribunal shall be arrived at by majority of members of the tribunal and shall be final and binding as between the parties to the dispute.[110]

104 ILA's Final Draft, Article 55.
105 *Ibid*, Article 56.
106 *Ibid*, Article 57 read with Article 11.
107 Article 58. Final Draft of the Revised Convention on the Settlement of Disputes related to Space Activities, International Law Association, Report of the 68th Conference, Taipei, Taiwan, Republic of China, 1998, pp. 249-267 [hereinafter ILA's Final Draft]
108 *Ibid*, Articles 59, 60, 61 and 62.
109 *Ibid*, Article 65.
110 *Ibid*, Articles 63 and 67.

(v) Arbitral Tribunal under the Convention

The Convention in ArticleV, lays down procedure for arbitration, similar to list of conciliators, a list of arbitrators has to be drawn up and maintained by the Secretary-General of the United Nations with each party entitled to nominate four arbitrators who are experienced in space law.[111] Arbitration proceedings are instituted by party giving a written notification to other party(ies) to the dispute, however institution of arbitration proceeding is prohibited if the parties by another agreement have submitted the dispute to another arbitration.[112]

The arbitral tribunal shall consist of five members, and the appointment of each of such member is to done preferably from the list drawn and maintained by Secretary-General of the United Nations (the "list"). The party instituting the proceeding shall appoint its one member chosen from the list and mention it in the notification so sent to the other party. On receipt of such notification, within 30 days, the other party is supposed to appoint one member according to its preference. Parties should appoint the other three members of the tribunal by agreement and also appoint a President of the arbitral tribunal among these three members. In case of several parties to dispute, parties of the same interest shall appoint one member jointly by agreement and if the interests are unclear they shall proceed with appointing one member each.[113]

If the parties have agreed, the appointment of the members can also be chosen to be done by a person or third State chosen by the parties, the President of the International Tribunal for Space Law and if not established then by the President of the International Court of Justice.[114] The Convention states that the procedure to be followed in the arbitration shall be determined by the tribunal itself, it also defines duties of

111 ILA's Final Draft, Article 2.
112 *Ibid,* Article 24.
113 *Ibid,* Article 26.
114 *Ibid,* Article 26(g).

the parties to provide all relevant documents, facilities and information and also assist to call witness or experts, receive evidence and visitations to locality to which the case relates.[115]

Further, the Convention enables the tribunal to proceed with arbitration where there are procedural difficulties like default of appearance and absence of less than half of the members of the tribunal, to reach a decision (award) which shall be final and without appeal unless the parties have agreed to appellate procedure.[116]

Permanent Court of Arbitration–Optional Rules for the Arbitration of Disputes Relating to Outer Space Activities[117]

Permanent Court of Arbitration (PCA) is an intergovernmental organization with 115 Member States[118] and facilitates dispute resolution majorly through arbitration. PCA is a forum open to combination of States, State entities, intergovernmental organizations, and private parties. In the year 2009, Administrative Council of the PCA, in order to address the lacunae of dispute settlement in space activities established an Advisory Group[119] of legal experts with mandate to "firstly... assess generally the need for a final and binding dispute-settlement mechanism for disputes involving the use of outer

115 ILA's Final Draft, Articles 28 and 29.

116 *Ibid,* Articles 31, 32 and 34.

117 Permanent Court of Arbitration—Optional Rules for Arbitration of Disputes Relating to Outer Space Activities, 6 December 2011, available at <http://www.pca-cpa.org/upload/files/Outer%20 Space%20Rules.pdf> [hereinafter "Outer Space Rules"].

118 As of July 2014. *See* Permanent Court of Arbitration, *Member States,* available at <http://www.pca-cpa.org/showpage.asp?pag_id=1038>.

119 Advisory group consisted of—Judge Fausto Pocar, (Chairperson), Dr. Tare Brisibe (Nigeria), Prof. Frans von de Dunk (Netherlands), Prof. Joanne Gabrynowicz (United States), Prof. Dr. Stephan Hobe (Germany), Dr. Ram Jakhu (Canada), Prof. ArmelKerrest (France), Mrs. Justine Limpitlaw (South Africa), Prof. Dr. Francis Lyall (United Kingdom), Prof. V.S. Mani (India), Mr. Jose Montserrat Filho (Brazil), Prof. Dr. Maureen Williams (United Kingdom/Argentina), and Prof. Haifeng Zhao (China).

space by States, intergovernmental organizations and private entities and, specifically, ... highlight the benefits of arbitration in this regard. Secondly, the Advisory Group will draw up optional rules to this end for inclusion in the PCA's set of arbitration rules".[120]

The Advisory Group noted the existing lacunae in the dispute resolution mechanisms in international space law, particularly the non-availability of settlement options to private parties. International space law being State-centric only offers dispute settlement methods to States as involvement of private players in space activities was not envisaged at the time of drafting of space treaties. In absence of such procedures private parties tend to resort to commercial arbitration which is governed by United Nations Commission on International Trade Law Arbitration Rules (UNCITRAL Rules) or the procedural rules of private arbitration institutions.[121] In the view of the ongoing discussion, Advisory Group arrived at a conclusion that international arbitration can prove to be advantageous for resolution of space-related activities.[122]

The Outer Space Rules are based on the 2010 UNCITRAL Arbitration Rules with changes in order to—

(*i*) synchronize the rules with dispute having outer space component involving the use of outer space by private and public, national and international entities;

(*ii*) reflect the public international law element of outer space activities;

120 F. Pocar, *An Introduction to the PCA's Optional Rules for Arbitration of Disputes Relating to Outer Space Activities*, Journal of Space Law, 2012, vol. 38, p. 174.

121 International Chamber of Commerce Rules of Arbitration, 2012, available at <http://www.iccwbo.org/court/arbitration/id4199/index.html>; or the London Court of International Arbitration Rules (1998), available at <http://www.lcia.org/Dispute_Resolution_Services/LCIA_Arbitration_Rules.aspx>.

122 F. Pocar, *An Introduction to the PCA's Optional Rules for Arbitration of Disputes Relating to Outer Space Activities*, Journal of Space Law, 2012, vol. 38, pp. 175-176.

(*iii*) to include the Secretary-General and the International Bureau of the Permanent Court of Arbitration (International Bureau) in such proceedings as and when required;

(*iv*) to allow parties to have one, three, or five member arbitral tribunals;

(*v*) to provide list of arbitrators and procedure for consultation with scientific and technical experts;

(*vi*) to provide procedures to ensure confidentiality.[123]

In order to analyze the Outer Space Rules briefly, attempt is made to touch upon the above six aspects which reflect the adaption of various PCA Models[124] to specificities of space/ space-related disputes.[125]

(i) Scope of Application

Article 1 lays down the scope of application of the optional rules and provides that *any* party can adopt these rules as procedure for settlement of dispute by consent. The scope of application by the use of phrase *"The characterization of the dispute as relating to outer space is not necessary for jurisdiction ..."*[126] is

123 Final Draft of the Revised Convention on the Settlement of Disputes related to Space Activities, International Law Association, *Report of the 68th Conference, Taipei, Taiwan, Republic of China,* 1998, pp. 249–267 [hereinafter ILA's Final Draft].

124 The 2010 UNCITRAL Arbitration Rules, the PCA Optional Rules of Procedure for Arbitrating Disputes between Two States (1992), the PCA Optional Rules for Arbitrating Disputes between Two Parties of Which Only One is a State (1993), the PCA Optional Rules for Arbitration between International Organizations and States (1996), and the PCA Optional Rules for Arbitration of Disputes between International Organizations and Private Parties (1996), PCA Optional Rules for Arbitration of Disputes Relating to Natural Resources and/ or the Environment (2001).

125 F. Pocar, *An Introduction to the PCA's Optional Rules for Arbitration of Disputes Relating to Outer Space Activities,* Journal of Space Law, 2012, vol. 38, pp. 180-181.

126 Article 1(1), Permanent Court of Arbitration—Optional Rules for Arbitration of Disputes Relating to Outer Space Activities, 6 December 2011, available at http://www.pca-cpa.org/upload/files/Outer%20 Space%20 Rules.pdf [hereinafter "Outer Space Rules"].

broadened and where doubts regarding whether the dispute relates to outer space in strict sense arise, this provision proves to include such dispute within its application. As discussed earlier, the problem with identification of the scope of term '*space activity*' appears to have been addressed in some sense by the drafters, however it was intentionally not defined by the drafters with intention to tackle the issue on case to case basis.[127] The "*ratione materiae* of Outer Space Rules, thus depends on the will of the parties [to submit dispute] and not on any conception of outer space."[128] Outer Space Rules further go beyond the conventional arbitration rules and waive of State immunity to jurisdiction once an agreement to arbitrate under Outer Space Rules has been contemplated. Article 1(2) provides that "Agreement by a party to arbitration.....constitutes a waiver of any right of immunity from jurisdiction, in respect of the dispute in question.."[129]

(ii) Party Autonomy, Number of Arbitrators and Use of Scientific & Technical Expertise

Outer Space Rules, preserving the essence of party autonomy, allow appointment of arbitrators by party themselves, and this is an important reason why parties prefer arbitration over adjudication. Under the Rules, to add to this advantage the parties are free to designate persons who are not member of the PCA and for this purpose the Secretary-General of the PCA is mandated to maintain a standing list of arbitrators with expertise in space field, from which and with assistance of the Secretary-General, the parties are supposed to choose their arbitrators.[130] This ensures high quality and high expertise of

127 Conversation with Prof. Dr. V.S. Mani.

128 F. Pocar, *An Introduction to the PCA's Optional Rules for Arbitration of Disputes Relating to Outer Space Activities,* Journal of Space Law, 2012, vol. 38, p. 181.

129 Article 1(2), Permanent Court of Arbitration–Optional Rules for Arbitration of Disputes Relating to Outer Space Activities, 6 December 2011, available at <http://www.pca-cpa.org/upload/files/Outer%20 Space%20 Rules.pdf> [hereinafter "Outer Space Rules"].

130 *Ibid,* Article 10(4).

arbitrators, as the list is drawn by nomination done by Member States of the PCA and proposed by the Secretary-General in consultation with the legal community in the relevant field.[131]

Outer Space Rules provide a default number of arbitrator to be three, in case where parties have not chosen to appoint sole arbitrator. In case of three arbitrators, each party shall appoint one arbitrator, and who shall then appoint the third arbitrator as president of the tribunal. If five arbitrators are to be appointed, the two party-appointed arbitrators shall choose the remaining three arbitrators and designate one of those three as the presiding arbitrator of the tribunal.[132]

Furthermore, where tribunal's scientific and technical expertise is felt to be insufficient, Outer Space Rules make provision for appointing more experts to assist the proceedings. Article 29(7) of the Rules requires the Secretary-General to formulate another list comprising of technical and scientific experts to facilitate the tribunal with expert opinion on disputed matters when required. The Outer Space Rules, in Article 27(4), further enable the tribunal with power to ask for "non-technical document summarizing and explaining the background to any scientific, technical or other specialized information which the arbitral tribunal considers to be necessary to understand fully the matters in dispute."[133]

(iii) Active Role of Secretary-General and the International Bureau of the PCA

Secretary-General plays an active role in appointing the arbitrators and maintaining the lists of arbitrators and other super-qualified experts. Article 6 states that Secretary-General is the default appointing authority and is further responsible to

131 F. Pocar, *An Introduction to the PCA's Optional Rules for Arbitration of Disputes Relating to Outer Space Activities*, Journal of Space Law, 2012, vol. 38, p. 182.

132 Articles 7 and 9, Permanent Court of Arbitration–Optional Rules for Arbitration of Disputes Relating to Outer Space Activities, 6 December 2011, available at <http://www.pccpa.org/upload/files/Outer%20 Space%20 Rules.pdf> [hereinafter "Outer Space Rules"].

133 *Ibid*, Article 27(4).

appoint, replace and decide challenges against arbitrators.[134] At the same time, increased role of International Bureau is reflected in Article 1(3), where the Bureau shall serve as registry for the proceedings and provide secretariat services.

(iv) **Confidentiality**

The Advisory Group recognized the "need for heightened confidentiality in space-related matters and the usual arbitral protections were expanded in the Outer Space Rules"[135] As per Article 17(8) of the Outer Space Rules, the arbitral tribunal at the request of a party or on its own motion can appoint a confidentiality adviser as an expert in accordance with Article 29 in order to provide it with confidential information on issues designated by tribunal. Such information is not disclosed either to the party from whom it does not originate or to the arbitral tribunal.

Conclusion

Analyzing the above discussion three primary observations can be drawn, *first,* international space law requires fundamental revision to address the definitional problems to do away with the perplexity in the application of law. *Secondly,* the lacuna in international space law to address the contemporary disputes involving diverse actors and interests needs to be filled up. *Thirdly,* there is a need for some form of mandatory and binding settlement mechanism to resolve disputes arising in space activities. It is thus pertinent that definitions of key terms in space law be identified and set out clearly and a multi forum system for dispute resolution be provided to the international actors including private entities, with an obligation to opt for

134 Articles 8(1), 9(2), 9(3), 10(3), 13(4) & 14(1), Permanent Court of Arbitration–Optional Rules for Arbitration of Disputes Relating to Outer Space Activities, 6 December 2011, available at <http://www.pccpa.org/upload/files/Outer%20Space%20Rules.pdf> [hereinafter "Outer Space Rules"].

135 F. Pocar, *An Introduction to the PCA's Optional Rules for Arbitration of Disputes Relating to Outer Space Activities,* Journal of Space Law, 2012, vol. 38, p. 183.

at least one mandatory and binding mechanism, and thus, in this regard ILA's Final Draft of the Revised Convention for the Settlement of Disputes Related to Space Activities comes close to what could be a solution to the above issues, however inclusion of private entities to opt for such mechanism is sought for a better mechanism in place.

Chapter 13

Regional Approaches to Space Cooperation– Creation of SASA (South Asian Space Agency)

VENKATACHALA G. HEGDE*

Introduction

South Asia accounts for nearly one-fifth of the global population. It also covers a large and diverse area comprising primarily eight countries.[1] The eight countries that constitute South Asia are – Afghanistan, Bangladesh, Bhutan, India, Maldives, Nepal, Pakistan and Sri Lanka. Economic and technological progress in some of the countries of South Asia is commendable despite several complex socio-political issues. In terms of scientific and technological progress India has a dominant position within the South Asian sub-continent.

In terms of economic and political issues all the South Asian countries are at different levels of development trajectory. India, considering its size, has a significant role to play. Despite several

* Associate Professor, South Asian University, New Delhi.

1 These eight countries are members of the South Asian Association of Regional Cooperation (SAARC). There is also a proposal to include Myanmar into SAARC. The SAARC Charter in its Preamble refers to all the eight countries. See, <http://saarc-sec.org/SAARC-Charter/5.> last visited on 27 February 2017. Australia, China, European Union (EU), Iran, Japan, Republic of Korea, Mauritius, Myanmar and the United States have been given the status as Observers. See, <http://saarc-sec.org/Cooperation-with-Observers/13/> last visited on 27 February 2017.

internal security problems both Pakistan and Sri Lanka have been attempting to put in place consistent economic and technological growth. China, Indonesia, Myanmar, Thailand and other Central Asian Republics (including Russia), who could be regarded as neighbours for South Asia, have a long standing historical relationship with the sub-continent. Some of these countries are part of another significant grouping, namely, Association of South East Asian Nations (ASEAN).[2] South Asian countries are part of the South Asian Association of Regional Cooperation (SAARC). Both ASEAN and SAARC, as regional organizations, occupy major part of Asia.

Economic development and its rational distribution is a key issue in South Asia. There are, of course, serious environmental and other related issues that need to be taken care as well. Besides these, there are issues relating to exploration and exploitation of natural resources in the South Asian sub-continent. This chapter seeks to argue that the use of science and space technology should be very helpful in this regard. Majority of the South Asian countries are rich in mineral resources as well. South Asian countries realize that the exploration and exploitation of these resources is the key for growth and development.[3] Space technology could be used for identifying these resources through remote sensing and other related technologies.

Besides this, there are also issues relating to various natural disasters in South Asia. Floods are a major problem in India, Pakistan, Nepal and Bangladesh. The Himalayan region of South

2 For an account on regional integration in South Asia and Southeast Asia, see Kripa Sridharan and T.C.A Srinivasa-Raghavan, *Reginal Cooperation in South Asia and Southeast Asia*, 2007, Institute of Southeast Asian Studies, Singapore.

3 The areas of cooperation within SAARC are many and diverse. In one sense, these areas of cooperation reflect the realities of South Asian region. These areas, briefly, include – agriculture and rural, biotechnology, culture, economic and trade, education, energy, environment, finance, funding mechanism, information, communication and media, people-to-people contacts, poverty alleviation, science and technology, security aspects, social development and tourism. See <http://saarc-sec.org/SAARC-Charter/5/#> last visited on 27 February 2017.

Asia continues to face on a regular basis flood-related calamity. Even India, Pakistan, Nepal and Bangladesh had rivers overflowing during rainy seasons causing calamitous flood resulting in huge loss of precious life and property. A decade ago an unprecedented *Tsunami* devastated coastal part of India. The regular onslaught of cyclones from Bay of Bengal to mainland of South Asia is also a serious problem. Some of these disasters in South Asia, as briefly chronicled above, could be predicted with the usage of space and other related technologies.[4]

This chapter seeks to argue that space technology could be used on a cooperative basis among South Asian countries to forecast accurately some of these impending disasters. India, for example, has put in place appropriate satellite-based technologies to predict *Tsunami*, cyclones and other similar natural disasters. Application of space and other technologies with its early warning mechanisms have contributed in recent years a great deal within India to avert some major disasters. There is a need to replicate this example in other parts of South Asia. This cooperation could be extended to other South Asian countries. As of now, this is not happening on a regular basis. The technological help, particularly space technology, is shared among countries more on a demand or need basis. It is also important to note that it is not entirely feasible, economically and otherwise, for the countries of the region to sustain and use the space technology on a regular basis. Cooperation is inevitable. There is no instrument of whatever kind, binding or non-binding, to guide the countries to do this on a regular and automatic basis in the SAARC region. The chapter, considering

4 Indian Prime Minister mooted and called upon Indian Space Research Organisation (ISRO) in 2014 to build and launch a SAARC Satellite as a 'gift' to all the neighbours. See, *Modi asks ISRO to develop a SAARC Satellite,* The Hindu, 30 June 2014; <http://www.thehindu.com/sci-tech/science/modi-asks-isro-to-develop-a-saarc-satellite/article6162823.ece>. It has been reported that India is to launch the South Asian Satellite (since Pakistan backed out of this it is not termed as 'SAARC Satellite') in March 2017; see, *ISRO Planning Launch of SAARC Satellite in March,* Indian Express, 16 February 2017, <http://indianexpress.com/article/technology/science/isro-planning-launch-of-saarc-satellite-in-march-4526312/>.

the South Asian regional complexities, proposes the creation of a regional space agency, namely the South Asian Space Agency (SASA) on the lines of European Space Agency (ESA).

The basic SAARC framework, through its Charter, provides for cooperative endeavours among countries.[5] There are several areas wherein such cooperation is taking place among SAARC countries.[6] Some are informal or what could be termed as 'soft law' instruments and there are other more formal legal instruments as well in the form of treaties and agreements. The chapter seeks to argue for the formulation and adoption of a SAARC Space Charter to facilitate sharing of space technology to help countries of the region to avert disasters and also to use it as a tool for development. This Space Charter could be the harbinger for the creation of South Asian Space Agency (SASA). The chapter looks at some of the legal and political constraints that exist among SAARC countries to evolve such an institutional framework so as to share such high-end space technology.[7] The chapter will examine some of these constraints and will attempt to outline the contours of a Space Agency in the shadow of a Space Charter that could be used as a non-binding tool to share technology. As an example, the SAARC already has an instrument that lists the areas of cooperation in the area of science and technology.[8]

The first part of the chapter outlines the broader cooperation in the context of SAARC Charter Framework. The second part

5 For the text of the SAARC Charter see <http://saarc-sec.org/SAARC-Charter/5/> last visited on 27 February 2017.

6 Science and Technology, Biotechnology, Food Bank are some of the key areas of cooperation within SAARC; See SAARC Areas of Cooperation <http://saarc-sec.org/SAARC-Charter/5/#> last visited on 27 February 2017.

7 Majority of the SAARC countries have been saddled with many bilateral contentious issues. These bilateral issues are not discussed within the SAARC forum. SAARC Charter specifically excludes such disputes. See Article X (General Provisions) of the SAARC Charter which, *inter alia*, provides that "1. Decisions at all levels shall be taken on the basis of unanimity; 2. Bilateral and contentious issues shall be excluded from the deliberations".

8 For a broader areas of SAARC Science and Technology Cooperation, see <http://saarc-sec.org/Cooperation-with-Observers/13/> last visited on 27 February 2017.

examines the role, capacity and participation of SAARC member countries in space affairs and space treaties. The third part, before concluding, examines the possible cooperative model in the form of a SASA and a Space Charter for South Asia largely drawing from the experience of the European Space Agency.

SAARC Framework

The basic SAARC broader cooperative framework is essentially based on its Charter. The Preamble of this Charter, *inter alia*, provides for "... fostering mutual understanding, good neighbourly relations and meaningful cooperation among Member States which are bound by ties of history and culture".[9] The Preamble further refers to the '... common problems, interests and aspirations of the peoples of South Asia ...' and that all these need a joint action, enhanced cooperation. All these cooperative efforts, as proposed in the Preamble, have to be achieved "within their respective political and economic systems and cultural traditions".[10] The SAARC Charter primarily emphasizes on the regional cooperation with specific focus on economic, social and technical cooperation with view to contributing to the national and collective self-reliance.

SAARC Charter framework is broad enough to accommodate all cooperative endeavours including a legal mandate to negotiate on a Space Charter. SAARC Member countries, however, should have the willingness and political climate to initiate such a negotiation. Space technologies, by themselves, are problematic as they are regarded as duel use technologies. There could possibly be some element of distrust among some of the SAARC countries in sharing or to allow their territorial limits to be

9 The basic SAARC Charter framework is based on the principles laid down in the United Nations Charter and it is "Desirous of promoting peace, stability, amity and progress in the region through strict adherence to the principles of United Nations Charter and Non-alignment, particularly respect for the principles of sovereign equality, territorial integrity, national independence, non-use of force and non-interference in the internal affairs of other States and peaceful settlement of all disputes". See SAARC Charter Preamble at <http://saarc-sec.org/SAARC-Charter/5/> last visited on 27 February 2017.

10 *Ibid*, Preamble of SAARC Charter.

used for remote sensing or any other similar usage for identification and exploration.

However, it should be noted that Article I of the SAARC Charter is broad enough to accommodate and to provide a legal basis for the negotiation of a 'soft law' instrument. A starting point could be a non-binding Space Charter that could facilitate use of space technology and satellites for identification and exploration. There are also issues relating to communication technologies. Member countries of the SAARC, as the SAARC Charter puts it, could promote active collaboration and mutual assistance in the economic, social, cultural, technical and scientific fields.[11] This cooperation within the region can also extend to international forums on matters of common interest. However, this is not an absolute right as it provides for a limitation. The limitation is that such cooperation should not be inconsistent with their respective bilateral and multilateral obligations.[12]

Institutional Framework

The SAARC Charter outlines an institutional framework for implementing its cooperative agenda. It provides for the Council of Ministers which is the highest decision-making body and it outlines the policy agenda.[13] It meets twice a year. However, there is a Standing Committee composed of Foreign Secretaries that meets on a regular basis and in fact it does take care of resource mobilization and identification of new areas for cooperation.[14] There are also Technical Committees that identify and implement Sectoral programmes.[15] The SAARC Secretariat

11 Article I(e) of the SAARC Charter. See <http://saarc-sec.org/SAARC-Charter/5/> last visited on 28 February 2017.

12 Article II(3) of the SAARC Charter. See <http://saarc-sec.org/SAARC-Charter/5/> last visited on 28 February 2017.

13 It is composed of Foreign Ministers. See Article IV of the SAARC Charter, <http://saarc-sec.org/SAARC-Charter/5/> last visited on 28 February 2017.

14 Article V of the SAARC Charter. See <http://saarc-sec.org/SAARC-Charter/5/> last visited on 28 February 2017.

15 Article VI of the SAARC Charter for the formation and procedures of Technical Committees, See <http://saarc-sec.org/SAARC-Charter/5/> last visited on 28 February 2017; also see SAARC Areas of Cooperation in the field of Science and Technology, <http://saarc-sec.org/areaofcooperation/cat-detail.php?cat_id=46> last visited on 28 February 2017.

located in Kathmandu, Nepal oversees and assists the work of these Committees.[16]

The areas of cooperation, as envisaged by the SAARC, in the above framework and context could be regarded as diverse. It extends to agriculture, biotechnology, culture, economic and trade (South Asian Free Trade Area and the earlier version of the South Asian Preferential Trading Arrangement), education, energy, environment, finance, information, communication and media, people-to-people contact, poverty alleviation and science and technology.[17] The scientific and technological aspect of cooperation also provides for three major components. These are: (*a*) sharing of scientific and technological expertise; (*b*) joint research and development; (*c*) industrial application of higher technologies. Reference also should be made here to the five agreements and conventions concluded by SAARC.[18]

The above list of areas of cooperation as listed within the SAARC framework is fairly broad as it includes several inter-linking areas such as environment, biotechnology, science, poverty alleviation, science and technology. Space technology could be of immense help in realizing the goals in some of these areas of cooperation. The role of SAARC Secretariat[19] is crucial in providing the necessary assistance and it help in

16 Article VIII, SAARC Charter. See <http://saarc-sec.org/SAARC-Charter/5/> last visited on 28 February 2017.

17 SAARC areas of cooperation, as mentioned above, touch many areas. For details see <http://saarc-sec.org/SAARC-Charter/5/# > last visited on 28 February 2017.

18 SAARC Agreements are in the areas of: (*i*) Arbitration Council; (*ii*) Avoidance of Double Taxation; (*iii*) Customs matters; (*iv*) SAARC Development Fund (SDF); (*v*) Food Bank: (*vi*) South Asian Free Trade Area (SAFTA); and (*vii*) Regional Standards Organisation. SAARC has five Conventions. These are: (*i*) SAARC Convention on Combating and Prevention of Trafficking in Woman and Children; (*ii*) Convention on Welfare of Children; (*iii*) Convention on Mutual Assistance in Criminal Matters; (*iv*) Convention relating to Narcotic Drugs; and (*v*) Regional Convention on Terrorism. See <http://saarc-sec.org/Agreements/69/> and <http://saarc-sec.org/SAARC-Conventions/63/> last visited on 28 February 2017.

19 Article VIII, SAARC Charter. See <http://saarc-sec.org/SAARC-Charter/5/#> last visited on 28 February 2017.

carrying out the cooperative mandate. Besides this, we should also take note of decision-making process within SAARC. Decisions are made on the basis of unanimity. The Charter also provides that bilateral and contentious issues must be kept out of the purview of functioning of the SAARC.[20]

Space Programmes–Asymmetries within South Asia

The need for space technology as a tool towards development and disaster management is noted and implemented by major South Asian countries. They are, however, not on the same scale in terms of research and development with regard to these technologies. There are noticeable asymmetries in pursuing space-related programmes by some of them considering the kind of investment needed in science-related activities. It may not entirely fit into their planning programmes as they would wish to pursue their other developmental priorities. Even then, the usefulness and effectiveness of this technology for their country is understood and accordingly some form of institutional mechanism is provided. However, some countries, especially India and Pakistan have full-fledged space technology programmes.[21]

The space technology programmes in India and Pakistan, according to one view, are pursued for a strategic reason. The evolution of space technology, for that matter in the global arena, evolved during cold war era to meet primarily strategic ends.[22]

20 Article X, SAARC Charter. See <http://saarc-sec.org/SAARC-Charter/5/#> last visited on 28 February 2017.

21 India, for example, has a budget of over 2 billion dollars and its programme has gone commercial by launching satellites of other countries. For this purpose, it has created a company called ANTRIX Corporation which is commercial wing of its Department of Space. For the ISRO budget profile see <http://www.isro.gov.in/budget-glance> last visited on 28 February 2017; Pakistan, although as a Space Agency, it does not speak about commercialization of its space activities; For Pakistan Space Agency details see <http://suparco.gov.pk/webroot/pages/intro.asp> last visited on 28 February 2017.

22 All major technological breakthroughs at the global level (particularly cold war era super powers) had evolved on account of their usage in the context of military. Even the widely used computer and other related technologies at the global level achieved more sophistication and compactness on account of research done in military-dominated research. See *50 Years of NASA History,* <https://www.nasa.gov/50th/50th_magazine/historyLetter.html> last visited on 28 February 2017.

However, according to another view some of these new technological inventions and related innovations, be it in space technology or otherwise are camouflaged into more dynamic developmental activities. This may, however, not entirely be true. The Indian space research programme is a self-reliance-driven programme, despite several sanctions against it.[23] The first of the Indian satellite series were primarily used for communication and related purposes.[24]

India, for instance through its Indian Space Research Organization (ISRO), has an ambitious space programme with the primary objective of promoting development and application of space science and technology to assist in all-round development of the nation.[25] Even Pakistan is pursuing space research and has broad based programme on remote sensing and other related areas of space science. The Pakistan Space

23 India was placed under strict sanctions by the international community on account of its detonation of nuclear material in 1998 and earlier in 1974. Pakistan also followed suit. Several of the European and North American countries placed both India and Pakistan under sanction, particularly for duel use technologies. Rocket technology was one such duel use technology. India had to realign its research in the area of developing cryogenic engines to launch rockets so as to place satellites on orbit; see Dan Balz and William Drozdiak, *ÜS Responds with Penalties, Persuasion,* Washington Post, 14 May 1998 <http://www.washingtonpost.com/wp-srv/inatl/longterm/southasia/stories/penalties051498.htm> last visited on 28 February 2017; also see Declaration on International Cooperation in the Exploration and Use of Outer Space for the Benefit and in the Interest of All States, Taking into Particular Account the Needs of Developing Countries, adopted on 13 December 1996 (Resolution 51/122) <http://www.un.org/documents/ga/res/51/a51r122.htm> last visited on 28 February 2017.

24 All major disarmament treaties, including Nuclear Non-Proliferation Treaty (NPT) authorized nuclear testing for peaceful purposes. Both India and Pakistan, though nuclear States, are not parties to NPT. India argues and maintain that NPT is discriminatory as it does not apply to certain States who had tested nuclear material before a designated date as mentioned in NPT. For Indian position on NPT see <http://www.idsa.in/idsastrategiccomments/IndiaandtheNPT%20_Manish_060605> last visited on 28 February 2017; also see Rajiv Nayan (Ed.) *The Nuclear Non-Proliferation Treaty and India,* 2012, (London: Routledge).

25 See <www.isro.org/scripts/satcom.aspx>.

and Upper Atmosphere Research Commission (SUPARCO) is the national space agency and its objective is to develop indigenous capabilities in space technology and promoting space application for socio-economic uplift of the country.[26]

ISRO activities provide its broad-based activities in the usage of space science. It outlines its areas of activities as – telecommunications, TV Broadcasting, DTH Services, business communications, rural area connectivity, tele-education, tele-medicine, village resource centres, search and rescue operations and emergency communications, disaster management systems (DMS).[27] It also works closely with its meteorological department for the purposes of weather forecasting. India is now launching its own satellites and also satellites of other countries. It has gone commercial with the establishment of ANTRIX Corporation which builds satellites and makes sub-systems and components for satellites; provides launch services and tracking facilities; and most importantly organizes training of manpower and software development. Pakistan's programme is yet to go on for commercialization.

Besides these two countries, the other countries in the region such as Sri Lanka and Bangladesh have been attempting to put in place some kind of space programmes. While Sri Lanka is yet to formally structure its space programme,[28] Bangladesh has in 1991 established the Bangladesh Space Research and Remote

26 See <www.suparco.gov.pk>.

27 See <www.isro.org>.

28 It was reported by The Hindu that "Notably, a Sri Lankan company, Supreme SAT (Pvt.) Ltd. signed an agreement with the Board of Investment of Sri Lanka in May 2012 to launch the telecommunication satellite at a cost of $320 million in partnership with China Great Wall Industry Corporation, a state-owned Chinese company. Subsequently, it was also decided to set up a space academy-cum satellite ground station at Kandy." Sandeep Joshi, *China-Sri Lanka Space Cooperation Worries India*. The Hindu, 21 March 2013, <http://www.thehindu.com/news/national/chinasri-lanka-space-cooperation-worries-india/article4530698.ece>; As Reuters reported on 27 November 2012 stating that China did launch a communication satellite for Sri Lanka see <http://in.reuters.com/article/sri-lanka-satellite-china-idINDEE8AQ 07320121127>.

Sensing Organization (SPARRSO).[29] The objective of this organization is towards the effective and peaceful application of space and Geo-Information Technology (GIT) for sustainable development and human safety, security for benefits.

Maldives, Nepal and Bhutan have no space programme or any specific agency, although India provides the necessary data and help to them on a regular basis. However, China is also an important player in the South Asian region. As mentioned above, it is stated that Sri Lankan proposed space programme is reliant on Chinese assistance. Similar cooperation is also envisaged between China and Pakistan, although there is no formal agreement on record so far.[30] There are many visits and exchange programmes that had taken place between some of these countries from China and other space-faring countries, particularly from European Space Agency. India, of course, views some of these developments with caution and concern as it seeks to keep its zone of influence in the South Asian region.

SAARC and Space Treaty Regime

It is clear from the above that SAARC Charter provides the legal basis and mandate for the countries to identify areas for cooperation in the arena of science and technology. Biotechnology is one of the thrust areas. Space and space-related technologies could also be regarded as a thrust area. However, it is important to examine as to how many of the South Asian countries are parties to the space treaties and what kind of domestic legal and institutional framework they have within their country. It is also important to outline the kind and extent of space programme the Member States of the SAARC have. The 1996 United Nations General Assembly Declaration on Outer Space with specific focus on developing countries in paragraph 3 specifically provides that "All States, particularly those with relevant space capabilities and with programmes for the

29 This Space Agency was established through legislation in 1991, see <https://www.sparrso.gov.bd/>.

30 Pakistani newspaper Dawn on 19 August 2015 has reported that both Pakistan and China would cooperate in space as part of Karamay Declaration, see <https://www.dawn.com/news/1201240> last visited on 28 February 2017.

exploration and use of outer space, should contribute to promoting and fostering international cooperation on an equitable and mutually acceptable basis. In this context, particular attention should be given to the benefit and the interests of developing countries and countries with incipient space programmes stemming from such international cooperation conducted with countries with more advanced space capabilities."[31] This Declaration also urges all those countries with capabilities of space technology to provide and facilitate developing countries with technical and financial assistance.

The five space treaties have been signed and ratified by some of the South Asian countries. It is not uniform and the reason or criteria for acceding to a specific space law convention is not clear. Maldives, for example, has acceded to the Rescue Convention and not others. India and Pakistan are parties to all major conventions. Majority of the South Asian countries are members of the Outer Space Treaty.[32] Except Bhutan and Maldives all the other six countries of the South Asia have acceded to the Outer Space Treaty.[33] The Outer Space Treaty 1967 provides and incorporates the basic principles for space law with specific focus on exploration and use of outer space. It also requires Member States to treat outer space as province of mankind and use it for peaceful purposes.[34] The exploration

31 Declaration on International Cooperation in the Exploration and Use of Outer Space for the Benefit and in the Interest of All States, Taking into Particular Account the Needs of Developing Countries, adopted on 13 December 1996 (UN General Assembly, A/RES/51/122). See <http://www.un.org/documents/ga/res/51/a51r122.htm> last visited on 28 February 2017.

32 Following South Asian Countries have acceded to the Outer Space Treaty: Afghanistan, Bangladesh, India, Nepal, Pakistan and Sri Lanka.

33 Treaty on Principles Governing the Activities of States in the Exploration and Use of Outer Space, including the Moon and Other Celestial Bodies (General Assembly resolution 2222 (XXI), annex)—adopted on 19 December 1966, opened for signature on 27 January 1967, entered into force on 10 October 1967 (herein after referred to as 'Outer Space Treaty'); Outer Space Treaty has been acceded to by 101 countries and 26 countries are signatories.

34 Article 1 of Outer Space Treaty 1967 provides that exploration and use of outer space is carried out for the benefit and in the interests of all countries and that it shall be the province of all mankind. Further

of the outer space is open to all countries despite differences in scientific development. The Outer Space Treaty embodies some of the basic international legal principles and norms relating to the use and exploration of space.

Among South Asian countries, India, Pakistan and Maldives are parties to Rescue Agreement. It is interesting to note that Maldives, though had not acceded to the Outer Space Treaty had acceded to the Rescue Agreement 1968.[35] Remaining South Asian countries are not parties to this Agreement. With regard to Liability Convention 1972[36] only India and Pakistan are parties and Nepal is a signatory. Similar position remains with the Registration Convention 1975[37] as well with India and Pakistan being the only parties from South Asia. As regards the Moon Agreement 1979[38] only Pakistan is a party to the Convention from South Asia and India had only signed the Convention.

---

it provides that outer space shall be free for exploration and use by all States without discrimination of any kind, on a basis of equality and in accordance with international law. All countries shall have freedom of scientific investigation in outer space. Article II provides that outer space is not subject to national appropriation by claim of sovereignty, by means of use or occupation, or by any other means.

35 Agreement on the Rescue of Astronauts, the Return of Astronauts and the Return of Objects Launched into Outer Space 1968 [resolution 2345 (XXII), annex]—adopted on 19 December 1967, opened for signature on 22 April 1968, entered into force on 3 December 1968; (hereinafter referred to as 'Rescue Agreement') it has 91 countries as parties and with 24 signatories. Like Outer Space Treaty it is also a widely accepted Convention.

36 Convention on International Liability for Damage Caused by Space Objects 1972 [resolution 2777 (XXVI), annex]—adopted on 29 November 1971, opened for signature on 29 March 1972, entered into force on September 1972 (hereinafter referred to as 'Liability Convention').

37 Convention on Registration of Objects Launched into Outer Space 1975 [resolution 3235 (XXIX), annex]—adopted on 12 November 1974, opened for signature on 14 January 1975, entered into force on 15 September 1976 (hereinafter referred to as 'Registration Convention').

38 Agreement Governing the Activities of States on the Moon and Other Celestial Bodies 1979 [resolution 34/68, annex]—adopted on 5 December 1979, opened for signature on 18 December 1979, entered into force on 11 July 1984 (hereinafter referred to as 'Moon Agreement').

India and Pakistan are members of the Committee on the Peaceful Uses of Outer Space (COPUS) for a very long time.[39] The other South Asian countries are not members of this Committee.

South Asian Space Agency–Evolving a Model

The South Asian Space Agency could be modeled on the lines of European Space Agency (ESA) which otherwise has been described as Europe's gateway to space with about 20 members.[40] The ESA took more three decades to formally evolve into a Convention with 12 countries as its Member States in 1980. ESA Convention while creating a multilateral space agency took care to carefully delineate the sovereign and delicate national security issues relating to space programmes out of the purview of multilateral obligations. The ESA established European Space Research Organization which is a European Organization for the development and construction of space vehicle launchers. The European Launch Development Organization (ELDO) was also established. Both were established during early years of 1960s.[41] It also seeks to integrate national programmes and sets out scientific purpose. It works on space research and technology and space applications

39 COPUS was set up by the United Nations General Assembly. For an account on the working of this Space Committee, see generally, <http://www.unoosa.org/oosa/en/ourwork/copuos/index.html> last visited on 1 March 2017.

40 The Convention for the Establishment of European Space Agency was concluded in May 1975 and entered into force on 30 October 1980. Unlike SAARC which has 8 Member States, ESA has 20 Member States and with increasing number of States joining European Union the membership of ESA is also likely to go up. The existing members are – Austria, Belgium, Czech Republic, Denmark, Finland, France, Germany, Greece, Ireland, Italy, Luxembourg, Netherlands, Norway, Poland, Portugal, Romania, Spain, Sweden, Switzerland and United Kingdom. See generally <http://www.esa.int/About_Us/Welcome_to_ESA/ESA_history> last visited on 1 March 2017.

41 The Convention establishing these two organisations, ESRO and ELDO was signed in 1964; all this began in the later part of 1950s when it was decided by some European countries to set up a 'purely scientific' joint organisation for space research; see generally *A History of European Space Agency, 1958-87* (2000), available at <www.esa.int/esapub/sp/sp1235/sp1235v1web.pdf> last visited on 28 February 2017.

with a view to being used for scientific purposes and for operational space application systems. It also provides for exchange of information and data, besides launching and other space transport systems.

The European Space Agency which seeks to coordinate space programmes of 20 different European countries could be taken as model for the development of SASA. It should be noted that it took almost three decades for the ESA to evolve. SAARC could make a beginning and gradually it could evolve into a viable institutional mechanism for cooperation in space programmes. The Convention establishing ESA was formally brought into existence in 1980. But, a modest beginning of a cooperative endevour in science was made in the 1960s. A similar effort could be made in the context of SAARC keeping in view the benefits it could accrue to the countries of the region. One of the reasons for ESA to come up was to manage the high costs of space technology. ESA began as a simple cooperative model and over the years it took a formal shape and finally through a multilateral convention.

The Preamble to the Convention establishing the ESA outlines the *raison d'être* for cooperation and notes that "...considering that the magnitude of the human, technical and financial resources required for activities in the space field is such that these resources lie beyond the means of any single European country."[42] However, Article I(3) of the ESA Convention makes it clear that "All Member States .... shall contribute to the fixed common costs of the Agency".[43]

For SAARC these basic reasons of ESA based on resource mobilization and utilization for concluding a Space Agency are

42 Preamble of the Convention Establishing the ESA reiterates this position through the same language. For the text of the Convention see <http://www.esa.int/About_Us/Law_at_ESA/ESA_Convention> last visited on 28 February 2017.

43 *Ibid.* Article II of the ESA Convention seeks to elaborate and implement long-term European space policy by recommending space objectives to the Member States. There is also reference to integration of national programmes with European programme. None of these provisions, as reflected in the language, create a binding obligation on the Member States.

no different. Even after three decades of ESA Convention these reasons remain valid. The European Convention also refers to the use of space technology for 'peaceful purposes' repeatedly in several places and thereby reiterates its main purpose for concluding such a multilateral convention aligning it with the obligations of Outer Space Treaty.[44] In Article II which outlines the purposes of concluding ESA, for example, it states that space technology is being used "... for exclusively peaceful purposes cooperation among European States in space research and technology and their space applications, with a view to their being used for scientific purposes and for operational space applications, systems".[45]

Besides some core obligations the ESA Convention provides for some basic, yet very important, softer obligations such as to facilitate exchange of scientific and technical information pertaining to space research and technology and their space application. The ESA Member States, however, are not required to communicate any information obtained outside the Agency if it considers that such communication would be inconsistent with the interests of its own security or its own agreements with third parties or the conditions under which such information has been obtained.[46]

ESA also has certain grey areas wherein intervention of Members States is required to decide upon certain matters. Some of these issues relate to accruing of certain rights such as for example rights of access, rights relating to disclosure and rights of use. There are also such issues as what would objects in space or on ground constitute the property of the Agency or would it remain within the domain of the national government. All these rights will have to be considered and decided by the Member States by voting and deciding upon two-thirds majority. SAARC countries could decide these issues on the basis of

44 *Ibid.* All the European countries who are members of the ESA are also members of the various space law treaties independently thereby agreeing to abide by those obligations.

45 Article II of the ESA Convention.

46 Article III(1) of the ESA Convention.

unanimity. This unanimity rule is integral to the SAARC system. However, on softer issues of exchange of information or data there could be agreement and on other issues of acquiring, use or transfer of space technology there could be no agreement.[47]

In order to overcome some of the contentious issues ESA has divided the activities and programmes into 'mandatory' and 'optional' activities.[48] 'Mandatory' activities relate to education, documentation, studies of future projects and technological research work. Cooperation and exchange in these areas mentioned above does not create any problems. The 'mandatory' areas relate to elaboration and execution of satellites and other space systems, collection of relevant information and dissemination to Member States, draw attention to gaps and duplication, advice on harmonization of national and international programmes and maintaining regular contact with the users of space techniques. The 'optional' activities relate to "design, development, construction, launching, placing in orbit and control of satellites and other space systems".[49] In all these activities, Member States participate "in equitable manner, having regard to their financial contributions".[50]

47 ESA has also dealt with the issue of exchange of persons concerned with work of Agency in Article IV. This will happen on the basis of respecting domestic laws and regulations for entry, stay in and departure. This could be a difficult area for SAARC to agree upon immediately, although future alignments in views could be a possibility.

48 Article V of the ESA Convention.

49 Article V of the ESA Convention. The Annexes to the Convention elaborate on the programmes and activities. Annex III provides for the detailed outline of optional programmes as per the requirements of Article V. Besides this, there are other Annexes relating to Privileges and Immunities (Annex I); Financial Provisions (Annex II); Internationalization of National Programmes (Annex IV).

50 Article VII of the ESA Convention; ESA Convention also provides for Institutional Mechanism. It has a Council where all Member States are represented (Article XI). The Council appoints the Director General and Staff (Article XII). The Council is also responsible for the adoption of Annual Programmes and Budget. The Council is also empowered to appoint a Science Programme Committee or any other such Committees as necessary.

Contours of SASA

The framework and the nature of the instrument in the context of SAARC at the initial period could be non-binding. It could be in the form of guidelines as it was done in the case of ESA at the initial stages during the decade of 1950s. The factors that need incorporation in the South Asian Space Agency need closer and careful scrutiny taking into account the diverse and complex socio-political nature of the South Asian region. The proposed instrument could perhaps begin by outlining the primary objectives of the space programmes with specific focus on dealing with peculiar problems that exists within South Asia. It could also draw upon the experiences and work of the space-faring countries like India. It also could elaborate and implement the long-term space policy of the region. While outlining these policies, it is important to adhere to or make references to some of the basic principles that have been part of the Outer Space Treaty. These principles are that the space technology should be used for peaceful purposes and that all countries should have equal opportunities in sharing the progress in space science. It would also require to incorporate certain principles relating sovereign equality of States, non-interference in the internal affairs and other related such principles.

Conclusions

Although SAARC shares a common historical and socio-cultural bonding among its population, asymmetries in terms of economic and technological growth and perception are clear. Strategic and security interests dominate the discourse on any common model proposed and it is not easy to overcome this problem. The interplay of law and politics with regard to the evolution of a space charter in the SAARC region is a real one. Space programmes, as outlined in this chapter, are not simply science and technology issues. States see these high technologies, particularly space technology as a weapon's programme and a potential threat. Communication and satellite technologies have, to a large extent, changed this perception. The cost of harnessing this technology is too high and it is just not possible for one country within the region to sustain the momentum, although India seems to be an exception. India, followed by Pakistan to an extent, has a very effective space programme. Other countries in the region are not in a position to maintain such a programme considering the cost involved. Even the ESA Convention, as shown in this chapter, agrees with it and mentions in its Preamble that financial resources required for activities in the space field is such that these resources lie beyond the means of any single European country. This is simply true of SAARC.

However, as argued in this chapter, there are several reasons why Member States of SAARC should attempt to put in place a cooperative model with regard to space activities. The ESA Convention establishing a common space charter for the European continent took almost five decades to evolve. The Convention establishing the ESA was finalized and brought into force only in 1980. The ESA model, as examined in this chapter, seeks to delineate the tough security and related issues from other softer issues wherein cooperation would go a long way in helping the countries of the region. Conclusion of a draft space charter for SAARC countries along with a space agency could mitigate the sufferings of people in the region. The nature of instrument, to begin with, in the SAARC context could be a non-binding one. This could facilitate cooperation in the field of research, education and other related areas. After gaining experience and trust, a more binding and detailed instrument could be evolved.

Identifying Basic Principles to Create SASA

In conclusion, it should be possible to draft the institutional structures of the South Asian Space Agency modeled on the following basic principles:

(*a*) basic principles and purposes enshrined in the United Nations Charter such as sovereign equality of States, friendly relations and cooperation, peaceful settlement of disputes, respecting territorial integrity, non-interference in the domestic affairs of another Member State;

(*b*) basic principles of the SAARC Charter as agreed and concluded by the SAARC Member States; no discussion on bilateral contentious issues and respecting the territorial and political independence of Member States;

(*c*) emphasis on the common historical and socio-cultural bonding in the region;

(*d*) the development of the SAARC region could be best achieved by cooperative endeavors among its Member States and that the science and technology play a vital role in realizing the developmental aspirations of the people of the Member States of the region;

(*e*) accepting the fact that SAARC Member States are at different stages of their economic development;

(*f*) also noting the fact that the potential for economic growth taking into account the abundant natural and human resources in the SAARC region;

(*g*) that there exists already a cooperative mechanism in various areas that had been agreed to by all Member States, particularly in the area of science and technology;

(*h*) also recognizing the asymmetries in the level of science and technology growth and its use within the SAARC region;

(*i*) that the SAARC region faces consistent natural and other disasters resulting in huge loss of life and property and that extent of loss of life and property could have been mitigated or averted by taking recourse to or sharing on a regular basis information and data on weather, atmospheric changes and other related issues;

(*j*) that majority of the SAARC Member States are parties or acceded to the United Nations Outer Space Treaty and other relevant treaties and protocols which outlines the basic principles and purposes relating to the conduct of space affairs;

(*k*) that the exploration and use of outer space should be carried on for the benefit of all people irrespective of the degree of their economic or scientific development; and lastly;

(*l*) South Asian States that have the capability and the technological know-how relating to forecasting some of the major changes that have been taking place through appropriate space technology and other related high technology to share with other SAARC Member States such information and data without infringing their security and other related concerns on a regular basis;

(*m*) with view to achieve and coordinate this aspect South Asian States on an urgent basis to identify and explore possibilities for creating avenues through new regional institutional instruments, such as SASA, to enhance cooperation in the field of space and related activities.

Chapter 14

Establishing International Space Organization– An Indian Vista

MALAY ADHIKARI*

Introduction

International Space Organization is not a new concept but contributing it from India is really a challenging task. In this era of globalization, it creates an extra pressure to think and plan different space activities under common umbrella. Alongside the costs and risks involved in each and every space mission, especially gigantic missions like Chandrayan and Mangalyaan, are very high. This is the main idea behind establishing an International Space Organization or alternatively called World Space Organization. The United Nations had some thoughts to establish it during UNISPACE–I session in Vienna (1968) followed by UNISPACE–II (1982).[1] The documents show that these thoughts were mainly proposed by space superpowers in western countries. In the mean time the current global space development scenario has been changed. This concept could be revisited from other countries or regions that have newly

* Assistant Professor, School of Law, SRM University, Tamil Nadu.

1 Simone Courteix, *Is it Necessary to Establish a World Space Organization?*, Proceedings of the 36th Colloquium on the Law of Outer Space, American Institute of Aeronautics and Astronautics, Washington, 1994, pp. 20-21 at p. 20.

achieved the status of space superpower like India or Asia-Pacific region. So how it would look like if the whole organizational process will be initiated from India? How it will be advanced stage by stage if India leads this concept? Or what benefits India will achieve in the long run?

Understandably, a significant query that may come up here is; why space lawyers are interested in this institutionalization process to establish international space organization? Is it related to the space law from any corner? Because when it comes to regulation of any field, generally people are attracted to make policies or legislation in that field. How building up an institution could be part of regulatory norms? The answer to this question is very significant because a country like India has so many policies and legislation, but their implementation is really a tough and challenging job. This is particularly observed in the domain of law related to technology where the development of latter is much faster than former. In such a scenario, how is it effective for India to institutionalize a high-end technology, like space technology, at international level? Does it make any sense in regulatory norms of India concerned with space? All these questions along with other ancillary questions are attempted to be answered in this chapter.

History of Institutionalization in India

Reasons for Institutionalization

Why and how India has developed its different organizations related with the term 'space' in modern times? The parallel way of tracking this roadmap is how India has institutionalized space activities which are reflected later on in building its current and dynamic national space programme. This process of institutionalization is very significant to know how India could contribute or take some major stake in developing International Space Organization. In other words, if any country had not been institutionalized properly in space, the country could not contribute too much in the mission of establishing World Space Organization.

Steps of Institutionalization

This process of institutionalization was first made by Indian Government though actors outside government were engaged indirectly. Later on some business associations, private bodies etc have participated. But the private bodies till now represent specific sectors of space activities. Here the big ones have formed associations where the small and medium sized business players have not so much contributions. Besides this national initiative, there is regional institutionalization process in Asia-Pacific region like APSCO (Asia-Pacific Space Co-operation Organization), APRSAF (Asia-Pacific Regional Space Agency Forum) etc along with proposal for SAARC Space Organization where India could take major role.

(A) Beginning Years or Pre-ISRO Period

All the queries have answers in the dedicated activities performed by the pioneering scientific institution builders in India like Prof. Meghnad Saha, Homi Bhabha, Vikram Sarabhai, Satish Dhawan and indirectly many more. It is not possible to cover up all others' contributions within the limited scope of this chapter. The most significant point to mention about all these great scientists is that they proved their brilliance not only in science but also in the concerned national institution building. Their process of institution buildings on space was mentored and supported by none other than Jawaharlal Nehru himself, the then Prime Minister of India, followed by his daughter and subsequent Prime Minister, Mrs. Indira Gandhi.[2] Since the purpose of this chapter is not to detail the historical landscape of Indian institutions concerned with space, the following discussions have only a brief sketch on how India has commenced this institutionalization process.

Introductory Institutionalization by Prof. Meghnad Saha

Initially, it was the individual contribution of Prof. Meghnad Saha. He first realized during 1937 the need to study

2 See more details in A. Parthasarathy, *Technology at Core-Science & Technology with Indira Gandhi*, 2007, p. 136 (Delhi: Pearson Longman).

astronomical observations from outside the Earth's atmosphere. He made a five member committee in 1945 to prepare a plan on astronomical and astrophysical observatories in India. A National Almanac Unit was formed in Kolkata in 1955. It was a follow-up of his individual effort. Later it was renamed as Positional Astronomy Centre in 1979. The objective of this unit was to provide scientific information to the traditional almanac makers in updating their astronomical elements.[3]

Institutionalization through IGY Programme in India

Besides this personal effort made by Prof. Saha, India started its space programme with the introduction of International Geophysical Year (IGY) (1957-58). It is to be noted that space was one of the agenda in IGY. This programme was planned to launch satellites in space to observe and get data of the upper atmosphere. In this view the IGY Indian national committee was made in 1955.[4] So it was the first national institute building process to regulate Indian space activities.

Institutionalization by Sarabhai

The then little known institution at Ahmedabad, Physical Research Laboratory (PRL), followed the above national programme in IGY.[5] It was basically a small laboratory of Vikram Sarabhai for cosmic ray research at his home (Ahmedabad) in 1947.[6] The government provided the fund and it was also supported by the Karmkshetra Educational Foundation and the Ahmedabad Education Society.[7] This was the informal establishment of the later Physical Research Laboratory

3 S.N. Sen, *Astronomy*, in D.M. Bose, *et al.* (eds.), *A Concise History of Science in India*, 1971, pp. 39-40 at p. 40 (New Delhi: Indian National Science Academy).

4 R. Kochar, *Science as a Symbol of New Nationhood: India and the International Geophysical Year 1957-58*, Current Science, 2008, vol. 94, No. 3, pp. 813-816 at p. 814.

5 See <http://www.prl.res.in/> last visited 24 May 2016.

6 See <http://www.prl.res.in/website_english1/about/hist.php> last visited 24 May 2016.

7 See <http://www.aes-ahmedabad.ac.in/index.html> last visited 24 May 2016.

(popularly known as PRL) that was officially inaugurated in 1954.[8] There are some interesting observations from these facts that the establishment of PRL is for moving towards the permanent foundation of space programme on establishing a national institute. It was also amazing that there were indirect contributions of two non-government actors on supporting the government institution PRL. But space was not so popular during that time. So it was rightly pointed out that PRL took place as the cradle of India's space programme.[9]

There were significant contributions from Sarabhai besides his interest on cosmic ray research at PRL. He made the satellite-tracking era of India during IGY more social than scientific. So Prof. Saha institutionalized space with scientific vision only whereas Sarabhai has the blend of science and society both; that is why our general understanding is that Sarabhai is the first Indian to institutionalize space. Hence, it can be simply said that though the government had started this organizational process, it was basically realized by an individual like Sarabhai.

Direct Involvement of Government of India in Institutionalization

(I) DAE Phase

The above institutional development was related to purely research purposes. The Government of India did not feel any necessity to regulate such researches because it was ultimately Sarabhai and his personal interest on space. To take this space programme like other national programme, the government would require some permanent set-up that is well regulated. Therefore, it was ultimately passed over to the Government of India under the mentorship of its Department of Atomic Energy (DAE). Subsequently Atomic Energy Commission (AEC) was formed within DAE. The Prime Minister was in charge of both the establishments. Another doyen of Indian science, Homi J Bhabha, was the first secretary of the DAE as well as the

8 See <http://www.prl.res.in/> last visited 24 May 2016.

9 Mrinalini Sarabhai, *The Voice of the Heart*, 2004, p. 149 (New Delhi: Harper Collins).

Chairman of AEC.[10] The AEC had the resources and freedom to create new scientific programmes like space and industrial programmes such as satellites. Now Bhabha had stepped into development of the national space programme through AEC and DAE. The ground made by Sarabhai became more solid.

At the outset, it is to be kept in mind that when India finalized its third Five Year Plan (FYP) (1961-66), there was no provision for space research. The government considered the responsibility of looking after space research and peaceful uses of outer space to the DAE in August, 1961 with Bhabha as the Secretary.[11] Its effect was observed in the fourth FYP. The provision has been made for INSAT-1, the proposed Indian-owned geo-synchronous satellite which was to provide a variety of meteorological data.[12] The Planning Commission took a major decision concerned with space for the first time. Therefore, institutionalization process for space programme within Planning Commission was started with this decision. Much later the 11th FYP onwards there was approach for planning of private actors within national space programme.[13] The on-going 12th FYP (2012-2017) has in-depth provision for national space programme with the increasing number of private actors in space all over the world.[14] Thus, the Planning Commission became an organization to develop national space programme.

(II) INCOSPAR PHASE

The post-DAE phase was taken by the Indian Committee on Space Research (INCOSPAR). The International Council of Scientific Unions (ICSU), now known as the International Council for Science (ICS) as well as one of the pioneer organizations for IGY programme established a Committee on

10 Department of Atomic Energy. See <http://dae.nic.in/> last visited 25 May 2016.

11 R.P. Kulkarni and V. Sarma, *Homi Bhabha Father of Nuclear Science in India*, 1969, p. 33 (Bombay: Popular Prakashan).

12 See <http://planningcommission.nic.in/plans/planrel/fiveyr/welcome.html> last visited 25 May 2016.

13 See <http://planningcommission.nic.in/aboutus/committee/wrkgrp11/wg11_subspace1.pdf > last visited 27 May 2016.

Space Research (COSPAR) in 1958 as its response to the launching of Sputnik.[15] So Bhabha thought it would be necessary to have similar national Committee of COSPAR. Accordingly the government created the Indian National Committee on Space Research (INCOSPAR) in February 1962 under the chairmanship of Sarabhai.[16] This Committee organized the responsibility for regulating national space programme for the first time in practical sense.

INCOSPAR only took the responsibility of space research from DAE. But this committee remained within DAE where Bhabha was the Director. The role of PRL was changed because of formation of INCOSPAR. The PRL was assigned the role for appropriate centre for research and development in space sciences. The funding agency became DAE as usual. The designation of Sarabhai also changed. He was introduced by Bhabha as one of the members of AEC in 1965. INCOSPAR had two purposes: (*i*) to promote international cooperation in space research and exploration and in the peaceful uses of outer space and (*ii*) to cooperate with COSPAR. INCOSPAR generally encourages and supports international activities likely to contribute to the peaceful uses of outer space.[17] Thus, INCOSPAR started a new institutionalization phase that was solely dedicated to build up national space programme.

The responsibility of INCOSPAR was carried forward by Thumba Equatorial Launching Station (TERLS) founded in 1963.[18] It was funded by DAE under the leadership of Bhabha. Later, United Nations General Assembly took the decision to sponsor the continuing operations here. So it was dedicated to

14 See 12th Five Year Plan of Department of Space, Report of Working Group, October 2011, p. 97, available at <http://planningcommission.nic.in/aboutus/committee/wrkgrp12/sandt/wg_dos2905.pdf> last visited 27 May 2016.

15 See <http://www.icsu.org/what-we-do/interdisciplinary-bodies/cospar> last visited 28 May 2016.

16 P.V. Manoranjan Rao and P. Radhakrishnan, *A Brief History of Rocketry and ISRO*, 2012, p. 5 (Hyderabad: University Press).

17 *Ibid.*

18 *Ibid.*

UN in 1965.[19] In this regard, INCOSPAR made an institutional bridge in launching for the first time between national and international space programme. It could also be said that opening up a launching facility from India (better say in the region of our neighbouring countries) for rest of the world in the decades of sixty is a solid ground stone to support India's current role in establishing International Space Organization.

Consequently, the Atomic Energy Commission (AEC) approved the Space Science and Technology Centre (SSTC) in 1965, which was opened at Thiruvananthapuram. The Centre was founded just beside the TERLS. Therefore, there was continuous expansion of 'space' within the 'atomic energy' family of organizations. It was said that in the eyes of Sarabhai, the DAE was 'the Ministry of Advanced Technologies'.[20] The SSTC was renamed as Vikram Sarabhai Space Centre (VSSC) after his death in 1971.[21]

(B) ISRO Period

The next institutionalization phase has been started with establishment of Indian Space Research Organization (ISRO). It was formed under the same parental body DAE on 15 August 1969.[22] Satish Dhawan was the man who transformed ISRO in new shape after the unfortunate death of Sarabhai. Dhawan institutionalized national space programme differently. The Space Commission and Department of Space (DoS) were formed in June 1972. ISRO was brought under DoS in September 1972.[23]

19 P.V. Manoranjan Rao and P. Radhakrishnan, *A Brief History of Rocketry and ISRO*, 2012, pp. 23-28 (Hyderabad: University Press).

20 Robert S. Anderson, *Nucleus and Nation: Scientists, International Networks, and Power in India*, 2010, p. 403 (Chicago: The University of Chicago Press).

21 See <http://www.vssc.gov.in/internet/compRepository/mediagallery/-1/Test/vssc.htm> last visited 24 May 2016.

22 See <http://www.isro.org/scripts/milestones.aspx> last visited 25 May 2016.

23 See <http://www.isro.org/pdf/Organisation.pdf> last visited 25 May 2016.

The hierarchy of bodies is the following to regulate the current system. The Prime Minister is at the top of this hierarchy as Minister-in-Charge for Department of Space.[24] There is one Minister of State in Department of Space.[25] The Space Commission is the highest as well as highly empowered body 'to formulate the policies and oversees the implementation of the Indian space programme to promote the development and application of space science and technology for the socio-economic benefit of the country'. The Chairman of ISRO is the Chairman of Space Commission by default. The other members are National Security Adviser; Principal Secretary to PM; Cabinet Secretary; Foreign Secretary, Government of India; Secretary, Department of Expenditure; Secretary to Government of India (GOI) as member-finance and three members from academic repute in space science. Additional Secretary of DoS is the secretary of Space Commission.[26] This is the first time that Foreign Secretary was introduced as member of Space Commission in 2015 when the government reconstituted the old structure.[27] So the government has taken stand that space is an issue in foreign affairs or policy of India. It implies that India is now in a position to negotiate any issue on space globally. Therefore, why India could not lead the idea of World Space Organization at least from region of neighbouring countries like Pakistan, Bangladesh, Nepal, Sri Lanka, Bhutan, Maldives etc. that are far behind in space activities?

The role of Department of Space (DoS) is simply implementation of the programmes planned by Space Commission through ISRO and other bodies. The DoS has the role to sanction the budget for space programmes as planned

24 See <http://dos.gov.in/node/79> last visited 25 May 2016.

25 See <http://cabsec.nic.in/showpdf.php?type=council_cabinet_cabinetministers> last visited 25 May 2016.

26 See <http://www.isro.gov.in/about-isro/space-commission> last visited 25 May 2016.

27 See <http://indianexpress.com/article/india/india-others/foreign-secy-included-in-space-commission/> last visited 25 May 2016.

by Space Commission.[28] The role of ISRO is confined to develop space technology and its application to various national needs.[29] The Antrix Corporation Limited is a wholly owned government company under the administrative control of the DoS. It was incorporated in 1992 as a private limited company owned by Government of India and marketing arm of ISRO.[30]

The governmental institutional mechanism discloses the fact that there are different bodies for different purposes. Ultimately, it is not the national space agency, ISRO, but the Prime Minister himself along with Space Commission takes care about the institutional mechanism and functioning from government side. Therefore, the Prime Minister individually becomes responsible to see India's face in global space programme like what Jawaharlal Nehru did in mentoring national space programme at the beginning. The individual scientific vision of the Prime Minister whoever may be is very much needed when it is considered that India could propagate the concept of World Space Organization from this region.

(C) Institutionalization by Non-governmental Organizations

There is another new turn during ISRO period. The institutionalization process of government follows non-governmental initiatives.

Society of India Aerospace Technologies and Industries (SIATI)

The first is Society of Indian Aerospace Technologies and Industries (SIATI).[31] Its mission is enhancement of private industry participation in aerospace sector. It also has association for working 'closely with Aero Society, FICCI, CII and such other industry associations for Government policy, formulations or modifications for the growth of Aerospace Technology and

28 See <http://www.isro.org/pdf/Organisation.pdf> last visited 25 May 2016. See also <http://www.isro.org/pdf/Outcome%20budget2013-14.pdf> last visited 1 June 2016.

29 *Ibid.*

30 See <http://www.antrix.gov.in/aboutus.html> last visited 24 May 2016.

31 See <http://www.siati.org/> last visited 29 May 2016.

business.'[32] It is empowered 'to interact with Government on offset and other policy and regulations'.[33] One of the objectives is 'Organizing interactions and deliberations between Government bodies, policy makers, regulatory authorities'.[34] Therefore, being the largest aerospace society having status of non-profit and non-commercial organizations, SIATI has tremendous role to contribute to institutionalize aerospace industry.

Confederation of India Industries (CII)

The next is Confederation of Indian Industries (CII) having status as a business association.[35] According to the information available, its contribution is till now visible as the major organizer of biggest space expo at Bengaluru since 2008.[36] The CII, being mainly an association of private business industries, takes the initiative to interact with different private actors over business dialogues in this expo. The exhibitors of 2014 expo are the renowned private actors in space, both from India and abroad.[37] CII started this commercial institutionalization process on space activities since 2008.[38]

Federation of Indian Chambers of Commerce and Industry (FICCI)

Another business body like Federation of Indian Chambers of Commerce and Industry (FICCI) intends to organize the geospatial industry. The FICCI Task Force on Geospatial Technologies is in charge of sending policy proposals to the government.[39] Moreover, the FICCI Inputs to 12th FYP has recommended incentivizing R & D in public and private sector.

32 See <http://www.siati.org/about.html> last visited 29 May 2016.
33 *Ibid.*
34 See <http://www.siati.org/objective.html> last visited 29 May 2016.
35 See <http://www.cii.in/about_us_History.aspx?enc=ns9fJzmNKJnsoQCyKqUmaQ==> last visited 29 May 2016.
36 See <http://www.bsxindia.com/index.asp> last visited 30 May 2016.
37 See <http://www.bsxindia.com/pdf/list_of_exhibitors-2014.pdf> last visited 30 May 2016.
38 <http://www.bsxindia.com/index.asp> last visited 30 May 2016.
39 See <http://www.ficci.com/sector-overview.asp?secid=85> last visited 30 May 2016.

So FICCI has started Lockheed Martin India Innovation Growth Programme (IIGP) for technology commercialization.[40] It is further recommended to concentrate its focus on public-private partnership models like knowledge parks and incubator programmes to promote the commercialization, transfer and diffusion of technology. In this line-up, space is one of the most suitable sectors because India is predominant in space research and development.[41] The FICCI inputs have also suggested the use of geospatial technology for developing geographical information system (GIS).[42] It is one of the pioneering organizations behind the National GI Policy.[43]

Association of Geospatial Industries (AGI)

The Association of Geospatial Industries (AGI) is another commercial consortium to organize the geospatial industries. But it is not as old as CII or FICCI.[44] Though AGI took the initiative to form a common platform to represent Indian geospatial industry, it is mainly a mouthpiece of the big corporate.

Cellular Operators Association of India (COAI)

The Cellular Operators Association of India (COAI) is a non-governmental society comprising of private telecommunication companies in India. It institutionalizes private telecommunication sector. The mission statement states 'Creating a facilitating ecosystem that provides a nurturing policy, regulatory and legal framework for the industry'.[45] The telecommunication sector in any country is a very vital one.

40 See <http://www.ficci.com/sector-policy-recommendations.asp?secid=85> last visited 30 May 2016.

41 P.V. Manoranjan Rao and P. Radhakrishnan, *A Brief History of Rocketry and ISRO*, 2012, p. 51 (Hyderabad: University Press).

42 *Ibid*, pp. 59-65.

43 See <http://www.ficci.com/sector-government.asp?secid=85> last visited 31 May 2016.

44 See <http://agiindia.com/about-us/objectives/>; <http:/agiindia.com/what-we-do/advisory-initiatives/> last visited 31 May 2016.

45 See <http://www.coai.com/About-Us/About-COAI> last visited 31 May 2016.

India being populous country is the destination of so many foreign telecommunication companies. Therefore, the activities of COAI have great impact on such companies. Perhaps when there are Indian dialogues on establishing International Space Organization, the private actors in telecommunication sector have tremendous role to lead. They are more commercially vibrant than other sectors in space. The other advantage is increasing their business revenue on sharing global telecommunication market with these foreign companies in India.

There are umpteen numbers of institutions or societies that contribute towards this national institutionalization process. Sometimes their impact is global but within very limited sphere. However, it appears that their key activities related to space science and technology has ample opportunities to contribute towards this global organization building process. In some cases, these bodies could contribute in real sense and in best way rather than a formal institution on space.[46] Unfortunately, India is lacking in assimilating all its institutional efforts on different issues concerned with space.

The above discussions disclose the fact how and why India has institutionalized its space activities. The construction of such an organization within some existing scientific body is a step forward for regulating space activities in the course of time. Its impact creates pre-regulatory or soft regulatory or sometimes regulatory norms. These are the institutions that raise their voices to regulate national or international space activities. Most probably, this is the major reason for attraction of space lawyers towards institutionalization process that is broadly reflected to develop the concept of World Space Organization.

46 Malay Adhikari, *Developing Space Law Education in India: Some Proposals*, Rostrum's Law Review, 2014, vol. 1(4). See <http://rostrumlegal.com/blog/developing-space-law-education-in-india-some-proposals-by-malay-adhikari/> last visited 3 June 2016.

Regional Institutionalization by India

In this background, where is India now to develop regional space organization, may be in Asia-Pacific or SAARC region? India is a member of Asia-Pacific Regional Space Agency Forum (APRSAF).[47] There are State and non-state actors representing India in this regional Forum. The actors are national space agency (ISRO), government institutions (National Remote Sensing Centre, Physical Research Laboratory), private companies (Sumitomo Corporation India Private Ltd.), policy group (Observer Research Foundation) and educational institutions (Manipal Institute of Technology, Manipal University).[48] Therefore, it is not only the interest of the Government of India but also the interest of different non-state actors from India which is reflected in building a regional institution.

Though it is hypothetical till now, this above trend may be repeated in International Space Organization. The presence of many non-government actors may be noticed from India. Especially, as discussed above, their presence is highly expected in telecommunication sector. They may be more proactive than government to develop this hypothetical concept of International Space Organization. At the same time their strategies behind such concept may be different. For commercial private actors from India, the strategy is to promote such concept to attract international commercial market in space, because space technology is such a high-end one that its commercial market could not be expected within national or regional boundaries. Space is always global and consequently, its market as well.

At the outset the proposal for SAARC Space Organization or similar of its kind in SAARC region is to be discussed. There was proposal from the Prime Minister of India to launch SAARC

47 See <https://www.aprsaf.org/participants/countries/india.php> last visited 19 February 2017.

48 *Ibid.*

satellite.[49] How and when it will be materialized is a different issue. It shows India's willingness to institutionalize space in SAARC region. India is already one step forward in regional cooperation when the country has its own navigational satellite system, that is, Indian Regional Navigation Satellite System (IRNSS). The full fledged functioning of seven satellites has been started from 2016. It primarily serves Indian region but the Prime Minister has welcomed the idea of serving the neighbouring countries.[50] It reflects India's strong standpoint on regional cooperation in space. The final message is that India would like to lead this institutionalization process in SAARC region through SAARC satellite or IRNSS or many other upcoming initiatives.

The country, which once had very humble beginning in space activities through the scientific activities of IGY, now tries to develop regional space organization. It proves India's immense capability for major contribution in World Space Organization with solid national infrastructure and strategic planning.

Conclusion

In concluding the discussion, the chapter would like to emphasize the following points that are very much required in future for effective development of International Space Organization from India.

First, institutionalization based on specific space sector must welcome dialogue from another space sector e.g. remote sensing sector with satellite communication sector (as these are the only two sectors that are commercially prominent). Secondly, consortium of organization should be established from such dialogue. Thirdly, even consortium in same space sector is much more needed. Fourthly, recommendation insists that industrial bodies should be attached to such consortiums because if the

49 See <http://www.thehindu.com/sci-tech/science/SAARC-satellite-to-be-launched-in-March-ISRO/article16440133.ece>, last visited 11 March 2017.

50 See <http://irnss.isro.gov.in/> last visited 11 March 2017.

institutions are not generating revenues directly or indirectly, such bodies will not exist in the long run. Fifth is to plan Indian Astronautical Congress like International Astronautical Congress. The sixth one is that in such Congress, a national committee should be made to lead India in proposed SAARC Space Organization or similar bodies. The seventh one proposes that on the next level, consortium of Asia-Pacific regional forum is needed. The last one is that Indian space law community should interact with other space community in and outside India to see strong national presence in proposed World Space Organization.

Chapter 15

Bangalore Declaration–
A Beacon for National Space Legislation for India

KUMAR ABHIJEET*

Introduction

Many rockets have roared into the cosmos that India has realized National Space Legislation is the need of the hour. A step in the right direction was the round table conference on "Commercialization and Privatization of Space: Issues for National Space Legislation" organized by the National Law School of India University, Bangalore on 18 July 2015. The conference came up with a one-page document titled as the 'Bangalore Declaration'.[1] The first part of the Declaration enumerates necessity for law and the second part prescribes minimum contents of national space legislation. Since India is in the process of drafting its National Space Act[2] it is expected the 'Bangalore Declaration' might enable the drafters to concretize the draft bill in a better manner guiding them on the

* Assistant Professor of Law, National Law School of India University, Bengaluru.

1 For text of the Bangalore Declaration refer published in Annexure 3 in R. Venkata Rao and Kumar Abhijeet (eds.), *Commercialization and Privatization of Space: Issues for National Space Legislation*, 2016, p. 158 (Knowledge World Publishers).

2 The Indian Space Research Organization has constituted a Draft Committee on National Space Act. The Committee organized a Workshop on the subject in discussion, 16-17 January 2015.

minimum contents to be covered. This chapter elaborates the Bangalore Declaration explaining the objectives behind laying the law and contents of the anticipated law.

Why a National Space Legislation?

As rightly pointed out in the Bangalore Declaration the need for law is in the light of private sector's participation. With India intending to grant access to space to its private participants it must prepare itself to combat plausible legal issues, so that the intended legislation truly becomes 'enabler of space commerce.' The Declaration has well defined the necessity of law in five lines.[3] The subsequent paragraph explains why a national Space Legislation is needed.

Commercialization and Privatization of Space

So far space activities in India has been within the governmental domain that has impressively achieved self-reliance both for societal needs and commercial activities but undoubtedly space activities are exorbitantly money syphoning activities heavily burdening the exchequer. Thus, there is a need to involve private sector that has demonstrated proven technological and financial capacity. With the advent of private sector in space, number of stakeholders is likely to increase and the nature of business contracts is inevitable to be complicated involving many-many legal issues. The immediate concern in the light of private sector participation includes[4] (*i*) liability for damage or injury resulting from space objects, (*ii*) ascertaining technical and financial risk, (*iii*) strict control of unauthorized space activities, (*iv*) ensuring safety and security of space assets, (*v*) incidental issues to

3 The Preamble of the Bangalore Declaration states, "Whereas with increasing commercialization and privatization in outer space several legal issues are likely; Realizing safety and security of India is of topmost priority; Knowing compliance with International obligations and Constitutional obligations is non-derogable; Recognizing the fundamental need to encourage investors in outer space; Appreciating the dire need for 'Rule of Law' in Outer Space."

4 V. Balakista Reddy, *Commercialisation of Space Activity: Need for a Law,* in Deccan Herald, 15 April 2015.

commercialization and privatization of space activities such as intellectual property rights, trade secrets, insurance, and indemnity, (*vi*) effective dispute resolution. These complex legal issues have been dealt further in the second part of the chapter.[5]

At present, commercial space activities in India are largely regulated through Remote Sensing Data Policy 2011 (RSDP) and Satellite Communication Policy 1997 (SATCOM Policy) that is grossly inadequate to cover the range of legal issues involved.

Safety and Security of India

All space activities are inherently dangerous. The immediate foreseeable commercial space activity in India include launch services, satellite communication and broadcasting, satellite navigation, remote sensing and others. Each of these space activities has its own distinct legal issues, which further leaves room for specific theme based future legislation. But the common concern among all space activities involves safety and security of life and property on earth.

By the year 2020, the first private rocket is expected to be launched from India.[6] Kaul and Jakhu[7] jointly have enumerated four types of risks that are typically involved in commercial launches whether such launches are procured from the private sector or from the governmental entity. "These are (*i*) possibility of damage or injury resulting from faulty launch manufacture or launch vehicle components; (*ii*) improper performance of the launch mission; (*iii*) mishaps occurring at the launch site in connection with the provisional launch services; and (*iv*) ancillary risks, including delay in performance of the launch mission and unauthorized dissemination of proprietary data." Security concerns pertaining to commercial launch services include[8] (*i*) export

5 Discussed under the heading *Contents of National Space Legislation.*

6 Raghu Krishnan & Alnoor Peermohamed, *India's First Private Rocket Set for Launch in 2020,* in Business Standard, 13 June 2016.

7 Ranjana Kaul and Ram S. Jakhu, *Regulation of Space Activities in India* in Ram S. Jakhu (eds.), *National Regulation of Space Activities,* 2010, pp. 153-198 at p. 164 (Springer).

8 *Ibid,* p. 166.

control regime to prevent proliferation of missile and dual use technologies; (*ii*) validation, certification and monitoring systems so as to prohibit access and use of missile and dual technologies by non-state parties, (*iii*) protection and defense of space assets and systems on ground and in the orbit.

Need not to discuss, remote sensing and satellite navigation have direct bearing on the safety and security issues.

Compliance with International Obligations and Constitutional Obligations

Though outer space is infinite but the domain of international space law is very limited. The Outer Space Treaty 1967 is widely considered to be the foundation of the international legal regime governing outer space activities.[9] Use of space for 'benefit and in the interest of all nations' for 'peaceful purpose' and 'non-appropriation' by any means are fundamental to any space activity/use.

Some of the provisions of the Outer Space Treaty have further been elaborated into four separate treaties *viz* the Rescue Agreement 1968, the Liability Convention 1972, the Registration Convention 1976 and the Moon Treaty 1979. In addition to these there are a number of United Nations General Assembly Resolutions.[10] India has ratified all the space treaties except for the Moon Treaty.

9 Ram Jakhu, *Legal Issues Relating to the Global Public Interest in Outer Space*, Journal of Space Law, 2006, vol. 32(1), pp. 31-110 at p. 31.

10 Principles Governing the Use by States of Artificial Earth Satellites for International Direct Television Broadcasting 1982; Principles Relating to Remote Sensing of the Earth from Outer Space 1986; Principles Relevant to the Use of Nuclear Power Sources in Outer Space 1992; Declaration on International Cooperation in the Exploration and Use of Outer Space for the Benefit and in the Interest of All States, Taking into Particular Account the Needs of Developing Countries 1996 Resolution on the Application of the Concept of the "Launching State" 2005; Resolution on Recommendations on Enhancing the Practice of States and International Intergovernmental Organizations in Registering Space Objects 2008; UNCOPUOS Space Debris Mitigation Guidelines 2007and Resolution on Recommendations on National Space Legislation Relevant to the Peaceful Exploration and Use of Outer Space 2013.

Article VI of the Outer Space Treaty has primarily been considered to be the basis for national space legislation.[11] It imposes international responsibility for national activities in outer space whether such activities are carried on by governmental agencies or by non-governmental entities. Further the activities of non-governmental entities require authorization and continuing supervision by the appropriate State party to the Treaty.[12] Authorization being a procedural aspect creates the fundamental basis for legislation. Besides authorization and supervision, States also bear the obligation to register their space objects in their national registry[13] and in the UN registry.[14]

It is the constitutional obligation of India to foster respect for international law and treaty obligations.[15] Although international treaties are binding but enforcement or implementation of treaties is not by itself. Unless municipal law is changed an international treaty does not bind.[16] It is only the municipal law that binds the courts.[17] The Supreme Court has observed, "International law today is not confined to regulating the relation between the States. Scope continues to extend . . . It is almost an accepted proposition of law that the rules of customary international law which are not contrary to the municipal law shall be deemed to be incorporated in the domestic law."[18]

In the absence of legislation, the constitutional mandate of Article 51, to respect international treaties, is generally implemented through the executive power of the Union of

11 Michael Gerhard, *Commentary on Article VI of OST* in Stephan Hobe, *et. al.* (eds.), *Cologne Commentary on Space Law*, 2009, vol. 1, pp. 103-124 at p. 120 (Carl Heymanns Verlag).

12 Article VI, the Outer Space Treaty 1967.

13 Article II of the Registration Convention.

14 Article IV of the Registration Convention.

15 Article 51(C) of the Constitution of India.

16 M.P. Jain, *Indian Constitutional Law*, 5th Ed., p. 1395 (Wadhwa & Company Publishers).

17 *Jolly George Varghese* v *Bank of Cochin* AIR 1980 SC 470.

18 *Peoples Union of Civil Liberties* v *Union of India* AIR 1997 SC 568; (1997) 1 SCC 301.

India.[19] But there are exceptions to this general provision where legislation is must like for the topic in discussion if treaty obligations provide for payment to a foreign entity that must be withdrawn from the consolidated fund of India.[20] The breach of international responsibility of Article VI of Outer Space Treaty may give rise to a claim for compensation that might have to be met from the Consolidated Fund of India. In the absence of a law no money can be appropriated out of the Consolidated Fund of India except in accordance with law and for the purposes and in the manner provided in the Constitution.[21]

As compliance with international and constitutional obligations is non-derogable, it is necessary that India enact its national space legislation.

Fundamental Need to Encourage Investors in Outer Space

Space activities in India started in 1963 from Thumba Equatorial Rocket Launching Centre and today it has a made a significant place amongst the space-faring nations contributing distinctively to nation's economy and security. The launch services and satellite application *viz* remote sensing and navigation are the predominant features of Indian space programme. With annual shoestring budget of USD1.2 billion the space programme has been outstanding.

Till date space activities has largely remained exclusive governmental activity but considering the heavy expenditure and need to further take space programme to new height, it has been felt to find alternate source of funding. A Public-Private venture in space will not only accelerate capacity and consequently increase the number of satellite manufacture and launch but will also decrease the cost to access to space. The

19 Article 53(1) of the Constitution of India – "The executive power of the Union shall be vested in the President and shall be exercised by him directly or through officers subordinate to him in accordance with this Constitution."

20 Article 266(3) of the Constitution of India.

21 *Moti Lal* v *Govt. of the State* AIR 1951 All 257; *also see* Article 266(3) of the Constitution of India.

growth of space activities depends upon the possibility of recovering investment.[22] Absence of legislation is likely to deter prospective space investors as the investors need to weigh the risk and investment before taking this fancy endeavor.

Legislation to that effect can define regulatory and procedural aspects that could encourage balance development to tap the potential of lucrative space commerce and industry.[23]

The need for 'Rule of Law' in Outer Space

The key challenge in commercialization of space[24] is first, compliance with international treaties and secondly, legal issues that inevitably arise when private sector participates. It is not disputed that these concerns might be safeguarded through non-legislative methods as well but considering the number of stake holders and legal issues it is in the interest of the nation to go for 'rule of law' as former might lead to arbitrariness and the later shall promote transparency and predictability that shall facilitate confidence building measures in the investors. It can provide a practical legal framework and help to formulate aims and priorities in the exploration and use of outer space.[25]

The pre-commercial space age regulations are inadequate to deal with complex and sophisticated legal issues revolving around private sector participation in outer space.[26] Advantages of enacting national space legilsation[27] are (*i*) provide norms

22 H.L. Van Traa-Engelman, *Commercial Utilization of Outer Space: Law and Practice*, 1993, p. 18 (Martinuss Nijhoff Publishers).

23 Ranjana Kaul and Ram S. Jakhu, *Regulation of Space Activities in India* in Ram S. Jakhu (eds.) *National Regulation of Space Activities*, 2010, p. 154 (Springer).

24 Ranjana Kaul and Ram S. Jakhu, *Regulation of Space Activities in India* in Ram S. Jakhu (eds.), *National Regulation of Space Activities*, 2010, p. 164 (Springer).

25 Irmgard Marboe, '*National Space Law*' in Frans von der Dunk with Fabio Tronchetti (eds.), *Handbook of Space Law*, 2015, pp. 127–204 at p. 138 (Edward Eligar Publishing).

26 J. Hermida, *Commercial Space Law: International, National and Contractual Aspects*, Ediciones Depalma, 1997, p. 17.

27 V.S. Mani, *Space Policy and Law in India its Relevance to the Pacific Rim*, Journal of Space Law, 2009, vol. 35, No. 2, pp. 615-633 at pp. 632-633.

and institutional mechanism to promote the policy goal; (*ii*) avoid problems of no-law *vis a vis* space liability; (*iii*) making legal obligation to facilitate interdepartmental co-ordination; (*iv*) smooth private participation in light of techno-legal complications involved in space activities; and (*v*) constitutional obligation to domestically implement international treaties.

Contents of National Space Legislation

Having discussed the objectives behind the national space legislation, subsequent part will now reflect upon the contents of such legislation. The Bangalore Declaration has identified fourteen issues, *inter alia* they are—space governance; licensing conditions; monitoring of space activities; liability for damages; protection of environment of space; registration of space objects; indemnification factors; insurance coverage; sale-transfer of space objects; incidental issues to commercialization and privatization of space activities–research and development, data protection and IPR, technology transfer, sanctions for breach and dispute resolution clause.

Space Governance

As discussed in the previous section, participation of non-governmental entity in outer space activity demands 'authorization' and 'continuing supervision' from the State.[28] Meaning there must be some authorizing body/licensing body to grant, renew or revoke licenses for private space activities. National Space Legislation must establish a statutory authorizing/licensing body prescribing its qualification and composition and procedure for licensing of space activities.[29]

While establishing this statutory body care must be taken for division of work. If we see the present space governance

28 Article VI, the Outer Space Treaty.

29 Sandeepa Bhat B., *On Drafting a Viable Model of National Space Legislation for India* in R. Venkata Rao & Kumar Abhijeet (eds.) *Commercialization and Privatization of Space Activities – Issues for National Space Legislation*, 2016, pp. 65-77 at p. 67 (Knowledge World Publishers).

regime, Department of Space (DoS) is the apex governing body directly under the Prime Minister of India Office (PMO) responsible for implementation of the space programme. In between the two is the Space Commission that formulates the space programme bridging the PMO and DoS. Under the DoS is the Indian Space Research Organization—whose vision is to "Harness space technology for national development, while pursuing space science research and planetary exploration."[30]

Though it appears there exists hierarchy in governance regime but at times it is the same person who have been entrusted different positions in various bodies. Such a model has worked so far as all space activities were within governmental domain but with advent of commercialization and privatization of space each statutory body must have its distinct defined role. This will avoid conflict of interest and ensure effective 'supervision of space activities' and establish good governance regime in space sector as well.

Licensing Conditions

Article VI of the Outer Space Treaty imposes an international obligation on States to authorize activities of non-governmental entities in outer space but it does not prescribe the conditions of such authorization. The conditions of such authorization are left to the discretion of States but it does prescribe two inherent conditions: *first*, assurance that space activities are in conformity with the provisions set forth in the Outer Space Treaty and *secondly*, assurance of the safety of the activity.[31] The licensing conditions shall assure that space activity is carried out in conformity with provisions set forth in the Outer Space Treaty.[32]

30 ISRO Vision Statement.

31 H.L. Van Traa-Engelman, *Commercial Utilization of Outer Space: Law and Practice*, 1993, p. 18 (Martinuss Nijhoff Publishers).

32 Manfred Lachs, *The Law of Outer Space: An Experience in Contemporary Law Making*, 1972, p. 122 (Martinus Nijhoff Publishers).

General conditions of license observed in the national legislation of space-faring nations are:[33] technological competence of operator; financial capacity of operator (adequate funding, insurance etc.); national interests and security; safety of persons and property; environmental safeguards including debris mitigation steps. The UNGA Resolution on national space legislation has recommended for including conditions of in-orbit transfer/sale of satellites as well.[34]

Monitoring of Space Activities

Article VI of the Outer Space Treaty also requires continuing supervision of non-governmental activities in outer space. This aims at ensuring that above-mentioned licensing conditions will be observed not only at the time of seeking licensing before an activity has begun, but also for the whole duration of the activity. The supervision and monitoring of space activities is essentially a procedural question that has not been addressed in the UN treaties but left to the discretion of States.[35]

In order to ensure continuing supervision, national legislation must provide adequate means for receiving information as well as other means for intervention or deterrence and punishment in case of non-conformity.[36] Some legislation empowers the authorities for inspection of the facilities[37] as well as for investigations[38] and requires the licensee to furnish information in case of change in initial conditions to licensing. In case of violation of licensing conditions, revocation, suspension or

33 Irmgard Marboe, Setsuko Aoki and Tare Brisibe, *The 2013 Resolution Recommendations on National Legislation Relevant to the Peaceful Exploration and Use of Outer Space* in Stephan Hobe, *et. al* (eds.), *Cologne Commentary on Space Law*, 2015, vol. 3, pp. 483-603 at p. 518 (Carl Heymanns Verlag).

34 UNGAR 68/74 of 2013 Recommendations on National Legislation Relevant to the Peaceful Exploration and Use of Outer Space.

35 Manfred Lachs, *The Law of Outer Space: An Experience in Contemporary Law Making*, 1972, p. 587 (Martinus Nijhoff Publishers).

36 *Ibid.*

37 See national legislation of UK, South Africa, France, Belgium and many others.

38 See national legislation of UK, Russia.

varying the term of the license as well as imposition of monetary penalty and imprisonment has also been seen.[39]

Liability for Damages

All space activities are inherently dangerous. Precisely for this reason for securing a reliable liability regime liability for damages caused by a space object is imputed upon the 'launching State'.[40] According to Article VII of the Outer Space Treaty, each State that launches, or procures the launching and each State from whose territory or facility an object is launched, is internationally liable for damage to another State or to its natural or juridical persons by such objects or its component parts. This concept of State liability that is 'unlimited in quantum, time, and territory'[41] is a strong incentive for State to take appropriate steps to minimize the risk of damage and avoid this liability from being invited.[42]

The Liability Convention[43] lays two fold liability regimes. It provides for absolute liability for damage caused by a space object on the surface of the earth or to the aircraft in flight[44] but fault liability in the event of damage being caused elsewhere.[45] National space legislation is desirable for States that

39 See national legislation of UK, South Africa, Sweden, Ukraine, Australia and many others.

40 Armel Kerrest, *Liability for Damage caused by Space Activities*, in Marietta Benkö/Kai-UweSchrogl (eds.), *Space Law: Current Problems and Perspectives for Future Regulation*, 2005, pp. 91-111 at p. 91-92 (Eleven International Publishing). Also see Armel Kerrest, *Sharing the Risk of Space Activities: Three Questions, Three Solutions* in Karl-Heinz Böckstiegel (ed.), *Project 2001–Legal Framework for the Commercial Use of Outer Space*, 2002, p. 136 (Carl Heymanns Verlag).

41 Stephan Hobe, *Harmonization of National Laws as an Answer to the Phenomenon of Globalization*, in K.H. Böckstiegel (eds.), *Project 2001–Legal Framework for the Commercial Use of Outer Space*, 2002 (Carl Heymanns Verlag).

42 Irmgard Marboe, *National Space Law* in Frans von der Dunk with Fabio Tronchetti (eds.), *Handbook of Space Law*, 2015, pp. 127–204 at p. 137 (Edward Eligar Publishing).

43 The Convention on International Liability for Damage Caused by Space Objects 1972.

44 The Liability Convention, Article II.

45 The Liability Convention, Article III.

involve private players in space activities. It is well-established principle that international liability, which has been fixed by treaties, cannot be changed through a domestic legislation. Therefore National space legislation in no way can alter the international liability regime but it can enable States to minimize risk by prescribing procedure for verification process and if in the remotest of possibility a State has to pay for damages caused by a space object operated by private players it can prescribe mechanism for recourse.[46] State practices suggest that States demand that operator take compulsory insurance in order to guarantee that the amount paid on their behalf is recoverable.[47]

Protection of Environment of Space

Presence of space debris[48] in outer space possesses a risk to access space and spacecraft in orbit. With increase in population of debris the probability of damage resulting from collisions proportionately increases. In addition, if they survive in re-entering earth's atmosphere there is also risk of damage on the ground. Article IX of the Outer Space Treaty may be considered as the basis for environmental protection of outer space and its preservation for peaceful uses.[49] It imposes obligation upon States to avoid harmful contamination and adverse changes in the environment of the earth resulting from introduction of extraterrestrial matter and demands to adopt appropriate measures for this purpose.

46 Irmgard Marboe, *National Space Law* in Frans von der Dunk with Fabio Tronchetti (eds.), *Handbook of Space Law*, 2015, pp. 127–204 at p. 138 (Edward Eligar Publishing).

47 Kumar Abhijeet, *State Practices Towards National Space Legislation* in R. Venkata Rao & Kumar Abhijeet (eds.), *Commercialization and Privatization of Space Activities – Issues for National Space Legislation*, 2016, pp. 79-86 at p. 82 (Knowledge World Publishers).

48 Background to the 2007 Space Debris Mitigation Guideline of COPUOS (UGAR 62/217) defines space debris "as all man-made objects, including fragments and elements thereof, in Earth orbit or re-entering the atmosphere, that are non-functional".

49 Sergio Marchiso, *Commentary on Article IX of OST* in Stephan Hobe, *et al.* (eds.), *Cologne Commentary on Space Law*, 2009, vol. 1, pp. 169-182 at p. 176 (Carl Heymanns Verlag).

National space legislation can prescribe mechanism for certification of quality assurance or 'space worthiness' for space object before they are launched. It can prescribe technical standards for space object so that they survive in the extreme temperatures of outer space.

It can also prescribe for compulsory environment impact assessment before and after launch,[50] and in case of re-entry of space objects. In addition it can prescribe for debris mitigation measures.[51]

Registration of Space Object

Ownership of objects launched into outer space is determined by the registration of space object. A State on whose registry an object launched into outer space is carried retains 'jurisdiction and control' over such object.[52] *Cologne Commentary on Space Law* has commented that "'jurisdiction' means the legislation and enforcement of laws and rules in relation to persons and objects and 'control' means the exclusive right and the actual possibility to supervise the activities of a space object, and if applicable the space object."[53]

The launching State has the obligation to register the space object both in their national registry[54] and in UN register[55] by furnishing information in the manner as prescribed by the Registration Convention. Provisions of the Registration Convention[56] apply only to States and not to private actors and so responsibility for registration of privately launched space object is also upon the launching State. Therefore obligation

50 Article 8, Law of the Activities of Launching, Flight Operations or Guidance of Space Objects 2005 (Belgium Space Act).
51 See Austrian Outer Space Act 2011.
52 Article VIII Outer Space Treaty.
53 Bernard Schmidt-Tedd and Stephan Mick, *Commentary on Article VIII OST* in Stephan Hobe, *et al.* (eds.), *Cologne Commentary on Space Law*, 2009, vol. 1, pp. 146-168 at p.157 (Carl Heymanns Verlag).
54 The Registration Convention, Article II.
55 The Registration Convention, Article IV.
56 The Convention on Registration of Objects Launched into Outer Space 1974.

for private actors to disclose information on non-governmental space activities for registration purposes has to be formulated within the respective national space legislation, and annexed to the licensing of such private activities, so as to enable the concerned State to register privately launched space object in accordance with Article VIII of the Outer Space Treaty and the provisions of the Registration Convention.[57]

Since by virtue of registration State will retain jurisdiction over private space objects as well, in the slightest possibility of non-compliance of licensing condition States can always take-over such activities.[58] Hence registration of space object shall be complimentary to fulfilling international responsibility under Article VI of the Outer Space Treaty.[59]

Indemnification Factors

It is clear that States bear international responsibility for non-governmental activities and may make them liable for compensation even for damages caused by private space objects. States often reserve their right for indemnification, should an occasion come for payment. Such a provision though safeguards State interests but may cause undue hardship on private players particular if all due diligence has been exercised by them. National space legislation while prescribing indemnification provisions must also prescribe indemnification factors as well. Whether State will have absolute right of indemnification or there can be exceptions? Whether State will seek full/partial indemnification or there can be a cap on the indemnification amount? Limiting the liability for private players may encourage them to invest in risky space business.

57 Bernard Schmidt-Tedd and Stephan Mick, *Commentary on Article VIII OST* in Stephan Hobe, *et al.* (eds.), *Cologne Commentary on Space Law*, 2009, vol. 1, pp. 146-168 at p. 153 (Carl Heymanns Verlag).

58 Kumar Abhijeet, *I Too Have a Road to Outer Space But Do I Need a Law? The Necessity for National Space Legislation*, Indian Journal of Air and Space Law, Volume: July-December, 2015, pp. 137-161 at p. 157.

59 *Ibid.*

Insurance Coverage

Reserving the right to seek indemnification may not be sufficient to safeguard financial interest of the State. There may be in a situation where a private player does not have capacity to repay. Since damages are future oriented unlimited in amount it will be in the interest of both the parties that private operators do take sufficient insurance towards third party damage.[60] Legislation to that effect can prescribe for compulsory insurance depending upon the risk evolved.[61]

Sale/Transfer of Space Objects

In a commercial era it is foreseeable that in orbit sale or transfer of satellites is likely. UN treaties do not provide any provision for transferring of liability or registration of a launching State to another State,[62] which leads to the conclusion that 'once a launching State forever a launching State.'[63] This is disadvantageous not only to the transferor State but also to the transferee State as the former having no further interest in the particular space object still owes the liability and later is interested in taking jurisdiction and control but is not permitted. To solve this dilemma, it is suggested national legislation prescribe for compulsory international agreement distributing rights and obligation in relation to space object with the consent

60 Armel Kerrest, *Liability for Damage caused by Space Activities,* in Marietta Benkö/Kai-UweSchrogl (eds.) *Space Law: Current Problems and Perspectives for Future Regulation,* 2005, pp. 91-111, p. 109 (Eleven International Publishing).

61 Recommendation on National Legislation Relevant to the Peaceful Use of Outer Space, 2013 (UNGAR 68/74 of 2013).

62 Irmgard Marboe, Setsuko Aoki and Tare Brisibe *The 2013 Resolution Recommendations on National Legislation Relevant to the Peaceful Exploration and Use of Outer Space* in Stephan Hobe *et. al* (eds.) *Cologne Commentary on Space Law,* 2015, vol. 3, pp. 483-603 at p. 502 (Carl Heymanns Verlag).

63 Henry Hertzfeld and Frans G. vonder Dunk, *Bridging Space Law into the Commercial World: Property Rights without Sovereignty,* Chicago Journal of International Law, 2005, vol. 5, pp. 89-90.

of initial licensing authority.[64] This makes it possible to fulfill obligation of Article VI, Outer Space Treaty 'continuing supervision of space activities' in the event of transfer of ownership and control of space objects.

Incidental Issues to Commercialization and Privatization of Space Activities

With commercialization and privatization of space activities issues of intellectual property right and data protection are inevitable as investors will always be interested in securing their commercial interests. Besides this law must also address issues of technology transfer and facilitate research and development for using space for betterment of mankind.

Sanctions are part of all legislation that gives teeth to the legislation. National laws often provide for civil penalties and imprisonment and fines. Some legislation have provided for criminal sanctions as well. As discussed earlier, sanction will significantly aid in ensuring effective continuing supervision and effective compliance with licensing conditions.

With increase in number of stakeholders in space activities disputes are also inevitable. For the success of space commerce it is essential that legislation prescribes for effective dispute resolution system giving space for alternate modes of dispute resolution as well.

Conclusion

National Space Legislation is of paramount importance, as it will not only ensure maximum returns for the investment incurred but will also ensure transparency and predictability boosting confidence amongst the various stakeholders and also blanket and insulate the dangers that outer space activities poses.

64 Michael Gerhard, *Transfer of Operation an Control with Respect to Space Objects: Problems of Responsibility and Liability of States,* German Journal of Air and Space Law, ZLW 51.Jg.4/2002, pp. 571-581. Also see, Michael Chatzipanagiotis, *Registration of Space Objects and Transfer of Ownership in Orbit,* German Journal of Air and Space Law, ZLW 56 Jg.2/2007, pp. 229-238.

The Bangalore Declaration has only flagged up the issues to be considered while drafting the legislation. It has enumerated that key issues for national space legislation include space governance, licensing conditions, monitoring of space activities, liability for damages, protection for environment of space, registration of space objects, indemnification factors, insurance, sale/transfer of space object, research and development, data protection and IPR, technology transfer, sanctions for breach and dispute resolution. But the challenge in drafting the legislation is giving a legal language to the issues highlighted which gives further scope for research on this topic.

Significant guidance in this regard can be sought from the model law on national space legislation proposed by the International Law Association.[65] Besides this around twenty-four nations have drafted their respective national space legislation. A study of existing legislation can significantly help in better shaping the intended legislation but it should be kept in mind that national space legislation of Indian should be drafted according to the Indian need suiting domestic requirements of India.[66]

---

65 Kumar Abhijeet, *Development of National Space Law for India,* in 14 Astropolitics, 2016, pp. 185-202 at p. 198.

66 Kumar Abhijeet, *State Practices Towards National Space Legislation* in R. Venkata Rao & Kumar Abhijeet (eds.), *Commercialization and Privatization of Space Activities–Issues for National Space Legislation*, 2016, p. 86 (Knowledge World Publishers).

Index